THE 100 BEST AGGRESSIVE STOCKS YOU CAN BUY 2012

BRIAN + BARB -
BEST WISHES FOR
A PROSPEROUS 2012!
KEEP BIKING!
Scott

THE 100 BEST AGGRESSIVE STOCKS YOU CAN BUY 2012

PETER SANDER AND SCOTT BOBO

AVON, MASSACHUSETTS

Published by
Adams Media, a division of F+W Media, Inc.
57 Littlefield Street, Avon, MA 02322. U.S.A.
www.adamsmedia.com

ISBN 10: 1-4405-2594-3
ISBN 13: 978-1-4405-2594-0
eISBN 10: 1-4405-2611-7
eISBN 13: 978-1-4405-2611-4

Printed in the United States of America.

10 9 8 7 6 5 4 3 2 1

Library of Congress Cataloging-in-Publication Data
is available from the publisher.

Contents

PART I

THE ART AND SCIENCE OF *AGGRESSIVE* STOCK INVESTING

The Art and Science of *Aggressive* Stock Investing

We welcome you to the intrepid, adventurous, and, if all works as intended, ultimately lucrative world of *aggressive* stock investing.

You are holding a copy of the first edition, the 2012 edition, of what we hope to be many to come for this new title, *The 100 Best Aggressive Stocks You Can Buy*. As the tired old cliché goes, life isn't just about the destination, it's about the journey. So true. But we won't bore you with tired old clichés; if you're a seeker of truth and light about individual, do-it-yourself investing, you've probably seen enough of them already.

That, in fact, is why we've put together this new series that we hope to update every year. In fact, we aim to offer not only a fresh perspective on one of the most difficult arenas in investing, but we also offer our picks, for 2012, of the best *aggressive* stocks to invest in. We offer fish *and* we teach you how to fish.

Okay, another tired cliché, perhaps. And perhaps, not even accurate, for the "fish" we offer aren't really cooked and ready to eat. The 100 "fish" we offer in the form of selected companies, their "stories," and their upside and downside potential are meant perhaps to be bait, not fish. They are ideas for you to pursue further, to research further. They are ideas to consider against your own interests, intuitions, and investing strategies. They are food for thought.

Okay, more clichés. Perhaps it's time to get down to business and talk about the phrase "*Best Aggressive*." What does "Best" mean? What does "Aggressive" mean? For that matter, just why are we doing this book?

The story starts with the "mother ship" from which this book sailed: *The 100 Best Stocks You Can Buy*. Many—perhaps most—of you have seen that book. You may have the 2012 edition already; you may have even purchased it along with this book. You may be one of the loyal readers who have followed *100 Best Stocks* and all of its lessons and recommendations from its inception fifteen years ago.

Mother or Sister Ship?

We are by no means setting out to replace *100 Best Stocks You Can Buy*. This is not some transition between an "old, tired approach" and some new sexy can't-miss secret sauce for investing. Both books have their place, and—forgive us for being bold—both books belong on your investing bookshelf. We'll explain this a bit more later.

The 100 Best Stocks You Can Buy 2012 and all previous editions set out to pick, and give you the knowledge and ability to pick, what we feel are the 100 overall best stocks you can own. They balance safety and current income with long-term success and growth. They represent the best of all worlds, companies you'll do well with primarily over the long term. They don't necessarily represent the *least* risk, but risk commensurate with the returns to be gained. They aren't investments you can make one day and ignore for twenty years; all investments these days must be watched and managed as you would manage a business. The world just changes too fast to do anything else.

Why Stock Investing Is Important

In our naturally biased opinion and worldview, we all should own some of the *100 Best Stocks*. They should be somewhere in our portfolio. In fact, perhaps they should comprise a large portion or even a majority of our portfolios.

In our worldview, one of the major premises of owning stocks is to keep up with economic progress. Buy a bond, and what are you doing? You are lending a company money to do something with it, and you'll eventually be paid back with interest. But do you participate in the growth of that company? Growth in its business? Productivity? Market share? Better ideas? New products? No, not at all. You get a fixed, predetermined return, the value of which may well be diminished by inflation, the interest rate climate, or God forbid, an all-out default if the company goes belly-up.

Put your money in a CD or some other fixed investment and you avoid the last risk, but still incur the first two. Buy a commodity or commodity future, and your success is left to the whims of supply and demand, with no management team or any other guidance working to make sure that things turn your way. And real estate? Well, we all know what happened with that one.

Not that these alternative investments are necessarily bad; they have their place. Companies have risks, too. Bad management, technology changes, poor response to competition—the list is long. Any shareholder in Enron, Eastman Kodak, or E*trade can tell you from experience.

But if you want to participate in growth—and that growth can come in the form of company value and in actual cash dividends returned (which can grow too, as so many forget), you should buy *companies*. That is, if you don't have the whim and wherewithal to start your own. (Or even if you do, for you shouldn't put all your business eggs in one basket.)

So, we feel that you should own at least some stocks. They offer not only the best chance to get ahead but also the best chance to keep up.

A Little Further, a Little Faster

Now, assuming you've come on board with the idea of hitching your wagon to companies, American companies primarily, to keep up with or even get a little ahead of the pack, the question arises: Do you participate in the real growth opportunities in today's economy? Technology? Productivity? Efficiency? New, cool technologies like digital music, digital photography, and alternative energy, or less sexy but still new ideas like plastic composite backyard decking? Do you participate in recently realized economic necessities like replacing old water, sewer, and electric infrastructure? Do you participate in new business models such as streaming video, mobile wallets, or Fresh Mex?

Life is expensive. And as many have found out the hard way, it gets more expensive the older you get. Health care costs rise through the roof. Ditto for college costs for those kids and grandkids. And until recently, housing costs steadily went up. While that is all going on, personal incomes have hardly kept pace. Ditto for interest rates, venture capital, and other fixed returns. You will not get ahead, and you may not even keep up, if you invest for modest returns, even in our *100 Best Stocks*. Life *demands* more wealth and hence greater returns, and at the same time, all things equal, it *produces* weaker ones.

That's where *100 Best Aggressive Stocks You Can Buy 2012* comes in. We, your authors (more on us shortly), have developed this book to help you invest a *little* more aggressively. Not across your entire portfolio, mind you, we don't recommend that at all. But for a portion of your investing base, your portfolio, *100 Best Aggressive Stocks* will give you some ideas for how to hitch your wagon to the future, to see, in hockey star Wayne Gretzky's favorite allegory for success, where the puck is going, in today's economy and lifestyle—and make some money in the process.

AMERICAN AS APPLE PIE?

If you read the last few paragraphs closely, you may have caught our phrase "American companies primarily." Now, with all the headlines you read today about growth in China and so forth, why would we stick to American companies?

While we acknowledge that many foreign economies are growing faster and that many foreign counterparts to American companies and American technological leadership are becoming more formidable, we still for the most part choose to "buy American" when it comes to investing. Why? Two reasons. First, American companies are easier to understand. Financial and accounting standards are better known and more consistent. Second, American companies with good products sell a lot—for many, more than half—of their products and services into foreign economies. So you get exposure to the "good" of foreign growth without many of the inherent risks.

A Sister *Ship*

So we come back to the question posed by the earlier header: mother, or sister ship? Did *100 Best Stocks You Can Buy* give birth to the *100 Best Aggressive Stocks You Can Buy*? In a sense, yes. There is plenty of *100 Best* DNA in *100 Best Aggressive Stocks*. If there weren't a *100 Best*, there probably wouldn't be a *100 Best Aggressive*. But for you as an investor, it makes more sense to treat the books as two sisters, one to help you with the foundations of your investing portfolio, the other to get more on board with emerging trends and to grow with the "fast" parts of the economy, and as a consequence, to jazz up your overall returns and investing outcomes.

Who Are We to Write This Book?

Well, okay, first of all, we're the authors and creators of *100 Best Stocks You Can Buy*, and have been since the 2010 edition. That qualifies us, right?

Yes, it does help. We understand how to craft useful tools for individual investors. We understand the idea of culling down thousands of stocks into a useful *100 Best* list serving a composite of investors with a composite of best company attributes aligned to the idea of investing for value.

We are value finders, regardless of how that value is delivered. The value may be anchored to safety and current cash returns, or it may come in the form of growth and growth potential. With the *100 Best Aggressive* list, we think we have found stocks of good businesses in good industries that can achieve aggressive investment objectives that also happen to be good values at today's prices.

We function as a team. But a team is made up of individuals, so here is a brief summary of who we are, where we came from, and how our experiences relate to bringing you the *100 Best Aggressive* stocks. If you read the sister *100 Best Stocks You Can Buy*, these bio sketches will look familiar.

About Peter Sander

Peter is an independent professional researcher, writer, and journalist specializing in personal finance, investing, and location reference, as well as other general business topics. He has written twenty-five books on these topics, done numerous financial columns, and independent privately contracted research and studies. He came from a background in the corporate world, having experienced a twenty-one-year career with a major West Coast technology firm.

He is most definitely an individual investor, and has been since the age of twelve, when his curiosity at the family breakfast table got the better of him. He started reading the stock pages with his parents. He had an opportunity during a one-week "project week" in the seventh grade to read about and learn about the stock market. He read Louis Engel's *How to Buy Stocks*, then the pre-eminent—and one of the only—books about investing available at the time (it first appeared in 1953; he thinks he read a 1962 paperback edition). He read Engel, picked stocks, and made graphs of their performance by hand with colored pens on real graph paper. He put his hard-earned savings into buying five shares of three different companies. He watched those stocks like a hawk and salted away the meager dividends to reinvest. He's been investing ever since, and in combination with twenty-eight years of home ownership and a rigorous, almost sacrificial savings regimen, he has done quite well in the net worth department, pretty much on his own.

Yes, he has an MBA from a top-rated university (Indiana University, Bloomington), but it isn't an MBA in finance. He also took the coursework and certification exam to become a Certified Financial Planner (CFP). But by design and choice, he has never worked in the financial profession. His goal has always been to share his knowledge and experience in an educational way, a way helpful for the individual as an investor and personal financier to make his or her own decisions.

He has never made money giving investment advice or managing money for others, nor does he intend to.

Outside of an occasional warm Friday evening at the harness race track or a nickel-dime-quarter poker game with former work buddies, Peter just doesn't gamble. Not that he thinks it's unethical; he just doesn't like to lose hard-earned money on games of chance. But when it comes to investing, Peter can be fairly aggressive. Not with all of his investments, but with a portion. He is a classic Buffetonian value investor in most ways, investing for value in businesses he understands. He occasionally will make a big bet on something that appears to be an obvious winner. A couple of his bigger bets can be found on the *100 Best Aggressive Stocks* list.

Scott Bobo

Scott is relatively new to the professional writing game but has been an investor since age fourteen, when he made the switch from analyzing baseball box scores to looking at the numbers and charts in the business section. Cautious from the start, his first stock purchase was an electric utility with a spicy dash of dividend reinvestment. Unfortunately, his investing career was cut short by a lack of investment capital, and eight years later his brokerage firm was nice enough to send him a letter asking him if he was still alive and would he mind terribly taking his business elsewhere. As it turned out, that early 1980s episode was the real start of his investing career, since he now had an income and lived five minutes from a brokerage with half a dozen open Quotron electronic quotation machines.

In his twenty-plus years in engineering and technology management, he's learned that a unique product value proposition is important to the success of any company, and has also learned (the hard way) that proper financial fundamentals are just as critical. From a development manager's perspective, comprehending a new product's risk/reward proposition is one of the keys to a company's success. From an investor's perspective, it's also one of the keys to successful value investing in a dynamic, innovation-driven market.

Like Peter, Scott has always been a value investor. Picking a company to buy based on momentum or popularity won't always result in a bad pick, it just *usually* does. And while there are plenty of companies out there that can point to a history of increasing stock prices, there are far fewer that can point to a future of the same. Looking hard at the numbers, picking through the pretenders, and finding the contenders based on their success in the *marketplace* is where Scott really adds his own value.

Scott plays poker too, and finds the atmosphere around a poker table to be a bit like the stock market. Everyone knows there's money to be made, but not everyone is willing to do the math. Rather than figure out if they've got a reasonable chance of achieving financial gain with the cards (or stocks) they see in front of them, some simply bet on a combination of hope and the theory that "if you don't bet, you can't win." And while that's true, it's also true that if you don't bet, you can't lose. You only have so much money to play with—make the most of it by understanding what you're betting on, where the opportunities are, and what you're up against. This is where this book can help.

What Does "Best Aggressive" Really Mean?

Sometimes, to understand what a book or a chapter is really about, it helps to take apart the title into its component words and phrases. We'll give it a try here—what do we mean by "Best Aggressive"? One word at a time, but in a slight twist, we'll describe "aggressive" first.

Aggressive Means Aggressive

According to the *Random House Dictionary of the English Language*, the word "aggressive" has two definitions. The first—characterized by or tending toward unprovoked offensives, attacks, invasions, or the like; militantly forward or menacing"—probably doesn't fit. Too warlike, too "offensive," too militaristic. When we invest in companies, we aren't trying to conquer, invade, or destroy anything.

The second definition comes closer: "vigorously energetic, especially in the use of initiative and forcefulness; boldly assertive and forward." Again, this definition has a hint of force, but also captures the ideas of vigor, energy, assertiveness, and forwardness—in our case, forward thinking. One of the synonyms offered is "enterprising"—we feel this gets close as well.

Perhaps another way to circle in on a definition is to describe what something isn't. Aggressive investing is not passive, complacent, or "stay with the pack" investing.

Goals, Strategies, and Tactics

But let's get on with it and home in on what aggressive investing really *does* mean. The goal of aggressive investing is simple: to achieve higher returns than market averages or "average" investments. It is to make more money faster.

That's the goal, but where the rubber really meets the road is the "how"—the strategies, tactics, and investment mentality deployed to meet the goal. For us, aggressive investing is about getting ahead of the pack, the investing public as it were. It means getting on board with newer technologies. But it means more than that. It means seeing "where the puck is going" not only with technology but also with business and business models in general.

For example, does Southwest Airlines succeed in capturing market share using technology? Hardly. The airplanes they fly are about as low-tech as airplanes come. Okay, they have a pretty good website, but its quality is in its simplicity, not its dancing doodads and fancy graphics. Instead, they "get it," far better than their competition in an extremely competitive industry. They see where the puck is going, especially with customer experience and operational efficiency, and they seem to always get there before their competitors, even though what they do seems as obvious in hindsight as a school bus in broad daylight. So investing aggressively means doing the homework, finding the leaders, and boarding in the front rows with those leaders.

Aggressive investing can also mean finding the *next* leader, the company soon to emerge from the pack. Or, the next revolution or serious evolution in technology, like Apple with digital music or Starbucks with excellent, intellectually stimulating "third places" to replace the corner tavern. It can, of course, mean hooking up with leaders and strong niche players in exciting, futuristic industries like alternative energy today or computer networking twenty years ago. A rising tide will float all boats, but in the business world some boats will rise faster than others.

But Isn't This Risky?

Note that we didn't mention risk in any of the above. So what about it? you might ask. Yes, there is a component of risk in investing in new technologies or new business models or reinvented old ones—they might not work, or your company might turn out not to have the best technology or solution. This does happen. Aggressive investments can mean taking on more risk, both in the success of the technology and the success of the company involved.

Additionally, leading companies in evolving industries tend to attract a lot of investor attention and may be expensive to buy. So yes, there often is more risk, and the aggressive investor should be willing to take more risk to achieve more return. But, just as in value investing, if you understand the company and the market, and you can determine that the company is a dominant player in a good business or good niche, the risk can be reduced considerably. Aggressive investing is not necessarily risky investing.

We'll repeat this, because it's important: *Aggressive investing is not necessarily risky investing.*

We'll discuss risk management a bit more later on.

Reasonable Expectations

With regard to *aggressive* investing, it's right to ask: What is a reasonable objective? Surely we all want to double, triple, quadruple our money. We're thrilled at the idea of the "ten-baggers" we've heard about at cocktail parties. But is that realistic? How many IBMs, Microsofts, Apples, or Starbucks are there? How many companies are so successful that their stocks just seem to keep on going, going, going to many multiples of their original offering price? As you know, not very many, and they're hard to find.

Many stocks gain 40 or 50 percent in a year, but these are hard to find and often come with risks many might not find acceptable. As a result, we choose not to "shoot the moon" with our picks. We're not trying to find the "can't miss" winners, the "glamour" stocks of the age that everyone is piling into, although some of our picks are inevitably popular.

Instead, we seek something more modest but still very lucrative to your portfolio. We search for stocks that we feel are well positioned to achieve a 20 percent return per year, and can perform in that range over a sustained period. These are not stocks that will double this year and lose 50 percent (back to zero return) the next. While these are not stocks you can buy and ignore for years or even months, we feel that if they're in your portfolio, you will, for the most part, be able to sleep at night.

If our picks as a whole achieve a 20 percent sustainable annual return, with at least some strength in a down market, we will feel that we've done our job.

20 PERCENT RETURNS—JUST HOW MUCH BETTER *IS* THAT?

Some may wonder why it's really so important to do better than "market" returns. After all, if you make money at all, that's a good thing, right? And your friends talk about doubling their money, hitting four-baggers (quadrupling it), ten baggers, and the like. So why did you just spend $16 on this book to try to get some portion of your portfolio up to a 20 percent annual return?

The answer lies in the sometimes subtle, sometimes not-so-subtle power of compounding, that is, the return on your money and the returns on the returns that materialize, at first slowly, then begin to snowball. Einstein once called it "the most powerful force in the universe."

If you earn more on your investment, and leave those earnings on the table to compound, the results can be staggering. Even a little more return will eventually produce some rather amazing returns. Check out Table 1.

TABLE 1: BENEFITS OF BEATING THE MARKET

Return	years:	1	2	5	10	15	20	30	40
Market return	5.0%	$1,050	$1,103	$1,276	$1,629	$2,079	$2,653	$4,322	$7,040
Beat by 5%	10.0%	$1,100	$1,210	$1,611	$2,594	$4,177	$6,727	$17,449	$45,259
Beat by 10%	15.0%	$1,150	$1,323	$2,011	$4,046	$8,137	$16,367	$66,212	$267,864
Beat by 15%	20.0%	$1,200	$1,440	$2,488	$6,192	$15,407	$38,388	$237,376	$1,469,772

If you invest $1,000 at a market return, say, 5 percent, you'll earn $50 after one year—simple enough. If you leave that money on the table, invested at 5 percent, the return on the original investment plus the earnings will grow nicely, more than doubling it in fifteen years and almost quintupling it to $4,322 in thirty years. If you invest, say, $100,000 now, that's $432,200 when you retire, perhaps, and that's if you don't add another dime to the kitty.

Now kick that rate of return up to 10, 15, or even 20 percent. What happens? At 20 percent annually for fifteen years, you would end up with fifteen times your original investment; at thirty years, you'd have 237 times your original investment! Now if you invested $100,000, that's what, $23 million? You can see why 20 percent is a big deal. And you can see why Warren Buffett, with his 30 percent returns over the course of forty years, is one of the world's top three net worth individuals.

Heck, we'd even take 5 percent better than market returns. Though less than our desired objective of 20 percent, a 10 percent return over thirty years still generates more than four times the cash nest egg as compared to a 5 percent "market" return.

Doesn't that $16 spent on this book look better now?

Best Means Best

Okay, back to that *Random House Dictionary* again—this time for a definition of "best":

Two definitions this time, both relevant: 1. of the highest quality, excellence or standing—*the best work, the best students*; 2. Most advantageous, suitable or desirable; *the best way.*

These definitions capture pretty well what we're trying to do with *100 Best Aggressive Stocks*. We're sifting through long lists of stocks and companies, both established and emerging, to come up with the best possible assortment. That assortment takes into account many characteristics, which boil down eventually into reward and risk. The characteristics, which will be illuminated a bit more later, combine hard facts and intangibles into a *story.*

It's a bit more complicated than this, but here's the bottom line: We've chosen the 100 companies with the most compelling story—the greatest potential to turn your invested dollars into sizeable returns without incurring too much risk.

Growth Versus Value?

Our approach to stock analysis and selection is still a "value" approach, even though many investing professionals don't associate "value" principles with growth stock investing. We think these professionals (and many financial journalists) are wrong, for a company's value can clearly be based on its growth, both in principle and in tangible calculations. As we just saw in the last sidebar, a stream of growing cash returns can have considerable value.

In case you think this flies in the face of the Buffettonian view of value, it doesn't. Unlike his predecessor and teacher, Benjamin Graham, who tended to count only a company's assets, liabilities, and current income in the value equation, Warren Buffett clearly includes growth in his intrinsic value equation.

In the sister book *100 Best Stocks You Can Buy* we identify what we feel to be the 100 best overall values. In this book, *The 100 Best Aggressive Stocks You Can Buy*, we are finding the 100 best values among stocks with a strong growth or turnaround story.

Best Aggressive Investing Strategies

Growth stock investing in general—and aggressive growth stock investing in particular—can be quite challenging. Why? Because most companies in their initial growth phases don't have a long, solid track record of financial, or for that matter, marketplace performance. It becomes more important to have a good crystal ball. The past doesn't predict the future, because there isn't very much "past" to go on.

As we explain in more detail in *The 100 Best Stocks You Can Buy*, analyzing a company for the purposes of investing is similar, if not the same, as analyzing the purchase of the entire business. You want to look at the number stuff—revenues, margins, profits, assets, cash flow. You also want to look at the intangibles—brand, marketplace acceptance, market share, management quality, channel excellence, and supply chain excellence—that lead to *future* financial excellence.

This model may oversimplify a bit, but essentially it calls for examining the *results*—the financials—and the *story*—the business model and intangibles that sell the goods and bring in the cash.

We carry this same thought process into *The 100 Best Aggressive Stocks You Can Buy*. But since most of the companies we analyze are young and are still waiting to some degree to be defined by their future, we place more emphasis on the intangibles, that is, the story. Not that we ignore the financials completely; we can't. We simply choose to look more into the future prospects for the company and less into the past results. You'll see that in the write-ups that follow.

Putting Yourself at the Helm

If you're reading this, you're probably a do-it-yourself investor. You may be an investor relying on others to make your investments, but you want to know what they're talking about. Either way, you're reading this because you want to get beyond throwing darts at stocks hoping to hit winners. You also want to get beyond relying on blind faith and throwing your investments over the wall to others.

So to do better than throwing darts, and to invest with a rational thought process and methodical approach, you need to have an investing *strategy*.

What Do We Mean by "Investing Strategy"?

Now, the notion of an "investing strategy" may sound kind of scary—weeks, months on end with highly paid consultants going over tools and techniques and four-quadrant grids and all sorts of things—expensive and, at the end of the day, so complex nobody can really use it, right? All of you working in large corporations or public or nonprofit organizations have probably seen this, right?

We feel that adherence to a few guiding investing principles is easier and more effective for an individual running his or her own investing show. Not absolute adherence, mind you—if that worked, you could simply write a PC or Mac program to do your investing for you and head to the white sands of the Cayman Islands. No, of course it isn't that simple. You knew that, right?

Here we offer what might be considered, rather than a full-blown strategy, a series of stand-alone stratagems, principles, or *rules* that an aggressive investor might follow. These principles help guide an *aggressive* investor to better stock picks, but—*disclaimer*—won't necessarily guarantee success. Followed as guidelines, they should produce better results with less pain and less risk.

Here, in no particular order or combination, are seven guiding principles.

Play Tailwinds

Anyone who has thrown a Frisbee or hit a golf ball knows that it's easier and faster to go downwind than upwind. Not that "upwind" is impossible, but it just works better to go the other way. And it's easier.

The same concept applies to investing. Why invest in a stock in a dying or out-of-favor industry? Why invest in a good homebuilder when homebuilding as a whole is going to heck in a handbasket? Sure, that one homebuilder may make a great product and may be poised to capture a lot of market share when the market rebounds, and you can make a case to buy that homebuilder (and yes, we picked a few stocks like that). But for the most part, picking growth stocks is easier if you pick a timely or "in favor" industry.

If an industry is in favor, a company within it is more likely to be in favor. More to the point, the industry itself is growing, and so the players within it will have an easier time meeting or exceeding growth expectations.

So part of the process in picking growth stocks involves identifying "tailwind" industries. Such "tailwind" industries can normally be categorized into one of three types:

1. *New or emerging industries.* These industries are where the technologies—and the key players—are still being sorted out. Today, alternative energy is an excellent example, and by way of illustration, personal computers were big in the 1980s and early 1990s, Internet stocks in the 1995–2001 era, and for that matter, railroad stocks in the 1870s through 1900.
2. *Strong growth-cycle industries.* These industries have risen beyond inception to be well understood and accepted by the market. Major players have already been sorted out, and these players are now enjoying the rising tide of the entire industry. Computer networking, design automation, and Internet retail are current examples, as were personal computing in the late 1990s and automakers perhaps in the 1950s. Care must be taken here to choose an industry with plenty of growth left, still operating well in advance of a maturing or consolidation phase (like PCs are in today) bound to hamper growth prospects for all.
3. *Re-emergent industries.* Makers of water pipes, water works, and major water infrastructure components were once a strong growth-cycle industry—in the 1880s to about 1910 or so. Millions of 1900-era dollars were spent putting water pipes underground to achieve today's indoor plumbing standards. What does that mean for today's investor? Not a heck of a lot—except that this old infrastructure is rapidly falling apart. What does that mean? Suppliers of water infrastructure materials and construction services—and for that matter, electrical grid materials and construction services, and so forth—are bound, in our humble opinions, to require considerable investments once again. There will be a new growth cycle for these industries, supplemented

> by new technologies like smart meters and other high-tech efficiencies that will be added when the replacement systems are installed. We see this in other industries too, even PCs as companies replace aging equipment, but the cycle must be larger and more pronounced to gain our attention.

The key is to identify economic megatrends, some of which may be obvious by simply listening and looking around. What is "hot" now? What is getting a lot of attention, and is on the verge of becoming a mainstream industry? We've all thought about putting solar panels on our roof or buying a hybrid vehicle, and as the economics start to make more sense, voilá, it goes mainstream. Someday you'll be able to buy solar panels at Home Depot and install them yourself in a weekend. We're not there yet, but wouldn't you like to be invested in photovoltaic (PV) technologies when that happens?

Here are a few "tailwind" industries we've already identified:

- Alternative energy/energy conservation
- Utility/infrastructure replacement
- Home networking and Internet media
- Health care information technology
- "Cloud" computing infrastructure
- LED lighting and manufacturing products

Many of our *100 Best Aggressive* stocks come from these industries.

Buy As If You're Buying a Business

For those of you readers who also read our *100 Best Stocks You Can Buy*, this and the next few sections will sound familiar. We've adapted them to the *aggressive* stock investing style.

Earlier in this introduction, we laid out one of the key tenets of our framework (and frame of mind, really)—that while this book is about "growth" investing, we still emphasize and use a "value" approach. The implied principle, of course, is that growth is part of the value equation. But that's not all—here are a few more components of our value thought process.

As with any value investing approach, you must think of buying shares in a company as buying the company itself; that is, buying the business. Particularly with emerging growth companies, you should put yourself in an entrepreneurial frame of mind well beyond a simple "investing" frame of mind. Would you want to own that business? Why or why not? That's the first and biggest question that must be answered.

Fundamentally, whether or not you want to own the business depends on two factors: first, the returns you expect to receive on your investment in the near and long term future, and second, the risk you'll take in generating those returns. Fortunately, the third factor the prospective entrepreneur must consider—"do I have the time for this?"—isn't typically a consideration, although as we'll point out later on, aggressive investing does and should take more of your time than plain old "*100 Best*" investing. Things change more and faster.

So you are looking for tangible value—tangible worth—for your precious, scarce, and hard-earned investment capital. That return doesn't have to be immediate in the form of dividends or a share of the assets, as many in the traditional "value school" suggest. For growth stocks, it will come in the form of enterprise growth for the longer term.

If you realize your return in the form of owning a share of a larger company eventually, that's still a legitimate return. Cash flow received later in the form of a higher share price or a takeover is still cash return, it is just less certain because of the forces of change that may take place in the interim. It may theoretically be worth less because of the nature of *discounting*—a dollar received tomorrow is worth more than a dollar received twenty years in the future. But future cash returns are what we all seek, and are what may be truly worth waiting for if we pick the "right" growth stock.

Value also implies safety. The safety comes in two forms. First is the fundamental quality and soundness of the firm's financial fundamentals, that is, income, cash flow, and the balance sheet. Value companies have plenty of reserves, a large enough margin of safety, to weather downturns and unforeseen events in the marketplace; but many typical "growth" companies do not enjoy such protection. Second, they can have strong enough intangibles—brands, market position, supply chain strength, etc.—to maintain their position in that marketplace and generate future returns. For example, we feel that Netflix and Redbox (Coinstar)—among our picks—have strong brands and reputations that have become part of their intrinsic value and add to their safety. These companies are safer than "no-brand" companies trying to compete in the same market.

If you're really practicing value investing principles, you buy these companies at reduced prices, when the markets are down and when the company is out of favor. You're looking for situations where the price is less than what you perceive to be the value, although calculating the value that precisely is difficult. When you "buy cheap" you provide another margin of safety; that margin makes it less likely that the stock will drop further. It gives you room for error if you turn out to be wrong about a choice. Again, it's much like buying a business of your own—you want to pay as little as possible in case things don't turn out as you'd expect.

So taking a strong "I'm buying this business" approach provides greater confidence and safety, and is more likely to get you through today's volatile business and investing cycles.

Focus on Financials, of Course

In *100 Best Stocks*, we called financials the "strategic fundamentals" that define, or keep score of, a company's success. We've identified eight strategic financial fundamentals below. They are "strategic" because they go beyond the typical revenues, earnings, cash flows, and so forth reported as snapshots of past financial performance; these "strategic indicators are designed to tell you what is *really* going on with a company. They are also, to an extent, leading indicators of future financial performance.

These eight strategic fundamentals are also cited in our *100 Best Stocks* book. They work the same way with growth stocks, but more emphasis may be placed on some, like profit margins and the generation of excess capital, and less on others like dividends. This list can be used as a checklist, although it's hard to find a company that shows excellence in all of these areas.

Are Gross and Operating Profit Margins Growing?

We like profitable companies; who doesn't? But what really counts is the size of the profit margin and especially the growth in that margin, especially with a new or rapidly growing company. If a company has a gross margin (sales minus costs of goods sold) exceeding that of its competitors, that shows that it's doing something right, probably with its customers and/or with its costs. If gross or operating margins are growing rapidly, so much the better—its products are really catching on with customers.

Competitive analysis is elusive, because direct "apples to apples" comparisons are hard to find, and there are no "industry standard" gross margins, particularly in emerging industries. It is best to look at the company's own history for valid comparisons.

While a growing gross margin signals that the company is doing something right, gross margin isn't a perfect indicator. The economy as a whole may have moved from boom to bust, and even excellent companies may report declines in gross and especially operating margins (sales – cost of goods sold – operating expenses) as workers are laid off and capacity is reduced. Still, in a steady-state environment, it makes sense to favor companies with growing margins. In a declining market, companies that can protect their margins will come out ahead.

Does a Company Produce More Capital than It Consumes?

Make no mistake about it—we like cash. And pure and simple—we like it when a company produces more cash than it consumes, particularly in the early phases of its growth, where that is particularly hard to do.

At the end of the day, cash generation is the simplest measure of whether a company is successful, especially over the long term. Sure, if a company buys an airplane or opens a factory or a bunch of stores in a given quarter, it will be cash-flow negative. But that should be a temporary thing; over the long haul, it should produce, not consume cash. Companies that continually have to borrow funds or sell shares to raise enough cash to stay in business are on the wrong track.

So how do you determine this? You'll have to become familiar with the Statement of Cash Flows or equivalent in a company's financial reports. "Cash flow from operations" is usually positive and represents cash booked from sales less cost of goods sold, with adjustments for non-cash items like depreciation and for increases or decreases in working capital. In simple terms, it's the cash going into the cash register from the business.

"Cash used for investing purposes" or a similar term is a bit of a misnomer, and represents net cash used to "invest" in the business—usually for capital expenditures but also for short term non-cash investments such as securities and a few other smaller items usually beyond the scope of a typical assessment. This figure is typically negative unless the company sells some part of its infrastructure. Over the long haul, cash generated from operations should well exceed cash used to invest in the business.

Companies in growth or expansion mode may not show such a surplus, and that's where "cash from financing activities" comes in. That's the cash generated from issuing debt or selling securities—or paying off debt or repurchasing shares, if things are going well, and dividends are included here as well. Again, a successful company will produce more cash—capital—from the business than it consumes, just as a successful household does the same, or else it goes into debt. Smart investors track this surplus over time.

Again, a company in an extreme growth phase can be expected to consume cash to finance business growth; the less the better, and if a company is self-funded in its early or rapid growth stages, so much the better.

Are Expenses under Control?

Again, just like your household, company expenses should be under control, and anything else, especially without explanation, is a yellow flag.

The best way to test this is to check whether selling, general, and administrative (SG&A) expenses are rising, and more to the point, rising faster than sales. If so, that's a yellow, though not necessarily a red, flag. For very rapidly growing companies, expense growth exceeding revenue growth may be tolerable in the very short term, as the company is building for growth, say, by adding a sales force. But if the excess expense growth continues, it suggests that something is out of control, and it will catch up with the company sooner or later. In the recent downturn, companies that were able to reduce their expenses to match revenue declines scored more points.

Is Non-Cash Working Capital under Control?

Working capital is a hard concept to grasp—even for small entrepreneurs who live with its ups and downs on a daily basis. Insufficient working capital is one of the biggest causes of death for small and growing businesses, and working capital, and especially changes in working capital, can signal success or trouble.

Using a simplistic analogy, working capital is the circulatory lifeblood of the business. Money comes in, money goes out; working capital is what circulates in the veins in between. In its purest sense, it is cash, receivables, and inventory, minus short-term debts. It's what you own minus what you owe aside from fixed assets like plant, stores, and equipment.

If receivables are increasing, that sounds like a good thing—more people owe you more money. But if receivables are rising and sales aren't, that suggests that people aren't paying their bills, or worse, the business has to finance more to achieve the same level of sales. Similarly, a rise in inventory without a rise in sales means that it costs the business more money—more working capital—to do the same amount of business. That costs twice, because unless the firm is lucky, more inventory means more obsolescence and potentially more write-offs down the road.

Such inventory growth in the short term may precede a growth spurt, but on the other hand, for a lot of the growth industries we cover, obsolescence is an extreme and usually underappraised risk. The amount of last year's computer parts or networking hardware found for sale at an electronics flea market will tell you all you need to know about obsolescence.

A sharp investor will check to see that major working capital items—receivables and inventory—aren't growing faster than sales; indeed, a company that generates more sales with a decrease in working capital is becoming more productive.

Is Debt in Line with Business Growth?

As is the case with many other "fundamentals" items, you can tear your hair out looking at debt figures and trying to decide whether they're in line with asset levels, equity levels, and industry norms. A simpler test is to check and see whether long-term debt is increasing or decreasing, and in particular, whether it is increasing faster than business growth. Gold stars go to companies with little to no debt and to companies able to grow without issuing mountains of long-term debt.

A sharp-eyed investor may also check out other items, such as capital leases, that are often hard to tease out of financial statements but are a "financing" activity just the same, though are not debt in its purest sense.

Is Earnings Growth Steady?

We enter the danger zone here, because the management of many companies have learned to "manage" earnings to provide a steady improvement, always "beating the street" by a penny or two. So stability is a good thing for all investors, and companies that can manage toward stability get extra points. It's worth checking for, but with the proverbial grain of salt.

Still, a company that is able to manage its sales, earnings, cash flow, and debt levels more consistently than competitors, and perhaps more consistently than what would be suggested by the ups and downs of the economy, or its competitors, is desirable—or at least more desirable than the alternatives.

Is Return on Equity Steady or Growing?

Return on equity (ROE) is another of those hard-to-grasp concepts and another subjective measure in valuing assets and earnings. But at the end of the day, it's what all investors really seek: returns on their capital investments.

Like many other figures derived from income statements and balance sheets, a pure number is hard to interpret—does a 26.7 percent ROE mean, in itself, that a company is excellent? The figure sounds healthy, to be sure—it's a heck of a lot better than investing your money in a CD or T-bill. But because earnings and asset values are subjective, it may not represent true success. In fact, a company can increase ROE simply by borrowing money (yes!) and investing it into the business, even if it isn't invested as productively as other previous funds invested. The math is complicated; we won't go into it here.

For a true test of ROE success, check whether it is steady or increasing. Increasing—that makes sense. Why steady? Because if a company makes profits in a previous period and reinvests them in the business, that amount of money becomes part of equity (retained earnings). If the company reinvests productively, it will produce more returns, and ROE will at least keep up. If the company can't reinvest those earnings productively, ROE will drop—and perhaps it should be paying the earnings to you as dividends instead of investing them unproductively in the business. So if ROE is steady, the company still has good investments to make, and management is probably doing the right thing.

For very new "growth" companies, ROE figures may be understated. First, if they have considerable cash on hand from initial financing, that is also part of their equity position; this cash earns little (almost nothing these days) but is being banked for future needs. This cash inflates the denominator and reduces the reported ROE. Similarly, most early-stage companies are financed by equity—stock sales, venture capital, and so forth—and tend to use relatively less debt, again reducing financial leverage and thus reported ROE.

Does the Company Pay a Dividend?

Those of you coming from *The 100 Best Stocks You Can Buy* recognize dividends as an important investing theme for the mainstream stocks. Aggressively growing companies—those with a good story, anyway—should be able to invest funds in their business with good results, and thus, as an investor, you should want them to do that. For any financially secure company, we like to see dividends as a gesture of appreciation and a "bird in the hand" to its investors. Similarly, we like to see dividends as payback to investors in growth companies, but we realize that it might not always make sense. A company with great and well-funded growth prospects and dividends is the best of both worlds and is to be admired, but if a growth company is paying dividends, one is always nagged by the question, "If the business is really growing and doing well, why can't these folks invest these funds for a greater return than I can get?"

Bottom line: We like dividends, but in the *Aggressive Stocks* arena, they are not always the thing you really want.

Price-to-Earnings-to-Growth Ratio

Finally, we'll tip our hats to one of the more standard and commonly used financial metrics applied well to growth stocks: the price-to-earnings-to-growth (PEG) ratio. The ratio is comprised of two parts: the conventional and ever-popular price-to-earnings ratio (P/E), and the growth rate, usually measured as the five-year growth rate in earnings per share or something similar. The ratio is arrived at by first calculating the P/E, then dividing that figure by the growth rate. The purpose of the ratio, along with its component P/E, is valuation; that is, to determine if a stock's price makes sense related to the level of earnings generated.

So if you have a growth stock with a P/E ratio of 20, that implies a 5 percent return (earnings of, say, $1 on a share price of $20)—a relatively low rate considering the risks involved but not too far out there (recently, the S&P 500 benchmark had a P/E ratio just exceeding 16). But that's not the whole story, especially for a growth stock.

A P/E of 20 is relatively high compared to the market—*if* there is little in the way of growth prospects for the company. Stated differently, the price paid is high relative to the earnings generated given that there is little growth prospect for the earnings. But if the earnings are growing at 20 percent per year, now what? Without going into the math details, those earnings will double in approximately four years. (If you want to learn the shorthand calculation for this—look up the "rule of 72" in a search engine.)

So now you can think of the P/E as being something closer to 10—in four years; that's pretty good. Or, turned around, if the stock price reflects this growth and the P/E ratio stays constant at 20, the price will be $40 in four years—$2 in earnings times a P/E of 20.

Many investors choose—wisely, we think—to use the PEG ratio to incorporate growth into the valuation exercise. The growth rate determines whether the P/E, and thus the stock price, really makes sense. Our $20 stock with a P/E of 20 and a growth rate of 20 percent would have a PEG ratio of 1. A stock with a $60 price and earnings of $1—P/E of 60 and a growth rate of 20 percent would have a PEG of 3. The 20 percent growth rate is nice, but it doesn't support a $60 stock price or the P/E of 60 currently experienced by the shareholders.

Generally, a PEG rate of 1 or less is considered reasonable, but a P/E of 3 is considered too high; that is, the growth rate does not really support the stock price as it is. PEG serves as a good and fast valuation benchmark, but there are two caveats. First, reported earnings may not reflect the true earning potential of the company because of one-time items and accounting tricks. Second, the growth rates, especially for new companies without a track record, may also be fickle and hard to project too far into the future.

Intangibles—Now More than Ever

Now we will turn our attention beyond the financial statements to those ephemeral, true, but hard-to-grasp qualities that make companies great now and in the future—the intangibles. Intangibles are sort of the "rest of the story" for all stocks, but a big part of the story for growth stocks. Why? Because the right combination of intangibles—the right "story"—will bring success and ultimately solid financial fundamentals down the road.

Intangibles can be thought of as the "secret sauce" that makes any company work. If the secret sauce is right, the company will vault past its competition and take full advantage of its growth opportunity. In extreme cases like Apple or Starbucks (a few years ago), the secret sauce will create the opportunity; that is, it will define new markets for products customers didn't even know they needed.

A Hundred Billion to Spend

When you look at any company, perhaps the bottom-line question follows the Buffett wisdom: If you had a hundred billion to spend (and we'll assume, the genius intellect to spend it right), could you re-create that company?

If the answer is "yes," it may still be a great company, but it may not be great enough to fend off competition and keep its customers forever. If the answer is "no," the company truly has something unique to offer in the marketplace, and that is difficult to duplicate at any cost. That distinctive competence, that sustainable competitive edge—whatever it is, a brand, a trade secret, a lock on distribution or supply channels—may be worth more than all the factories and high-rise office buildings and cash in the bank it could ever have.

The intangibles are the "soft" factors that make companies unique, the factors that add up to more than the sum of their parts, the factors that ultimately drive future revenues. Intangibles not only define excellence, they define the future, while most financial fundamentals mainly define the past. Here are seven key intangible categories to think about in any company or industry.

Does the Company Have a Moat?

A business "moat" performs much the same role as the medieval castle equivalent—it protects the business from competition. Whatever factors (some are discussed below) create the moat, ultimately, those are the factors that prevent you, with your $100 billion, from taking their business. Moats are usually a combination of brand, product technology, design, marketing and distribution channels, and customer loyalty all working together to protect a company. A moat doesn't just protect the existence of a company, it helps it command higher prices and earn higher profits now and in the future.

Moats are a particularly important concept for growth companies. They can be very dynamic and even fleeting, and even more difficult to assess. A new company in a new industry, say, LED lighting, may have a moat right out of the gate, because they come into the market, as Civil War general Nathan Bedford Forrest famously said, "first with the most." They enjoy initial success because of their "first mover" advantage, but this advantage quickly dissipates as other competitors—some with new and better technologies or manufacturing processes or marketing channels, etc.—hit the market. The moat can dry up, so to speak, so determining the *permanence* of the moat becomes the imperative.

Other companies may come into a market with no moat at all—but they acquire one because they have a better way of doing something. CarMax, which we'll come back to in a second—might qualify here.

Whether a company has a "narrow" moat, a "wide" moat, or none at all is a subjective assessment for you to make. You can get some help at Morningstar (*www.morningstar.com*), whose stock ratings include an assessment of a company's moat.

Coca-Cola has a moat because of the sheer impossibility of surpassing its brand and brand recognition worldwide. CarMax has *built* a moat because it is further along in putting retail-style dealerships on the ground and applying management information technologies to its business than anyone else; it would take years for a competitor to catch up. As in our *100 Best Stocks* book, we have a "Moat Stars" list to identify the top ten stocks with a solid and sustainable competitive advantage (see Table 7).

Does the Company Have an Excellent Brand?

It's hard to say enough about brand, especially in today's fast-moving, highly packaged, highly national and international culture. A strong brand means consistency and a promise to consumers, and consumers sold on a brand will prefer it over any other, almost regardless of price. People still buy Tide, and although there's been a slowdown lately, Starbucks is still synonymous with high quality and a posh, progressive ambience.

Good brands command higher prices, and foster loyalty and identity and even customer "love." Again, using the Starbucks example, websites appeared soliciting customer appeals to not close stores during the recent store-closing initiative; when has anyone (other than a worker) offered so much resistance to closing a U.S. auto plant? Once a company has created a dominant brand (or brands, in the case of P&G) in the marketplace, aside from some major faux pas, they will endure and continue to create value for shareholders for years to come; a good brand is one of the most valuable (yet hard to value) long-term assets around.

Ask yourself if a company has a sought-after brand, a brand customers would pay extra to buy or align with, a brand that would be difficult to duplicate at any cost. Would customers rather fight than switch? Think about Starbucks, Coca-Cola, Tiffany, or Under Armour as company brands; think about iPod, iTunes, QuickBooks, Redbox or, again, Under Armour as *product* brands. And don't just think about consumer brands—industry brands in the business-to-business world are important too.

Is the Company a Market Leader?

Market leadership usually—but not always—goes hand in hand with brand. The trick is to decide whether a company really leads in its industry. Often—but not always—that's a factor of size. The market leader usually has the highest market share, and the important point is that it calls the shots with regards to price, technology, marketing message, and so forth—other companies must play catch-up and often discount their prices to keep up. Apple is a market leader in digital music, Intel is the market leader in microprocessors, Toyota is emerging as the market leader in automobiles.

Market leaders may be leaders in smaller, or niche, markets—it still works. Mentor Graphic is the leader in electronic design automation, Healthstream is the leader in computer-based health-care learning tools, and Cree leads the way in LED lighting and components.

Excellent companies tend to be market leaders, and market leaders tend to be excellent companies. But this relationship doesn't always hold true—sometimes the nimble but smaller competitor is the excellent company—and will likely assume market leadership eventually. Examples such as Nucor, Discover Financial Services, and Peet's Coffee & Tea can be found on our list.

Does the Company Have Channel Excellence?

"Channels" in business parlance refers to the chain of players engaged to sell and distribute a company's products. These players might be stores, they might be other industrial companies, they might be independent sales forces or distributors. If a company is considered a top supplier in a particular channel, or a company has especially good relations with its channel, that's a plus.

Excellent companies develop solid channel relationships and become the preferred supplier in those channels. Companies such as Fair Isaac, First Solar, Johnson Controls, MetroPCS, Nike, or Trex could all have excellent relationships with their channels through which they sell their product. Or they might *be* the channel, as is the case with Arrow Electronics, Costco, McKesson, Overstock.com, and Tractor Supply, and simply do it better than anyone else.

Does the Company Have Supply Chain Excellence?

Like distribution channels, excellent companies develop excellent and low-cost supply channels. They are seldom caught off-guard by supply shortages and tend to get favorable and stable prices for whatever they buy. This is often not an easy assessment unless you know something about a particular industry. Companies such as Dell, Nike, and perhaps Target and Costco succeed because they manage their supply chains well.

Does the Company Have Excellent Management?

Well, it's not hard to grasp what happens if a company doesn't have good management; performance fails and few inside or outside the company respect the company. It's not easy for an investor to determine if a management team does a good job or acts in shareholder interests.

Clues can include candor and honesty, and the ability of company management to speak in accessible, easily understood terms about the company and company performance (it's worth listening to conference calls as a resource). A management team that admits errors and eschews other forms of arrogance and entitlement (i.e., luxury perks, office suites, aircraft) is probably tilting their interests toward shareholders, as is the management team that is financially prudent and refrains from excess expenditure or temptation arising from an abundance of early cash invested in the business.

This may be the most subjective and elusive assessment of all, as few investors work with these folks on a daily basis. Still, over time, you can garner a strong hunch about whether a management team is effective and on your side. When company managers are known and respected as industry leaders, that's a good sign.

Are There Signs of Innovation Excellence?

This question seems pretty obvious, especially for growth companies. Innovation, and the effective management of innovation, is key to new or emerging companies, and even "re-emerging" companies, building their market presence. "Innovation"—as differentiated from its oft-interchanged word "invention"—implies not only the creative capacity and effort to create new products—but also to *bring them to market* in a way to satisfy or delight *customers*. The italicized parts of the last sentence are key to determining the quality and value of a company's innovation. Innovations must be about things customers want or need or even about a better customer experience, and they must be real and available in the marketplace to succeed.

Innovation is not just about the products a company sells. True, if the company is leading the industry in innovation, that's usually a good thing, for "first to market" and "best to market" clearly offer business advantages.

The less obvious part of this question is whether the company makes the best use of technology to make operations and customer interfaces as efficient and effective as possible. Southwest Airlines certainly didn't invent discount air travel. But they do make our list in terms of innovation excellence. Why? Simply because, after all of these years, amazingly, they still have the best, simplest, easiest-to-use flight booking, boarding, and other customer-experience processes in the industry. Sometimes these sorts of innovations mean a lot more than bringing new fancy products and bells and whistles to the market. And one can look to Apple, Google, and CarMax on our list for some of the more obvious examples.

Be Streetwise

One savvy guiding principle advanced through the years, especially by Fidelity Magellan fund manager and investing guru Peter Lynch, but also by Buffett and others, is to observe what's happening "on the street" to gain an investing advantage.

In the view of Lynch, Buffett, and others (including ourselves) it is important to gain as good a knowledge as possible about a business before investing in it. Again, it's like buying the whole business for yourself—why would you do it if you didn't understand it? The principle goes further: You can often gain the best insight into a business simply by watching what goes on "on the street."

Stop, Look, and Listen

We're talking "Main Street" here, not "Wall Street." Watching a business "in person" means watching customers go in and out, engaging with the business yourself, or if they make high-tech 3D vision components for integrated circuit manufacturing, something you wouldn't normally be able to see on the street, find out more by reading about it or networking with those who do see it.

The idea is to gain a real, on-the-ground understanding of the marketplace, and how the company performs in it. Is the customer experience right? Do customers respond well? Does the business seem to be growing, and managing its growth effectively? When we see three Home Depots within three miles of each other, we start wondering about that, and wondering whether management really sees through to customer needs and operational costs at the ground level, or whether decisions are being made on some other basis.

We advise watching, listening, reading, networking, and gaining personal experiences with a company wherever possible. Buffett once watched the number of railroad tank cars being switched in and out of a chemical company to get some investing insight. You may or may not wish to go this far, but if you're a Starbucks investor, why not go to a Starbucks at least once in a while to gauge activity, customer service, and customer response? Or if you're investing in the alternative energy industry, semiconductors, or some such, watch the financial press and especially the trade press on these industries as much as possible. You might consider getting a quote on a solar-panel system for your home; not only might this make sense for your utility bills and home value, but it would also help your understanding of this emerging industry.

Keep It Simple . . .

A corollary principle, again spearheaded by Buffett, is to follow and invest in what you know and understand. With aggressive stocks, this principle may break down a bit as many new technologies defy thorough knowledge, especially by those individuals outside the industry. Buffett might have trouble with aggressive stock investing, at least the way we approach it, because it is doubtful that neither he, nor very many other people, would be able to *thoroughly* understand the technologies and businesses built around them.

As a result, you can choose to find some creative ways to stay on board, again through networks or industry journals and such, or you can choose to stay away from the more esoteric businesses altogether. There are plenty of "simple" businesses even in the aggressive space.

Manage Risk with a Tiered Portfolio

Although *The 100 Best Aggressive Stocks You Can Buy* is designed to help you pick the best of the best growth stocks to buy, investing by nature goes well beyond simply buying stocks, just like owning an automobile goes far beyond buying it. Just as clearly, this book isn't about investing strategy, nor about the personal financial strategies necessary to ensure retirement or a prosperous future. That said, we think a few words on investing strategy are in order. We find that many investors lose the forest in the trees, spending all of their energy trying to find individual stocks or funds without putting enough consideration into their overall investing framework. If they look at the big picture at all, they look at the formulaic covenants of asset allocation, a favorite subject of the financial planning and advisory community, as though the difference between 50 percent equities and 60 percent equities makes all the different in the world. Sure, it might in the world of pension funds and other institutional investments, where a 10 percent adjustment could move millions into or out of a particular asset class and more or less toward safety, but what about a $100,000 portfolio? Does $10,000 more or less in stocks, bonds, or cash make that much difference?

Perhaps not. And of course, there's more to that story—doesn't it matter more which equities you invest in than just the fact that you're 60 percent in equities? While asset allocation models make for nice pie charts, we prefer to approach big-picture portfolio constructs differently.

Moreover, in connecting *100 Best* with *100 Best Aggressive* stocks, the question becomes what percentage of your portfolio should be allocated to each (as well as other assets, like fixed income, real estate, gold, etc.). Rather than make hard and fast rules, such as "20 percent of your portfolio should be in aggressive stocks," it makes sense to put some thought into your overall portfolio and the *components* of that portfolio and how they all fit together.

Start with a Portfolio in Mind

First, we'll make an assumption: You are not a professional investor. You have other things to do with your time, and time is of the essence. You cannot spend forty, fifty, or sixty hours a week glued to a computer screen analyzing your investments.

To that assumption, we'll add another: that, as an individual investor, you're looking to beat the market. Not by a ton—20 percent sustained returns simply aren't possible *for all of your portfolio* without taking outlandish risks. But perhaps if the market is up 4 percent in a year, you'd like to achieve, 6, perhaps 7 or 8 percent without taking excessive risks. Or if the market is down 20 percent, perhaps you cut your losses at 5 or 10 percent. You're looking to do *somewhat better* than the market.

Because of time constraints, and owing to your objective to do slightly better than average, and because you have *The 100 Best Aggressive Stocks*

You Can Buy already at your fingertips, we suggest taking a tiered approach to your portfolio. The tiers aren't based on the type of assets; they're based on the amount of activity and attention you want to pay to different parts of your portfolio. It's a strategic portfolio approach you would probably take if you were managing a small business—put most of your focus on the products and customers who might bring the greatest new return to your business; let the rest of your slow, steady customer base function as it has for the long term.

To do this, we suggest breaking up your portfolio into three tiers, or segments. This can be done by setting up specific accounts; or less formally by simply applying the model as a thought process.

We can't go much further without defining the three segments:

Active Portfolio Segmentation

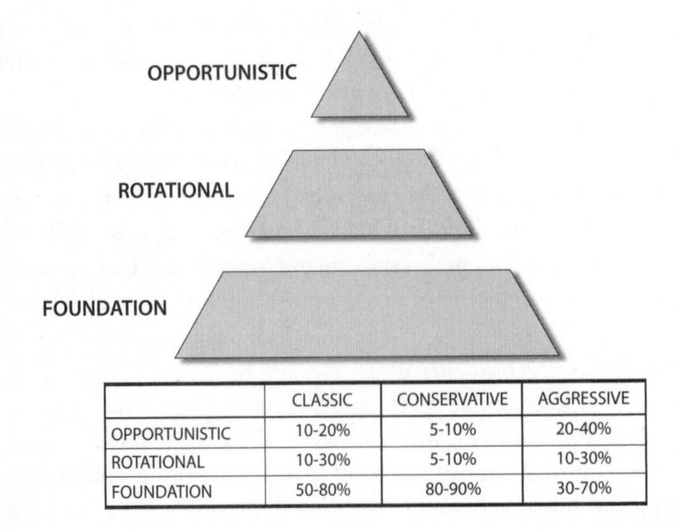

	CLASSIC	CONSERVATIVE	AGGRESSIVE
OPPORTUNISTIC	10-20%	5-10%	20-40%
ROTATIONAL	10-30%	5-10%	10-30%
FOUNDATION	50-80%	80-90%	30-70%

The Foundation Portfolio

In this construct, each investor defines and manages a cornerstone foundation portfolio, which is long-term in nature and requires relatively less active management. Frequently, the foundation portfolio consists of retirement accounts (the paradigmatic long-term investment) and may include your personal residence or other long-lived personal or family assets, such as trusts, collectibles, and so forth.

The typical foundation portfolio is invested to achieve at least average market returns through index funds, quality mutual funds, and some income-producing assets such as bonds held to maturity. A foundation portfolio may contain some long-term plays in commodities or real estate to defend against inflation, particularly in such commodities as energy, precious metals, and real estate trusts. The foundation portfolio is largely left alone, although as with all investments it is important to check at least once in a while to make sure performance—and managers if involved—are keeping up with expectations.

The stock selections in our sister book, *The 100 Best Stocks You Can Buy*, are generally well suited for this portfolio segment—although they can be used to populate all three portfolio segments at times.

The Rotational Portfolio

The second segment, the rotational portfolio, is managed fairly actively to keep up with changes in business cycles and conditions. It is likely in a set of stocks or funds that might be rotated or remixed occasionally to reflect business conditions or to get a little more offensive or defensive.

More than the other portfolios, this portfolio follows the rotation of market preference among different kinds of businesses and business assets. The portfolio is managed to redeploy assets among market or business sectors, between aggressive and defensive business assets, from "large cap" to "small cap" companies, from companies with international exposure to those with little of same, from companies in favor versus out of favor, from stocks to bonds to commodities, and so forth. Sector-specific exchange-traded funds are a favorite component of these portfolios, as are cyclical and commodity-based stocks like gold mining stocks.

Is this about "market timing"? Let's call it "intelligent" or "educated" market timing. Studies telling us that it is impossible to effectively time market moves have been around for years. It is impossible to catch highs and lows in particular investments, market sectors, or even the market as a whole. Nobody can find exact tops or bottoms. But by watching economic indicators and the pulse of business and the marketplace, long-term market performance can be boosted by well-rationalized and timely sector rotation. The key word is "timely." The agile, active investor has enough of a finger on the pulse to see the signs and invest accordingly.

While the idea isn't new, the advent of "low-friction" exchange traded funds (ETFs) and other index portfolios makes it a lot more practical for the individual investors. (See our forthcoming *The 100 Best Exchange-Traded*

Funds You Can Buy.) What does "low-friction" mean? They trade like a single stock—one order, one discounted commission. You don't have to liquidate or acquire a whole basket full of investments on your own to follow a sector. We should note that it's been possible to rotate assets in mutual fund families for years with a single phone call, but most funds in these families are less "pure" plays in their sector, and most fund families do not cover all sectors.

The Opportunistic Portfolio

Here is where this book, *The 100 Best Aggressive Stocks You Can Buy*, is most likely to find a home.

The opportunistic portfolio is the most actively traded portion of an active, self-directed investor's total portfolio. The opportunistic portfolio looks for stocks or other investments that seem to be notably under- or overvalued at a particular time, or for more aggressive plays to boost the returns of the overall portfolio.

The opportunistic portfolio may be used to generate short-term income or cash through short-term trading, or "swing" trading, or through short-term equity option strategies. These topics are beyond our scope here. And this part of the portfolio—or if you prefer to look at it as two separate "twin peaks" on your investing "mountain"—can also be used to layer in some aggressive plays. Perhaps you allocate 20 percent of your portfolio to aggressive stock plays, to be held for a year to a few years, and another 10 percent to short-term swing trades to be held for a few days or a few weeks. It depends on the investing styles you're comfortable with, and how much time you have to manage your investments.

ARE RETIREMENT ACCOUNTS ALWAYS PART OF THE FOUNDATION?

The long-term objectives and nature of retirement accounts suggest normal inclusion as part of the foundation portfolio. In fact, retirement assets can be deployed as part of either the rotational or opportunistic portfolio. And in fact, it might make a lot of sense. Why? Because returns generated are tax free, at least until withdrawn. Tax-free returns can compound much faster. Because of the importance of these assets, one should only commit a small portion to an actively managed opportunistic portfolio, but it can be a good way to "juice" the growth of this important asset base.

Make the Time Commitment

This final investing "principle" refers more to personal strategy than investing strategy. Many otherwise-savvy investors lose it because they simply don't have the time to do the homework—the investing due diligence—to manage their portfolios, especially with the rapid changes in business and investing sentiment inherent in today's markets.

We've said all along that buying a stock is like buying a business. Anyone who owns their own business knows about the time commitment involved to manage *one* business, let alone several. The good news, though, is that you have professional management teams in place to manage each of the businesses in your portfolio. Thank goodness.

Still, now you're in the position of a Warren Buffett or some other manager of a collection of businesses or a conglomerate. You must devote some time to each. You must keep track of what each is up to, and you must be able to, usually on a moment's notice, decide whether to invest more in that business or to liquidate some or all of that business. You must keep track of all that *changes* in that business, and all that changes in the marketplace that business operates in.

That's not a simple task if you own, say, twenty different businesses in ten different industries. You'll need to put your time into it. You'll need to segment your time strategically, too: to spend the most time watching the businesses that change the most and selecting new businesses to "acquire," while letting the stable parts of your business portfolio ride. But don't let them ride too long; we all know what can happen.

We can't give you a precise formula for how much time to spend on what. But we can tell you that most investors don't spend enough time managing their portfolios. They don't evaluate companies as though they plan to buy them or own them, and they don't "come back to the trough" often enough to see what has changed. If this sounds scary, it's why many investors throw their investing over the wall to professionals and fund managers. You may choose to do this for part of your portfolio as well.

Most who seek professional help will throw their foundational portfolio components over the wall or simply buy index funds or ETFs. But you may also choose to let professionals manage your opportunistic portfolio, your *aggressive* portfolio, too. Just be aware that professionals in this space charge more and that their "follow the crowd" tendencies can really hurt in this arena.

In producing *The 100 Best Aggressive Stocks You Can Buy*, we hope to save you enough time to continue to manage this part of your investing portfolio yourself.

Selecting Stocks for the 2012 List

So now the moment you all have been waiting for. Drum roll, please. What are the *100 Best Aggressive Stocks You Can Buy*, and how did we come up with the list?

You've read a lot of philosophy and about our thought process. But how do we turn those more abstract principles and thought processes into actual stock picks? How do we come up with a list of *100 Best Aggressive* stocks out of the 10,000-plus names to choose from?

If you're looking for an instantly replicable formula or list of selection criteria, you're out of luck. Stock picking simply defies fixed formulas. As we've already discussed, companies aren't just about numbers, and the factors beyond numbers create synergies for the present and future far beyond the capability of any black box model to analyze. If that were not the case, we'd all be buying "QuickStocks" or some other magic software program, and we'd all be investing in the same stocks—and a lot of fund managers and other investment professionals would be looking at jobs.

We do use some quantitative tools to narrow down the choices for further research. Then, we simply dive into all the company, industry, and marketplace information we can get. Sure, we start with the financials. But the real test is whether or not the rest of the story shouts out "Winner!" to us. There is no way we can precisely describe to you what makes that happen. Winners have great stories. The whole is greater than the sum of the parts. Many or most of the strategic financials and strategic intangibles are positive. Beyond that, there is nothing else to say.

Stock Screens: Ya Gotta Start Somewhere

Stock screeners serve as useful filters to narrow down the list for further research. Despite the increased complexity and scope (number of variables) available with today's screeners, they will never be suitable for final picks. They will, however, whittle 10,000 companies down to 200 or 300 to look more closely at. Suffice it to say, this book would be next to impossible without them.

We used Fidelity's stock screener (the more advanced one you can get to if you have an account). But there are others out there in the Yahoo! and Google financial portals, among others.

We ran several screens—some of the canned screens like GARP (growth at a reasonable price) and "Mo Plus Grow." We also made up a few of our own. By way of illustration, here are a few of our favorite criteria:

- Market Cap: > $200M
- Share price: > $5
- Daily volume: > 50,000 shares
- Cash Flow Growth Rate: highest 20 percent of selected group
- EPS Growth Rate, projected current year vs. last year: highest 20 percent of group, or >15 percent
- EPS Growth Rate, projected next five years: highest 20 percent of group, or > 15 percent
- Price Earnings to Growth (PEG) ratio: < 2.0

These criteria were run in various combinations with each other and with certain other criteria, to build a "master" list for further research.

Incorporating Investing "Themes"

Remember the "tailwind" principle we laid out earlier? We identified a few megatrends and industries likely to benefit from them—alternative energy/energy conservation, utility/infrastructure replacement, home networking and Internet media, health care information technology, "cloud" computing infrastructure, and LED lighting and manufacturing products.

Here is a brief description of each "theme:"

- **Alternative energy/energy conservation.** The rationale and market need for products that wean us as a nation and as a people from hydrocarbon fuels is obvious. What is not so obvious is how to make money doing this. We feel we've picked some of the more rational and market tested companies in solar, smart metering technologies, and the like. It should be noted from Table 3 that the abundance of "semiconductor" companies on the list includes companies that make silicon photovoltaic panels, which technically are semiconductors, but the business emphasis is really alternative energy.
- **Utility/infrastructure replacement.** We commented earlier on the need to replace old, worn-out infrastructure, particularly in the water, sewer, and electrical grids. While strained public budgets might slow this down in the short term, we feel that these replacements will have to happen eventually. Our companies make materials or offer construction

services; some, like Digi International and Itron bring new efficiency technologies to the party.

- **Home networking and Internet media.** We feel that mass adoption of streaming entertainment media, such as on-demand movies, is just around the corner. Our companies play in the technology and media delivery in that rapidly emerging space.
- **Health care information technology.** While health care providers have been fast to adopt medical technologies (and make us all pay for them), they are way behind the curve in using IT, automated diagnostic systems, and the like to standardize and digitize patient records, care regimens, and information useful to medical professionals. It's a huge market, and prodded along by the Obama administration, this should be a strong growth area for innovative companies.
- **"Cloud" computing infrastructure.** We've all heard about it—servers and data will move out of corporate and small business data centers and into the cloud, so that companies can now purchase just the amount of IT they need, keep software up to date, keep data intact, and compute from anywhere. How all of this is going to work still hasn't been sorted out, but we've identified some key players in the development of the necessary "plumbing."
- **LED lighting and manufacturing products.** Arguably this could be a subset of alternative energy/energy conservation, but we think it is so important that it should stand alone, and we also think it hasn't received the consideration it deserves. Energy-efficient and virtually indestructible LED lighting is slowly making its way into a broad base of applications, including vehicle lights, flashlights and other portable lights, and accent lights for architectural applications. We feel this list will expand rapidly, and companies that support the manufacturing of these products will flourish. Don't you wish you had been among the first investors in the incandescent light bulb?

From this list, we either knew of or could identify at least one or two companies in each of these industries. To build a list of companies in an industry, we used tools like Google Finance. Google Finance (*www.finance.google.com*) gives a list of ten "Related Companies"; from that list, we could build a list of companies in more or less the same business. Where it made sense, we also used trade publications, articles, and various searches to fill in industry players. In some cases, such as alternative energy, we had to build a few subgroups; e.g., solar, wind, and battery technology.

It would have been nice if all of our "theme" companies also happened to be picked up by the screeners, but that only happened occasionally. Obviously if a stock fit a theme and met the screening criteria, it is a bright prospect. Beyond that, we added some (not all, in most cases) "theme" stocks to our list for further analysis.

▼ Table 2: Investing Themes

THEME: ALTERATIVE ENERGY/ENERGY CONSERVATION

Company	Symbol	Sector	Industry	Business
Brookfield Asset Management	BAM	Financial	Investment Services	Property, power, and infrastructure asset manager
Digi International	DGII	Technology	Computer Hardware	Remote monitoring and control systems, smart meters
First Solar	FSLR	Technology	Semiconductors	Thin-film PV solar modules
General Electric	GE	Financial	Consumer Financial Services	Diversified technology, media, financial services
GT Solar	SOLR	Technology	Semiconductors	PV manufacturing services and materials for solar
Johnson Controls	JCI	Consumer Cyclical	Auto and Truck Parts	Auto interiors, building energy controls, EV batteries
OM Group	OMG	Basic Materials	Chemical Manufacturing	Specialty chemicals, electrochemical energy storage
Ormat Technologies	ORA	Utilities	Electric Utilities	Geothermal power plants
Power-One	PWER	Technology	Electronic Instruments & Controls	Energy-efficient power management solutions

THEME: UTILITY, INFRASTRUCTURE REPLACEMENT

Company	Symbol	Sector	Industry	Business
Digi International	DGII	Technology	Computer Hardware	Remote monitoring and control systems, smart meters
General Electric	GE	Financial	Consumer Financial Services	Diversified technology, media, financial services
Itron	ITRI	Technology	Electronic Instruments & Controls	Metering, data collection, and software for utilities
Layne Christensen	LAYN	Capital Goods	Construction Services	Water infrastructure, mineral exploration contractor

THEME: UTILITY, INFRASTRUCTURE REPLACEMENT (continued)

Company	Symbol	Sector	Industry	Business
Nucor	NUE	Basic Materials	Iron and Steel	Steel and steel products
Valmont	VMI	Capital Goods	Construction—Supplies & Fixtures	Metal products—irrigation, utility, roadway infrastructure

THEME: HOME INTERNET MEDIA

Company	Symbol	Sector	Industry	Business
Apple	AAPL	Technology	Computer Hardware	Personal computers, mobile and digital music devices
Cirrus Logic	CRUS	Technology	Integrated Circuits	Integrated circuitry for most audio and video products
Coinstar	CSTR	Services	Recreational Products	Automated retail solutions
Entropic Communications	ENTR	Technology	Semiconductors	Home networking, connected home entertainment
Google	GOOG	Technology	Computer Services	Online search and advertising, mobile operating systems
Netflix	NFLX	Services	Broadcasting & Cable TV	DVD subscriptions, streaming Internet movies and shows
SeaChange	SEAC	Technology	Communications Equipment	Digital video equipment, content

THEME: HEALTH CARE INFORMATION TECHNOLOGY

Company	Symbol	Sector	Industry	Business
Affymetrix	AFFX	Technology	Scientific and Technical Instruments	Genetic analysis systems
HealthStream	HSTM	Technology	Computer Services	Learning tools of health care industry
McKesson	MCK	Health Care	Biotechnology and Drugs	Pharmaceutical distributor, health care management systems
Standard Register	SR	Consumer (Non-Cyclical)	Office Supplies	Business documents supplier
WebMD	WBMD	Technology	Computer Services	Online consumer, professional health information portal

THEME: CLOUD COMPUTING

Company	Symbol	Sector	Industry	Business
8x8	EGHT	Services	Communications Services	IP telephony, video, web-based conferencing
Insight Enterprises	NSIT	Technology	Computer Hardware	IT services provider, outsourcing
NetApp	NTAP	Technology	Computer Storage Devices	Enterprise network storage and data management
Radware	RDWR	Technology	Communications Equipment	Network management solutions, security
Riverbed	RVBD	Technology	Communications Equipment	Distributed computer, "cloud" products
VMware	VMW	Technology	Software and Programming	Virtualization solutions, cloud applications

THEME: LED LIGHTING AND MANUFACTURING TECHNOLOGY

Company	Symbol	Sector	Industry	Business
Brooks Automation	BRKS	Technology	Semiconductors	Semiconductor, LED manufacturing, capital equipment
Cree	CREE	Technology	Semiconductors	LED components, chips, lighting, RF products
Ultratech	UTEK	Technology	Semiconductors	Equipment for specialty manufacture—LEDs, nanotech

Testing, Testing

Using the combined list as a starting point, we researched each company further. We looked at financials, websites, company communications (press releases, annual and quarterly reports, etc.), company websites, conference call transcripts, analyst commentary, comments on forums, and trade press materials where available. We looked at research reports from Value Line, Reuters, and others. Usually we started by reading research reports from the Value Line Investing Survey where available.

We examined items on our Strategic Financials list and used the various media mentioned above to get an idea of the intangibles. We looked for sustainable success and sustainable competitive advantages throughout. We looked for that certain something, that special quality that sets the company apart from the others. All through the process, we asked ourselves whether we'd want to own the company.

About the 2012 List

From here, we will deal with results—that is, we'll talk more about the *100 Best Aggressive Stocks* list developed through our analysis. First is a summary in Tables 3 and 4 of how the companies line up by sectors and industries. Next is a list of the eighteen "crossover" stocks that appear on *both* the *100 Best* and *100 Best Aggressive* lists (Table 5), and the four stocks that *moved* from the 2011 *100 Best* list to the *100 Best Aggressive* list for this year (Table 6).

From there, in Tables 7–10, we identify our "stars"—the best of the best in building a moat to fend off completion; the best in identifying, occupying, and taking advantage of a market niche; the best innovators; and the companies with the strongest and most advantageous brands.

Finally, in Table 11, we present the complete *100 Best Aggressive Stocks You Can Buy* list.

Sectors and Industries

▼ Table 3: Sector Analysis

Sector	# of companies
Technology	40
Services	17
Basic Materials	9
Consumer Cyclical	9
Consumer Non-Cyclical	5
Health Care	5
Capital Goods	4
Energy	3
Financial	3
Transportation	2
Conglomerates	1
Utilities	1

▼ Table 4: Top 5 Industries

Industry	# of companies
Retail	11
Semiconductors	10
Software and Programming	7
Communications Equipment	5
Computer Services	5

100 Best Stocks Crossovers

Especially for those of you who have read *The 100 Best Stocks You Can Buy*, it's interesting to note the "crossover"—that is, stocks appearing on *both* lists. Obviously, stocks appearing on both lists represented some of the more aggressive choices on the standard *100 Best* list. However, while more aggressive, we feel these eighteen companies are solid enough and strong enough to make sense on both lists.

▼ Table 5: Crossovers—Companies also on *100 Best Stocks 2012* List

Company	Symbol	Category	Sector
Apple	AAPL	Technology	Computer Hardware
Bed Bath & Beyond	BBBY	Services	Retail (Specialty)
Best Buy	BBY	Services	Retail (Technology)
CarMax	KMX	Services	Retail (Specialty)
Costco	COST	Services	Retail (Warehouse Club)
Fair Isaac	FICO	Technology	Software and Programming
Google	GOOG	Technology	Computer Services
Johnson Controls	JCI	Consumer (Cyclical)	Auto and Truck Parts
McKesson	MCK	Health Care	Biotechnology and Drugs
Nike	NKE	Consumer (Cyclical)	Footwear
Nucor	NUE	Basic Materials	Iron and Steel
Oracle	ORCL	Technology	Software and Programming
Perrigo	PRGO	Health Care	Biotechnology and Drugs

▼ Table 5: Crossovers—Companies also on *100 Best Stocks 2012* List (continued)

Company	Symbol	Category	Sector
Southwest Airlines	LUV	Transportation	Airline
Starbucks	SBUX	Consumer (Non-Cyclical)	Restaurants
Target	TGT	Services	Retail (Department and Discount)
Tractor Supply	TSCO	Services	Retail (Home Improvement)
Valmont	VMI	Capital Goods	Construction—Supplies and Fixtures

100 Best Stocks Movers

When we prepared the 2011 edition of *100 Best Stocks*, we included a few companies that might have been a bit too aggressive (or pricey) to really fit that list. We were concerned, but since this book didn't exist, we had no place else to put them. Now we do, and we've moved four stocks from the 2011 *100 Best* list to the 2012 *100 Best Aggressive* list—Chipotle Mexican Grill, NetApp, Panera Bread, and Peet's Coffee & Tea. Particularly in the case of Chipotle and Panera, we think these are "best" companies still, but the recent high prices make them a bit more of a risk. They have found a better home on the *100 Best Aggressive* list.

It's interesting to note that three of the four of these movers are in the "Restaurants" sector. That isn't entirely a coincidence—with the possible exception of McDonald's and a few others, most restaurants enjoy a rapid rise in popularity, stay at the top of their game for a short time, then begin to fade as consumer tastes (or food quality) changes.

▼ Table 6: Movers—Companies Transferred from *Best Stocks 2011* List

Company	Symbol	Category	Sector
Chipotle Mexican Grill	CMG	Aggressive Growth	Restaurants
NetApp	NTAP	Aggressive Growth	Technology
Panera	PNRA	Aggressive Growth	Restaurants
Peet's	PEET	Aggressive Growth	Restaurants

The Brightest Stars in the Sky

Next, we get to one of the favorite parts of these books. People often ask us: "So you've identified the *100 Best Aggressive* stocks. That's nice, but I want to know what you think the best one is, or maybe the best five or ten. Can you share that with me?"

Short answer: no. Identifying the best of the best is a futile exercise, because things change and because different stocks or characteristics appeal to different investors. So our approach is to create "star" lists—lists of companies we feel excel in at least one important area for consideration.

Moat Stars

Moat stars, as we said earlier, are companies that have built a significant "moat" around their business. The moat serves to defend them from competition or create a gap that makes it hard for current or potential competition to enter the market or keep up. Moats can be based on technology or the use of technology (Apple, CarMax), the cost of entering the business (Alumina, Titanium Metals), or the sheer value of the brand (as in the Coke example described earlier). We didn't include brand moats here because we have a brand stars list below.

▼ Table 7: Moat Stars

Company	Symbol	Sector	Industry	Business
Alumina Ltd.	AWC	Basic Materials	Metal Mining	Holding company—aluminum refining and smelting
Apple	AAPL	Technology	Computer Hardware	Personal computers, mobile and digital music devices
Baidu	BIDU	Technology	Computer Services	Chinese Internet search provider
CarMax	KMX	Services	Retail (Specialty)	Used-car superstores
Fair Isaac	FICO	Technology	Software and Programming	Analytic software, credit-scoring services
Titanium Metals	TIE	Basic Materials	Metal Mining	Titanium metal, milled products

Niche Stars

Niche stars have identified a niche—a specialized market or customer base within a market—and have served it so well that they have come to dominate it. In turn, they can use this dominance to control price, costs, profitability, and the pace and nature of technology development. A niche may be small, and its dominator may be a small company—but it's the "800-pound gorilla" in that space. Constant Contact has a straightforward product—e-mail marketing services—but they dominate in the small business and small organization space. Chico's FAS has wisely figured out that the middle-aged professional woman was underserved, and now dominates that niche among specialty retailers. Penn Gaming has found its way into lucrative geographic niches.

Niche players, by way of dominating their niches, have built something of a moat around their businesses. But describing them as niche players gives a more complete and accurate description of their strengths.

▼ Table 8: Niche Stars

Company	Symbol	Sector	Industry	Business
Adobe	ADBE	Technology	Software and Programming	Content management and development software
Brookfield Asset Management	BAM	Financial	Investment Services	Property, power, and infrastructure asset manager
Chico's FAS	CHS	Services	Retail (Apparel)	Private brand clothing retailer, age 35+ women
Constant Contact	CTCT	Technology	Computer Services	E-mail marketing services for small businesses
Cree	CREE	Technology	Semiconductors	LED components, chips, lighting, RF products
Globe Specialty Metals	GSM	Capital Goods	Construction Supplies and Fixtures	Produces silicon metal and alloys
Layne Christensen	LAYN	Capital Goods	Construction Services	Water infrastructure, mineral exploration contractor
Mentor Graphics	MENT	Technology	Software and Programming	Hardware and software electronics design systems
Ormat Technologies	ORA	Utilities	Electric Utilities	Geothermal power plants
Penn Gaming	PENN	Services	Casinos and Gaming	Regional casinos, pari-mutuel properties

Innovation Stars

As mentioned earlier in this narrative, true innovation—as opposed to basic invention—is key for many growing businesses. Innovation is customer focused, and brings products or services to market in ways that are truly embraced by the market. Innovations may be about technology and product but also about customer service and customer experience; many companies (and many investors) forget that. CarMax has completely re-engineered the used-car buying customer experience, as has Southwest the buying tickets and flying experience. Apple, and to a lesser extent Google, have become among the most successful and recognized innovators in history.

▼ Table 9: Innovation Stars

Company	Symbol	Sector	Industry	Business
Accuray	ARAY	Health Care	Medical Equipment and Supplies	Oncology and radiology
Apple	AAPL	Technology	Computer Hardware	Personal computers, mobile and digital music devices
CarMax	KMX	Services	Retail (Specialty)	Used-car superstores
Coinstar	CSTR	Services	Recreational Products	Automated retail solutions, "Redbox"
Exact Sciences	EXAS	Health Care	Biotechnology and Drugs	Molecular diagnostics for colorectal cancer detection
Google	GOOG	Technology	Computer Services	Online search and advertising, mobile operating systems
Orbotech	ORBK	Technology	PCB Manufacturing	Design and manufacturing tools for printed circuit boards
Riverbed	RVBD	Technology	Communications Equipment	Distributed computing, "cloud" products
Southwest Airlines	LUV	Transportation	Airline	Discount air carrier

Brand Stars

Then we get to the companies that have built a good brand for themselves and have leveraged that brand to improve their experience. Good brands have good reputations with customers; those customers tend to stay loyal and pay more for a company's products or services—and they tend to do it again when the company brings something new to the marketplace. Brands are not just names, they are images, such as Tiffany's blue boxes and design simplicity and Under Armour's active and high-quality sports apparel. They become words in the language, like Kleenex, used to describe a product that may not even be theirs, as Trex has for manufactured composite decking materials.

For companies like Starbucks, the brand is probably half the company's value. Don't forget that it isn't just the companies that have brands—the products do too. Many wouldn't recognize Intuit—but they would recognize Quicken, Quickbooks, and TurboTax. Brands can have broad appeal, or they can be the end-all within a niche, as Adobe's Photoshop is to professional photographers.

▼ Table 10: Brand Stars

Company	Symbol	Sector	Industry	Business
Apple	AAPL	Technology	Computer Hardware	Personal computers, mobile and digital music devices
Google	GOOG	Technology	Computer Services	Online search and advertising, mobile operating systems
Nike	NKE	Consumer (Cyclical)	Footwear	Footwear, apparel, athletic products
Southwest Airlines	LUV	Transportation	Airline	Discount air carrier
Starbucks	SBUX	Consumer (Non-Cyclical)	Restaurants	National specialty coffee chain, coffee products
Target	TGT	Services	Retail (Department and Discount)	Discount large-format retail stores
Tiffany	TIF	Services	Retail (Specialty)	Fine jewelry manufacturer, retailer
Trex	TREX	Basic Materials	Forestry and Wood Products	Wood/plastic composite decking, railing, fencing
Under Armour	UA	Consumer (Cyclical)	Apparel/Accessories	Performance and athletic apparel

And Now, Presenting . . .

We've just about said all we can say about it, so here's the list of the *100 Best Aggressive Stocks You Can Buy.*

Good luck with your investing. We'll see you in a year or so. We'll review how these picks fared and present another list for the 2013 investing season.

Part II

THE 100 BEST AGGRESSIVE STOCKS YOU CAN BUY

The 100 Best Aggressive Stocks You Can Buy

Index of Stocks by Category

Company	Ticker	Sector	Industry	Business
8x8	EGHT	Services	Communications Services	IP telephony, video, web-based conferencing
Accuray	ARAY	Health Care	Medical Equipment and Supplies	Radiosurgical equipment and supplies
Adobe	ADBE	Technology	Software and Programming	Content management and development software
Affymetrix	AFFX	Technology	Scientific and Technical Instruments	Genetic analysis systems
Alumina Limited	AWC	Basic Materials	Metal Mining	Bauxite mining, alumina refining, and aluminum smelting
Analog Devices	ADI	Technology	Semiconductors	Analog/mixed/digital signal processing ICs
Apple	AAPL	Technology	Consumer Electronics	Personal computers, mobile and digital music devices
Arrow Electronics	ARW	Technology	Electronic Instruments and Controls	Electronic components distributor
Autoliv	ALV	Consumer Cyclical	Auto and Truck Parts	Automotive safety systems, airbag components
Baidu	BIDU	Technology	Computer Services	Chinese Internet service provider
Bed Bath & Beyond	BBBY	Services	Retail (Specialty)	Housewares and domestic retailer
Best Buy	BBY	Services	Retail (Technology)	Consumer electronics superstores
Brookfield Asset Management	BAM	Financial	Investment Services	Property, power, and infrastructure asset manager
Brooks Automation	BRKS	Technology	Semiconductors	Semiconductor, LED manufacturing capital equipment
Callaway Golf	ELY	Consumer Cyclical	Recreational Products	Golf equipment
Calumet	CLMT	Energy,	Oil and Gas Operations	Specialty petrochemicals, lubricants

Company	Ticker	Sector	Industry	Business
CarMax	KMX	Services	Retail (Specialty)	Used-car superstores
Celestica	CLS	Technology	Electronic Instruments and Controls	Contract electronics manufacturer
Celgene	CELG	Health Care	Biotechnology and Drugs	Biopharma manufacturing of cancer and immune therapy drugs
Chico's FAS	CHS	Services	Retail (Apparel)	Private brand clothing retailer, age 35+ women
Chipotle Mexican Grill	CMG	Services	Restaurants	Mexican-themed restaurants
Cirrus Logic	CRUS	Technology	Semiconductors	Application-specific circuits for audio and energy markets
Coherent	COHR	Technology	Semiconductors	Lasers, photonics products, and components
Coinstar	CSTR	Services	Recreational products	Automated retail solutions, "Redbox"
Constant Contact	CTCT	Technology	Computer Services	E-mail marketing services for small businesses
Costco	COST	Services	Retail (Warehouse Club)	Warehouse club stores
Cree	CREE	Technology	Semiconductors	LED components, chips, lighting, RF products
Deckers	DECK	Consumer Cyclical	Footwear	Footwear and accessories
Dell	DELL	Technology	Computer Hardware	Personal computers, servers, and related technology
Digi International	DGII	Technology	Computer Hardware	Remote monitoring and control systems, smart meters
Discover Financial Services	DFS	Financial	Consumer Financial Services	Credit card, payment services
Eastman Chemical	EMN	Basic Materials	Chemicals (Plastics and Rubber)	Plastics, inks, polymers, coatings, adhesives
Entropic Communications	ENTR	Technology	Semiconductors	Home networking, connected home entertainment
Exact Sciences	EXAS	Health Care	Biotechnology and Drugs	Molecular diagnostics for colorectal cancer detection
Fair Isaac	FICO	Technology	Software and Programming	Analytic software, credit-scoring services

Company	Ticker	Sector	Industry	Business
Faro Technologies, Inc.	FARO	Technology	Scientific and Technical Instruments	Three-dimensional measurement, imaging systems
First Solar	FSLR	Technology	Semiconductors	Thin-film PV solar modules
Flow Int.	FLOW	Capital Goods	Misc. Capital Goods	Waterjet cutting, cleaning, surface prep solutions
General Electric	GE	Financial	Consumer Financial Services	Diversified technology, media, financial services
General Motors	GM	Consumer Cyclical	Auto and Truck Manufacturers	Auto and truck manufacturing, financing
Globe Specialty Metals	GSM	Capital Goods	Construction Supplies and Fixtures	Produces silicon metal and alloys
Google	GOOG	Technology	Computer Services	Online search and advertising, mobile operating systems
GT Solar	SOLR	Technology	Semiconductors	PV manufacturing services and materials for solar
HealthStream	HSTM	Technology	Computer Services	Learning tools for health care industry
Hecla Mining	HL	Basic Materials	Gold and Silver	Silver, gold, lead, zinc mining
Insight Enterprises	NSIT	Technology	Computer Hardware	IT services provider, outsourcing
Intuit	INTU	Technology	Software and Programming	Accounting and tax software for small business, consumers
Itron	ITRI	Technology	Electronic Instruments and Controls	Metering, data collection, and software for utilities
JetBlue Airways	JBLU	Transportation	Airline	Discount air carrier
Johnson Controls	JCI	Consumer Cyclical	Auto and Truck Parts	Auto interiors, building energy controls, EV batteries
Layne Christensen	LAYN	Capital Goods	Construction Services	Water infrastructure, mineral exploration contractor
Lufkin	LUFK	Energy	Oil Well Services & Equipment	Oil field, power transmission systems
McKesson	MCK	Health Care	Biotechnology and Drugs	Pharmaceutical distributor, health care management systems

Company	Ticker	Sector	Industry	Business
Mentor Graphics	MENT	Technology	Software and Programming	Hardware and software electronics design systems
MetroPCS	PCS	Services	Communication Services	Paid-in-advance wireless services provider
Motorola Mobility Solutions	MMI	Technology	Communications Equipment	Wireless handsets, accessories, entertainment devices
NetApp	NTAP	Technology	Computer Storage Devices	Enterprise network storage and data management
Netflix	NFLX	Services	Broadcasting and Cable TV	DVD subscriptions, streaming Internet movies and shows
Nike	NKE	Consumer Cyclical	Footwear	Footwear, apparel, athletic products
Nucor	NUE	Basic Materials	Iron and Steel	Steel and steel products
OM Group	OMG	Basic Materials	Chemical Manufacturing	Specialty chemicals, electrochemical energy storage
Oracle	ORCL	Technology	Software and Programming	Enterprise database and application software, systems
Orbotech	ORBK	Technology	PCB Manufacturing	High-precision tools
Ormat Technologies	ORA	Utilities	Electric Utilities	Geothermal power plants
Overstock.com	OSTK	Services	Retail (Catalog and Mail Order)	Online retailer, closeout, and discount merchandise
PACCAR	PCAR	Consumer Cyclical	Auto and Truck Manufacturers	Light, medium, and heavy-duty trucks
Panasonic	PC	Consumer Cyclical	Audio and Video Equipment	Consumer and industrial electronic products
Peet's	PEET	Consumer Non-Cyclical	Restaurants	Specialty coffee roaster stores
Penn National Gaming	PENN	Services	Casinos and Gaming	Regional casinos, pari-mutuel properties
The Pep Boys—Manny, Moe & Jack	PBY	Services	Retail (Specialty)	Auto parts manufacturer
Perrigo	PRGO	Health Care	Biotechnology and Drugs	Generic prescription pharmaceuticals, active ingredients

Company	Ticker	Sector	Industry	Business
Power Integrations	POWI	Technology	Semiconductors	High-voltage ICs for power supplies
Power-One	PWER	Technology	Electronic Instruments and Controls	Energy-efficient power management solutions
Powerwave	PWAV	Technology	Communications Equipment	Wireless communications network devices
Radware	RDWR	Technology	Communications Equipment	Network management solutions, security
Red Hat	RHT	Technology	Software and Programming	Linux operating system services
Riverbed	RVBD	Technology	Communications Equipment	Distributed computing, "cloud" products
SanDisk	SNDK	Technology	Computer Storage Devices	Storage devices, memory cards
Schnitzer Steel	SCHN	Basic Materials	Iron and Steel	Ferrous and nonferrous scrap recycler
SeaChange	SEAC	Technology	Communications Equipment	Digital video systems, content
Smithfield Foods	SFD	Consumer Non-Cyclical	Food Processing	Fresh and packaged meat products
Southwest Airlines	LUV	Transportation	Airline	Discount air carrier
Standard Register	SR	Consumer Non-Cyclical	Office Supplies	Business documents supplier
Starbucks	SBUX	Consumer Non-Cyclical	Restaurants	National specialty coffee chain, coffee products
Target	TGT	Services	Retail (Department and Discount)	Discount large-format retail stores
Temple-Inland	TIN	Basic Materials	Paper and Paper Products	Corrugated paper products, building materials
Textron	TXT	Conglomerates	Conglomerates	Aircraft, helicopters, defense, industrial businesses
Tiffany	TIF	Retail	Retail (Specialty)	Fine jewelry manufacturer, retailer
Titanium Metals	TIE	Basic Materials	Metal Mining	Titanium metal, miller products
Tractor Supply	TSCO	Services	Retail (Home Improvement)	Large-format retail farm and ranch stores

Company	Ticker	Sector	Industry	Business
Trex	TREX	Basic Materials	Forestry and Wood Products	Wood/plastic composite decking, railing, fencing
TTMI Technologies	TTMI	Technology	Electronic Instruments and Controls	Specialty printed circuit boards for defense, others
Ultratech	UTEK	Technology	Semiconductors	Equipment for specialty manufacture—LEDs, nanotech
Under Armour	UA	Consumer Cyclical	Apparel/Accessories	Performance and athletic apparel
Valero	VLO	Energy	Oil and Gas Operations	Refiner, marketer, retail gas stations
Valmont	VMI	Capital Goods	Construction—Supplies and Fixtures	Metal products—irrigation, utility, roadway infrastructure
VMWare	VMW	Technology	Software and Programming	Virtualization solutions, "cloud" applications
WebMD	WBMD	Technology	Computer Services	Online consumer, professional health information portal
Western Digital	WDC	Technology	Computer Storage Devices	Computer, digital video hard drives
Whole Foods Market	WFMI	Services	Retail (Grocery)	Natural and organic foods supermarkets

AGGRESSIVE GROWTH

8x8, Inc.

Ticker symbol: EGHT (NASDAQ) ❑ S&P rating: NA ❑ Value Line financial strength rating: NA ❑ Current yield: Nil

Who Are They?

It is a relatively small company with a very unusual name. It provides point-to-point and cloud-based telephony, Internet-based video communications, and IT services to consumers and businesses. It has been around longer than one might assume, given its relatively small size (242 employees) and revenues ($63 million in 2010). The company was founded in 1987, went public in 1997, and has been unprofitable until this past year, when it earned $4 million.

The company originally was established as a supplier of IP telephone services, back when Skype, Vonage, and others were also just getting started. At the time, voiceover-IP was competing mainly with POTS (plain-old-telephone-service) providers, so the list of features was fairly spartan. 8x8's telephony product line now, however, is broad and deep with very sophisticated functionality. Its target market is still the small to medium business, but the services available are well beyond what was available even ten years ago.

By the way, the name 8x8 refers to a technical aspect of video data compression (as if you didn't already know).

Why Should I Care?

For most of 8x8's history as a public company, it was supplying chips and software to the VoIP market. It later entered the consumer VoIP market with a service called Packet8. This market turned into a race to the bottom with the entry of a number of large players. Recently the company has focused its efforts on the small-to-medium business market and has found real opportunity, to say nothing of some earnings. As the company exits the residential market, some of the losses in residential are masking earnings in the commercial market. We believe the commercial gains will become more apparent soon, as comparisons to Vonage's residential business tend to show 8x8 in a more favorable light. 8x8 spends $825 to acquire each subscriber but collects $200 per month, for a four-month payback. The corresponding numbers at Vonage show an eight-month payback. 8x8 has also bettered Vonage's operating margins: Where both companies had 65 percent operating margins in 2009, 8x8's most recent four quarters have produced a 68 percent margin, while Vonage is still at 65 percent. 8x8 will have positive earnings again in 2011, whereas Vonage has yet to make a profit.

Key to the company's success are the "net neutrality" discussions taking place in the halls of the FCC and elsewhere. Net neutrality refers to a condition wherein the operators of a particular branch of the Internet infrastructure allows all traffic to pass without impediment, regardless of the type of traffic, its source, or destination. Smaller service providers such as 8x8 compete directly with companies like AT&T, which also happens to operate large portions of the Internet, including the critical "last mile," the length of wire between the customer and the branch exchange. If an ISP such as AT&T is permitted to block, throttle, or apply fees to time-critical data (such as telephony), the consequences for smaller competitors such as 8x8 could be dire. In the two major court cases that have touched on this issue, the rulings have been in favor of a neutral approach.

How's Business?

Good. The company should close FY2011 with nearly $6 million in earnings on nearly $70 million in revenue. That's a 50 percent increase in earnings for a 10 percent bump in revenue—pretty good leverage. Its client base increased approximately 15 percent during 2010 and churn (cancellation divided by client base) fell half a percent to 2.2 percent.

Upside

- Positive earnings momentum
- Exiting costly consumer market
- Superior small business offerings

Downside

- Nearest competitor is ten times its size
- Regulatory uncertainty risk
- Volume sensitivity of earnings

Just the Facts

INDUSTRY: **Communications Services**
BETA COEFFICIENT: **1.66**
5-YEAR COMPOUND EARNINGS-PER-SHARE GROWTH: **NA**

		2006	2007	2008	2009	2010
Revenues (Mil)		31.9	53.1	61.7	64.7	63.4
Net Income (Mil)		(-23.3)	(-9.93)	0.03	(-2.5)	3.88
Price:	high	2.04	1.67	1.26	1.60	3.15
	low	0.70	0.86	0.42	0.45	1.17

8x8, Inc.
810 Maude Avenue
Sunnyvale, CA 94085
(408) 727-1885
Website: ***www.8x8.com***

AGGRESSIVE GROWTH

Accuray Inc.

Ticker symbol: ARAY (NASDAQ) ❑ S&P rating: NA ❑ Value Line financial strength rating: NA ❑ Current yield: Nil

Who Are They?

Accuray is a technology leader in the radiation therapy market, specifically in the area of radiosurgery. The company's products provide a non-invasive, non-surgical treatment option for cancers and other tumors in areas difficult to treat surgically. Its flagship product, the CyberKnife system, destroys targeted tissues through the application of energetic particles (electrons, in this case) from a device outside the patient's body. No surgery or anesthetic is required for the procedure (although you might need a drink or two when you get the bill), and recovery time is negligible.

The company was founded by a team of Stanford researchers in 1990. The first approval for the system's use was in Japan in 1996; FDA approval came in 1999. The company completed its IPO in 2007.

Why Should I Care?

Once used almost exclusively for cranial procedures (brain tumors, basically), the CyberKnife system is now approved for the treatment of tumors anywhere in the body, including the spine, lung, prostate, liver, and pancreas. These "extra-cranial" applications represent over half of all CyberKnife procedures and are the fastest growing area for the current installed base of over 200 machines.

There are other radiation treatment products on the market, most of them made by much larger companies. What sets the CyberKnife product apart is its positioning system, which relies on radiological data to initially map the tumor and then to compensate in real-time for any movement of the tumor due to the patient's breathing or pulse. The robotic positioning system is unique in that it allows the electron source to be moved into almost any position with respect to the patient.

The accuracy of the positioning is critical to the success of the procedure. Most radiation treatments have to use a relatively low dosage in order to minimize damage to adjacent healthy structures. The accuracy of the CyberKnife's positioning system allows for the application of a much higher and far more effective dosage. Because each dosage is so much higher, the CyberKnife procedure typically requires just one to five separate treatments, whereas conventional radiation procedures can require thirty to forty separate patient visits.

And whereas most radiation treatments are used as a follow-up or an adjunct to surgery, the CyberKnife procedure can often be used to replace conventional surgery.

How's Business?

The results from second quarter 2011 were encouraging. Income beat expectations, and although revenue dipped to $54.2 million, the company reaffirmed its outlook for $210–$225 million for the fiscal year. Gross margins rose 900 basis points year-to-year as operating expenses declined significantly, and the company ended the quarter with $152 million in cash and equivalents, with no debt. On the down side, the company's inability to deliver against backlog in a timely fashion resulted in the cancellation of four orders.

The company announced in March that it plans to acquire a smaller rival in the radiation therapy system market, TomoTherapy Inc., for $277 million in a cash and stock deal. TomoTherapy's 2010 revenues were just over $180 million. Accuray's CEO anticipates cost synergies of $15–$25 million per year in the companies' combined operations, and expects EPS accretion beginning in July 2012.

Upside

- R&D is well funded
- $410 million in backlog
- Profitable

Downside

- Aging backlog
- TomoTherapy purchase could be burdensome
- Barely profitable

Just the Facts

INDUSTRY: **Medical Equipment & Supplies**
BETA COEFFICIENT: **1.15**
5-YEAR COMPOUND EARNINGS-PER-SHARE GROWTH: **NA**

		2006	2007	2008	2009	2010
Revenues (Mil)		—	141	210	234	222
Net Income (Mil)		—	(-5.6)	5.4	0.6	2.84
Price:	high	—	29.3	17.8	8.0	7.5
	low	—	13.2	4.1	4.1	5.9

Accuray, Inc.
1310 Chesapeake Terrace
Sunnyvale, CA 94089
(408) 716-4600
Website: ***www.accuray.com***

AGGRESSIVE GROWTH

Adobe Systems, Inc.

Ticker symbol: ADBE (NASDAQ) ❑ S&P rating: BBB+ ❑ Value Line financial strength rating: A+ ❑ Current yield: Nil

Who Are They?

Adobe Systems develops computer software used for the creation and printing of images and documents. It also develops tools to assist in the creation and support of websites of all sizes and types. Its products are used on desktops, servers, and mobile devices by developers, consumers, and enterprises for creating, managing, and delivering content across multiple operating systems, devices, and media.

Products include the Creative Suite, for the production of print and web-based designs, websites, and high-end video; the Acrobat line, for the creation and editing of cross-platform, visually complex documents; the Photoshop family, used in the production and manipulation of still and video images; the Online Marketing suite, which allows users to track and characterize the performance and usage patterns of a monitored Internet website; and Flash, an application programming interface that allows for the delivery of content across multiple platforms with one content development effort.

Adobe's products are sold through its own sales channel and through a network of independent retailers, OEMs, VARs, and system integrators. Its software is also licensed through hardware manufacturers, software developers, and service providers.

Why Should I Care?

You have to acknowledge any company whose product name has become a verb. Xerox, FedEx, and now Photoshop are all part of our daily lexicon as legitimate substitutes for "copy," "send," and "Dude, make me look like George Clooney." Several of Adobe's products, in fact, have achieved ubiquity in our modern technical life. Photoshop is the most popular image processing software in the world; Flash is the most widely used multimedia platform for personal computers; Acrobat is the most widely used document viewing platform for personal computers; and its PDF format is by far the most widely used document distribution and printing format in the world.

Adobe has been around so long and has been so successful at what it does that many people no longer associate the products with the company but rather assume that PDF and Flash just "are" (in fact, PDF has recently moved into the public domain and is now an ISO standard). Adobe has taken pains in recent years to make sure its brand is closely associated with the products it develops and supports (such as the name change from Acrobat Reader to Adobe Reader), and it's a move we applaud.

As a software company, Adobe's incremental revenues are highly leveraged. In the first quarter of FY2011, for example, revenues increased a modest 9 percent over the previous year. Earnings for the same period, however, grew 45 percent with no extraordinary financial events skewing the results. This is a very good ratio on incremental revenues, and the second quarter of 2011 is on track to produce even more dramatic results.

How's Business?

The company is rebounding extremely well from a weak 2009 with numbers in 2010 that exceeded expectations, with particular strength in the fourth quarter. The 2011 per share earnings should be as much as 20 percent higher than the company's previous record high. Growth in Japan, the company's second-largest geographic market, has been negatively affected somewhat by the problems there.

Upside

- Recent acquisitions contributing quickly
- Good financials for more acquisitions
- Highly regarded products

Downside

- Dominant market share reduces potential for growth
- Creative Suite may be overdue for a refresh
- No native support for Flash on iPhone

Just the Facts

INDUSTRY: **Software and Programming**

BETA COEFFICIENT: **1.20**

5-YEAR COMPOUND EARNINGS-PER-SHARE GROWTH: **12.5%**

		2006	2007	2008	2009	2010
Revenues (Mil)		2,575	3,158	3,580	2,946	3,800
Net Income (Mil)		506	724	872	387	775
Price:	high	43.2	48.5	46.4	38.2	37.8
	low	26.0	37.2	19.5	15.7	25.5

Adobe Systems, Inc.
345 Park Avenue
San Jose, CA 95110-2704
(408) 536-6000
Website: ***www.adobe.com***

AGGRESSIVE GROWTH

Affymetrix

Ticker symbol: AFFX (NASDAQ) ❑ S&P rating: NA ❑ Value Line financial strength rating: B ❑ Current yield: Nil

Who Are They?

Affymetrix develops, manufactures, and markets consumables and systems for genetic analysis in the life sciences and clinical health care markets. It also sells analysis services using its own equipment. The company's GeneChip system and related microarray technology is used to acquire, analyze, and manage complex genetic information. These products are used mainly as tools to better understand the role of genetic factors in disease and the effectiveness and safety of therapies.

The GeneChip system cleverly integrates semiconductor fabrication techniques and common laboratory chemical processes to produce a single "chip" with as many as 500,000 test sites on its surface. This chip (it is not an electronic device, but rather a passive array of chemical structures), which is a consumable in the test process, is the company's revenue mainstay, consistently accounting for over 80 percent of its annual sales.

The company sells its products directly to pharmaceutical, biotechnology, agrichemical, diagnostics, and consumer products companies as well as academic research centers, government research laboratories, private foundation laboratories, and clinical reference laboratories in North America and Europe. The company also sells some of its products through authorized distributors in Latin America, India, the Middle East, and Asia-Pacific regions, including China.

Why Should I Care?

Affymetrix was once one of the shining stars of the genomics research market, but it fell on hard times and has been languishing while rivals such as Illumina have grown to many times Affymetrix's size. So why is Affymetrix in this book and not one of the other players? Well, for one thing, Affymetrix isn't trading at multiples approaching 100, like some of its rivals. Yes, it is losing money at the moment, but 2011 is expected to be profitable, and its share price is in the mid-single digits, so it will actually *have* a multiple soon. This is one of the reasons we like it—a company that's turned itself around has demonstrated that it has a plan for success.

Affymetrix's plan includes the development of new markets, such as the personal DNA scanning market. In this business, individuals pay up to $1,000 each for a DNA scan for various genetic markers indicative of hereditary diseases. This is a service that has been doing well as of late, and Affymetrix has already signed up a screening customer for its hardware. Another area of focus is the routine testing and validation businesses, which management feels will grow faster than the overall research market in 2011–2012. The company is also expanding its product line into cancer assays, with new tools for pathologists and oncologists.

Lastly, the company has retired significant portions of its debt and has reduced expenses and manufacturing costs for its highest volume products.

How's Business?

The company's first quarter 2011 was encouraging. Revenues were down 10 percent versus 2010, but cost of goods sold fell 18 percent, leading to a bump in gross margins from 61 percent to 65 percent. Expenses fell 13 percent, as well. An increase in gross margins in the face of declining revenue is a very good sign for profitability when sales pick up.

Upside

- Share price is fully laundered
- Product interest in China
- New products in pipeline despite downturn

Downside

- Promise of technology not quite fulfilled
- Some revenue tied to NIH funding
- Certain key components are sole-sourced

Just the Facts

INDUSTRY: **Scientific & Technical Instruments**
BETA COEFFICIENT: **1.35**
5-YEAR COMPOUND EARNINGS-PER-SHARE GROWTH: —

		2006	2007	2008	2009	2010
Revenues (Mil)		355	371	320	327	311
Net Income (Mil)		(-2.1)	24.5	(-32.2)	(-23.9)	(-10.2)
Price:	high	48.0	32.0	23.8	10.1	8.4
	low	17.5	20.0	2.0	1.8	3.8

Affymetrix, Inc.
3420 Central Expressway
Santa Clara, CA 95051
(408) 731-5000
Website: ***www.affymetrix.com***

AGGRESSIVE GROWTH

Alumina Limited

Ticker symbol: AWC (NYSE) ❑ S&P rating: NA ❑ Value Line financial strength rating: NA ❑ Current yield: 2.7%

Who Are They?

Alumina Limited holds investments worldwide in bauxite mining, alumina refining, and aluminum smelting through its 40 percent ownership of Alcoa World Alumina & Chemicals (AWAC). With a production capacity of over 17 million tons per year, AWAC is the world's largest alumina business, representing approximately 17 percent of the world's alumina production. Alumina is the primary raw material used in the production of aluminum and has uses as an abrasive/polishing material, a chemical catalyst, and as filler in plastics.

Alumina Limited is based in Victoria, Australia, and was formed in 2002 in a de-merger from Western Mining Corporation. Its shares trade on the NYSE as American Depository Receipts (ADRs).

The company itself has no employees or production facilities, but is simply a board of directors who represent a 40 percent share of AWAC and advise Alcoa on behalf of AWC shareholders.

Why Should I Care?

Other than playing the futures market or buying raw aluminum billet, this may be the purest play on aluminum in the world. AWAC does not produce foil or other processed raw aluminum, nor does it produce castings or other follow-on aluminum products. It mines ore, refines it into alumina, and smelts the alumina into aluminum. A very small percentage of the raw alumina is sold into other markets, but by far the largest use is for aluminum production. During the recent financial crisis, however, that focus came back to haunt AWC, as the rapid and steep fall-off in industrial production led to greatly reduced demand for all commodities, particularly steel and aluminum. Aluminum, for example, is now trading in the range of $2,500 per ton, but at its low point it 2009 it was trading for just over $1,200 per ton. Production facilities around the world had been idled. The good news is that in early 2011, Alcoa has decided to restart three of its larger aluminum smelters in order to meet anticipated demand, and these facilities will require between 200,000 and 400,000 metric tons of alumina per year.

Although aluminum prices and aluminum demand are back to nearly pre-crash levels, AWC's stock price is still lagging. In May 2008, it was trading in the $20–$30 range, but in March 2011 it could be had for less than $9 per share.

How's Business?

While coal, steel, and aluminum prices have already firmed up as the economic recovery picks up steam, some commodity plays (like AWC) are still relatively cheap. Global demand for alumina is projected to increase 12 percent in 2011, in part due to rising demand from independent smelters, including many in China. This should return AWAC alumina production to near-peak output levels, last achieved in 2008.

Upside

- Stock is trading at all-time low in a growth economy
- Chinese demand still strong
- Two new mines coming on-line

Downside

- Full recovery expected to be a year away
- New Brazilian refinery costlier than anticipated
- High volatility versus market

Just the Facts

INDUSTRY: **Metal Mining**

BETA COEFFICIENT: **2.0**

5-YEAR COMPOUND EARNINGS-PER-SHARE GROWTH: **-43.4%**

		2006	2007	2008	2009	2010
Revenues (Mil)*		—	2.8	3.9	20.4	1.4
Net Income (Mil)		511	436	168	(-26.0)	34.6
Price:	high	24.4	29.9	24.7	7.2	10.3
	low	18.0	19.0	2.7	2.5	5.4

Alumina Limited
GPO Box 5411, Melbourne
Victoria 3001 Australia
61 03 8699 2600
Website: ***www.aluminalimited.com***

**Note—as these are ADRs, income is correct, but revenues shown are not reflective of operations.*

AGGRESSIVE GROWTH

Analog Devices, Inc.

Ticker symbol: ADI (NYSE) ❑ S&P rating: A- ❑ Value Line financial strength rating: A+ ❑ Current yield: 2.2%

Who Are They?

Analog Devices designs, manufactures, and markets high-performance analog, mixed-signal, and digital signal processing chips used in a multitude of electronic equipment. It does not make large-scale microprocessors, discrete digital logic, or memory but concentrates instead in the area of real-time signal processing (both analog and digital), front-end signal acquisition, conversion, and amplification. Its high value-add components find their way into products such as medical imaging equipment, cellular base stations, digital cameras and televisions, industrial process controls, defense electronics, factory automation systems, and automobiles. In all, the company derives nearly half its revenue from the industrial market, with communications, automotive, and consumer markets accounting for the other half. The company has a small and declining business in the computer market. It makes thousands of products, with the ten highest revenue products in total accounting for just under 9 percent of revenues.

The company fabricates many of its own analog parts at either of its two fabs, located in Massachusetts and Limerick, Ireland. ADI also employs third-part suppliers (primarily TSMC in Taiwan) for fabrication of its sub-micron CMOS die. The company closed its wafer fabrication facility in Massachusetts at the end of fiscal 2009 and now sources its blank wafers from third parties.

Why Should I Care?

Analog chip suppliers tend to hold design wins and customers for the life of a customer's product. In critical circuits, in particular, products are designed with the characteristics of key components in mind, and a change of suppliers for those key components often necessitates a redesign or a re-spec of the final product. For this reason, ADI's earnings are quite a bit more reliable than that of the suppliers of commodity ICs.

Fab ownership is a double-edged sword. If the fab is not fully utilized during a down cycle in the economy, the higher fixed costs lead to lower operating margins. As someone once said, "It's like owning a bunch of elephants—you can get a lot of work done, but they have to eat." During an up cycle, however, you're paying yourself rather than someone else to build your dies, effectively capturing what would have gone out the door to a vendor. In the end, fabs are nearly always a net positive if kept fully utilized. Owning the fab also means you can control and modify its operation very specifically to get the most out of your product designs. This is a real benefit to a maker of analog parts, as fab tuning for analog processes tends to be as much art as it is science.

How's Business?

The company recently announced the offering of $375 million in notes at 3 percent, with payments representing roughly 8 percent of 2011 cash flow through 2016. The company has very little debt and the share base has already declined by 20 percent over the last five years, so we think it's safe to assume ADI is going shopping. Likely targets might include companies with unique high-voltage IP for the energy management field.

Upside

- Strong margins
- Healthy(ier) automotive sector
- Captive fab capacity

Downside

- Communications sector still in recovery
- Top-line growth only moderate
- TI purchase of NatSemi bodes ill for ADI bargain hunters

Just the Facts

INDUSTRY: **Semiconductors**
BETA COEFFICIENT: **0.90**
5-YEAR COMPOUND EARNINGS-PER-SHARE GROWTH: **7.5%**

		2006	2007	2008	2009	2010
Revenues (Mil)		2,573	2,511	2,583	2,015	2,762
Net Income (Mil)		533	474	525	285	712
Price:	high	41.5	41.1	36.3	31.9	38.6
	low	26.1	30.2	15.3	17.8	26.3

Analog Devices, Inc.
One Technology Way
Norwood, MA 02062-9106
(781) 329-4700
Website: *www.analog.com*

AGGRESSIVE GROWTH

Apple Inc.

Ticker symbol: AAPL (NASDAQ) ❑ S&P rating: not rated ❑ Value Line financial strength rating: A++ ❑ Current yield: NA

Who Are They?

Apple Inc. designs, manufactures, and markets personal computers, portable music players, cell phones, and related software, peripherals, and services. It sells these products through its retail stores, online stores, and third-party and value-added resellers. The company also sells a variety of third-party compatible products such as printers, storage devices, and other accessories through its online and retail stores and digital content through its iTunes store.

The company's products have become household names: The iPad, iPhone, iPod, and MacBook are just some of the company's hardware products. And while the software may be less well known, iTunes, QuickTime, and OSX are important segments of the business, each with their own revenue streams.

The company was incorporated in 1977 as Apple Computer but has since changed its name to simply Apple Inc. The name change in 2007 was the last step in a ten-year retooling that had already changed the company from a personal computer also-ran into one of the most recognizable and profitable consumer electronics brands in the world.

Why Should I Care?

It's hard to imagine the current consumer tech landscape without Apple's presence at the top of the heap. Its iconic products have become so successful and its marketing so ubiquitous that if the company didn't exist, it seems that we would have to invent something very much like it to fill in the void. Its product line, while comparatively narrow, is focused on areas where the user interface is highly valued, and Apple has leveraged this focus on the user experience into a business that is far and away the most profitable in the industry.

Enhancing the user experience is the industrial design. The Apple design ethic is extraordinarily well executed and is a large part of the value proposition for every product they release. Many of Apple's customers are uncomfortable with any tech product *not* designed around the company's common content management interface. This overall focus on the user experience has been instrumental in creating an extremely loyal customer base and a brand cachet unequaled in the consumer electronics business. Apple was able to weather the downturn in consumer spending so well in part because many of its customers will forgo other expenditures in order to afford their next Apple purchase.

How's Business?

For the past five years, Apple has been the 800-pound gorilla of the consumer electronics space. Scratch that—it has been King Kong. Since 2006, revenues have more than tripled and profit has increased over seven-fold. While we here at *100 Best* tend to look favorably on a company that increases its margin by 20–30 basis points per year, Apple, over the five-year period, has increased its net margin by over 1,250 basis points (an average of 250 points per year).

How are they doing this? A look at the cell phone market tells the story. The iPhone launched in mid-2006 and has grown market share at a fairly steady pace, to the point where it now constitutes 3 percent of the total market unit share. What does this rather modest market share contribute to the bottom line? Merely 65 percent of all handset profits worldwide. That's right—with only 3 percent of the market, the iPhone's earnings before interest and tax (EBIT) dollars exceed the entire rest of the market by nearly a factor of two.

That's the power of user-centric design. That's the power of cool.

Upside

- Extremely strong brand and reputation
- Excellent, customer-centered innovation
- Continuing sales model through iTunes, apps, etc.

Downsides

- Everyone has them in their sights
- High stock price and valuation
- Steve Jobs health concerns

Just the Facts

INDUSTRY: **Consumer Electronics**

BETA COEFFICIENT: **1.05**

5-YEAR COMPOUND EARNINGS-PER-SHARE GROWTH: **70%**

	2006	2007	2008	2009	2010
Revenues (Mil)	19,315	24,006	32,479	36,537	65,225
Net Income (Mil)	1,989	3,496	4,834	5,704	14,013
Price: high	93.2	203	200.3	214	326.7
low	50.2	81.9	79.1	78.2	190.3

Apple Inc.
1 Infinite Loop
Cupertino, CA 95014
(408) 996-1010
Website: ***www.apple.com***

AGGRESSIVE GROWTH

Arrow Electronics

Ticker symbol: ARW (NYSE) ❑ S&P rating: BBB- ❑ Value Line financial strength rating: B+ ❑ Current yield: Nil

Who Are They?

New York–based Arrow Electronics is one of the world's largest distributors of electronic components and computing products. The company sources products from over 1,200 suppliers and distributes them to over 115,000 customers through its 340 locations across fifty-two countries and territories. Arrow also employs sales representatives who sell in the field and by telephone. The customer base includes original equipment manufacturers (OEMs), contract manufacturers (CMs), value-added resellers (VARs), and other commercial users. The company's products are primarily targeted at the industrial sector: typically, companies manufacturing computing, telecom, automotive, aerospace, and scientific and medical devices. ARW has a broad customer base, with no single customer generating more than 2 percent of the total sales. Competition comes from other electronics product distributors such as Avnet, Bell Microproducts, AVX Corporation, and Future Electronics.

Arrow operates two business segments, differentiated by product type: Electronic Components and Enterprise Computing Solutions. The Electronic Components segment supplies all of the lower-level components used to build circuits, to build circuits into assemblies, and to build assemblies into products. They also sell tools, test equipment, and embedded solutions for integrated products. The Enterprise Computing Solutions segment supplies computing hardware, software, training, and other services directed at the IT professional, and the software and systems development markets.

In 2010, approximately half the company's products were sold into the Americas, and the Components segment accounted for 70 percent of sales. Supporting these sales is a sophisticated global inventory system that the company claims provides real-time visibility to inventory levels at any location, anywhere in the world.

Why Should I Care?

As a supplier to such a broad market with a very large customer base, Arrow is a reliable bellwether for the industrial sector as a whole. When Arrow is selling, everyone is building. Consequently, Arrow tends not to have one or two good quarters in a row, but rather several good years in a row as industrial growth cycles ramp up, sustain, and wind down over longer periods of time.

Since April 2010, Arrow has acquired no fewer than eleven companies in North America, Europe, and Asia. All of these acquisitions are supplementary to its current businesses; acquisition is a very common practice in the distribution business, and Arrow's growth plans often require a purchase in order to get access to specific lines, geographies, or customers. The resources the company can bring to bear in down-market cycles should not be discounted—Arrow can spread like wildfire, particularly when the smaller firms are gasping for air.

The company's most recent acquisitions have been higher value-add service-based companies that still provide opportunities for sell-through of Arrow's lines. We like this move as a business multiplier and as a way to improve the quality of the cash flow.

How's Business?

Arrow's first quarter 2011 results were very encouraging. The company turned in record first-quarter sales ($5.22 billion), income ($136 million), and per share earnings ($1.18) and gave guidance for further record performance in the second quarter, with strong year-to-year growth. The company is well positioned for both acquisitions and organic growth over the next two years.

Upside

- Recovery on track at Arrow
- Shares are still reasonably priced
- Big fish in a big pond

Downside

- Acquisitions always chew up some capital
- Attractive takeover target
- Price could move up quickly

Just the Facts

INDUSTRY: **Electronic Instruments & Controls**
BETA COEFFICIENT: **1.15**
5-YEAR COMPOUND EARNINGS-PER-SHARE GROWTH: **12.5%**

		2006	2007	2008	2009	2010
Revenues (Mil)		13,577	15,985	16,761	14,684	18,745
Net Income (Mil)		361	408	356	202	494
Price:	high	36.9	44.9	39.4	30.1	35.0
	low	25.9	32.0	11.7	15.0	21.8

Arrow Electronics, Inc.
50 Marcus Drive
Melville, NY 11747
(631) 847-2000
Website: ***www.arrow.com***

AGGRESSIVE GROWTH

Autoliv

Ticker symbol: ALV (NYSE) ❑ S&P rating: BBB+ ❑ Value Line financial strength rating: B++ ❑ Current yield: 2.3%

Who Are They?

Autoliv, Inc., is the world leader in automotive safety systems. It develops and builds systems in-house for all the major automotive manufacturers. Together with its joint ventures, Autoliv has eighty facilities with nearly 43,000 employees in twenty-eight vehicle-producing countries. The company also has ten technical centers and twenty-one test tracks in nine countries around the world.

The company produces passenger safety devices such as seat belts, airbags, and steering and night vision systems, in addition to equipment for specialized applications. The bulk of its production is in restraints (seatbelts and airbags), where it is far and away the leading supplier, with just over one-third of this $18 billion market. Autoliv invented the side airbag and still has 40 percent of this market worldwide. Europe and North America are its two largest markets, followed by Japan and China. The company's top five customers account for just over half of 2010 sales, with the rest going to more than two dozen customers.

Why Should I Care?

Frontal airbags reduce driver and passenger deaths in frontal impacts by 20–30 percent and have been mandated in many markets where they're in use. These volumes are not going away as long as there's a demand for automobiles, and the volumes reduce the costs for follow-on products such as side curtain and rear passenger airbags. Customer demand for airbags has increased significantly; in 2005 the average number of airbags per vehicle was just over one, but in 2013 it is expected to be 2.8 per vehicle, and total airbag demand for 2013 will be five times higher than that of 2008.

Automobile and truck production in the rest of the world (outside of North America, Europe, and Japan) now makes up 18 percent of the global market. Autoliv has been well positioned there and as a result has seen its shipments increase 300 percent to the region. It expects further growth in market share in the region as its two major rivals (TRW and Takata) have a minor presence there. In 2010, the company grew sales 60 percent in China and began construction of a completely new manufacturing facility, doubling the size of the older plant it replaces.

Autoliv supports its customers with local supply; the company builds components for its products in a number of centralized locations, shipping lower-level components for stocking at local assembly facilities. When needed, finished products are assembled and delivered to customers. In this scenario, Autoliv can provide a two-to-five hour delivery on customer orders, keeping the customer's just in time (JIT) manufacturing process on schedule.

How's Business?

For the first quarter of 2011, the company reported record sales, operating income, net income, and earnings per share. Organic sales were up 14 percent, significantly ahead of global light vehicle production, which grew only 5 percent. Autoliv is growing market share and protecting margins at the same time, not an easy thing to do. The numbers would have been better had it not been for the effects of the tsunami in Japan, where light vehicle production was down 23 percent.

Upside

- Pricing power in several markets
- Leading technology
- Three consecutive blockbuster quarters

Downside

- Japanese downturn will last at least another quarter
- Heavy R&D spend on new "active safety" products
- Two top competitors

Just the Facts

INDUSTRY: **Automotive & Truck Parts**
BETA COEFFICIENT: **1.25**
5-YEAR COMPOUND EARNINGS-PER-SHARE GROWTH: **0.5%**

		2006	**2007**	**2008**	**2009**	**2010**
Revenues (Mil)		6,188	6,769	6,473	5,120	7,171
Net Income (Mil)		305	308	214	108	591
Price:	high	61.0	65.1	62.6	44.5	82.0
	low	45.1	51.3	14.5	12.0	40.3

Autoliv, Inc.
World Trade Center, Klarabergsviadukten 70
Section E, SE-107 24, Stockholm, Sweden
46-8-587-20-600
Website: *www.autoliv.com*

AGGRESSIVE GROWTH

Baidu, Inc.

Ticker symbol: BIDU (NASDAQ) ❑ S&P rating: NA ❑ Value Line financial strength rating: A ❑ Current yield: Nil

Who Are They?

Baidu is the owner of the website *www.baidu.com*, the most widely used Chinese-language search engine on the Internet. As of January 2010, it had a 63 percent market share of all searches originating within China, a country with over 450 million Internet users (amazingly, roughly double that of the United States). Its product and business models closely parallel those of Google. The search engine provides the bulk of the revenue, with paid advertisements embedded in search results, bidding for priority placements, and partnerships with key retailing sites. The company also provides apps for desktop and mobile devices, including context-specific search, entertainment, and mapping.

The company was established in 2000 and went public in August 2005, with Goldman Sachs and Credit Suisse First Boston handling the underwriting.

The name "Baidu," by the way, translates to "a persistent search for the ideal."

Why Should I Care?

A pictographic language such as Chinese is not made for rapid, easy searching. There are thousands and thousands of unique characters, and even very well educated users do not know how to construct many of the words they have to use from time to time. The development of an easy-to-use search engine that provides useful and predictable results has been the goal of many Chinese developers and, just as Google did with Alta Vista and others, Baidu has built a very strong lead on the rest of the market, based largely on its proprietary technology. In particular, its advanced search capability puts it far ahead of its competitors.

As an example, it's impossible to search on a keyword when you don't know what the keyword looks like, so Baidu has developed a search protocol that permits users to search for Chinese keyword characters using a Baidu-developed phonetic language and an English keyboard. Yes, in some cases, Chinese has to be translated into English phonemes before it can be used to search for Chinese characters. Call it The Great Leap Sideways.

It's worth mentioning that although China has a number of mutually unintelligible spoken dialects, the written language (Modern Standard Chinese) is common across mainland China, Taiwan, Singapore, and basically anywhere else Chinese dialects are spoken. Since the Internet provides a forum primarily for written language, a significant aspect of the Internet's momentum in China is in its role as a cultural unifier. Baidu.com, as the most frequently visited Chinese website, gets a free ride on this wave and, significantly, gets to steer it a little as well. As such, we feel Baidu.com has the potential to be not just "the Chinese Google" but also a central player in a modern, unified Chinese identity. Getting back to the numbers, this translates into brand loyalty, trust, and a ready acceptance of Baidu.com as the standard for search for nearly a billion eyeballs.

How's Business?

Baidu's market cap has increased approximately 100-fold since the IPO. Margin growth is tapering "somewhat," but is still at 45 percent net. The company has more than $1.1 billion in cash and no debt.

Upside

- Enormous market
- Prohibitive favorite in a culture that embraces its favorites
- The government wants to build out your infrastructure

Downside

- It's not exactly cheap at 60-plus P/E
- Can the great firewall be good for business long-term?
- The government wants to be your partner

Just the Facts

INDUSTRY: **Computer Services**

BETA COEFFICIENT: **1.3**

5-YEAR COMPOUND EARNINGS-PER-SHARE GROWTH: **138%**

		2006	2007	2008	2009	2010
Revenues (Mil)		123	256	469	652	1,199
Net Income (Mil)		43.6	92.3	154	218	537
Price:	high	12.9	42.9	39.8	44.3	115.0
	low	4.4	9.3	10.0	10.5	38.5

Baidu, Inc.
Baidu Campus No. 10, Shangdi 10th Street
Haidian District, Beijing 100085, The People's Republic of China
8610-5992-8886
Website: *www.baidu.com*

AGGRESSIVE GROWTH

Bed Bath & Beyond Inc.

Ticker symbol: BBBY (NASDAQ) ❑ S&P rating: BBB ❑ Value Line financial strength rating: A++ ❑ Current yield: Nil

Who Are They?

Founded in 1971, Bed Bath & Beyond and its subsidiaries sell a wide assortment of goods, primarily domestics merchandise and home furnishings, but including food, giftware, health and beauty care items, and infant and toddler merchandise. With over 1,100 stores in the United States, Canada, and Mexico, the company has strong geographic coverage—its goal is to be the customer's first choice for the merchandise categories offered. BB&B competes on the breadth and depth of its product offerings, its customer service, new merchandise offerings, and everyday low prices.

The company also owns (through acquisition) and operates three other retail chain concepts: CTS (Christmas Tree Stores, sixty-one stores in fifteen states), Harmon (forty-five stores in three states), and buybuy BABY (twenty-nine stores in fourteen states). The buybuy BABY stores offer over 20,000 products for infants and toddlers, including cribs, dressers, car seats, strollers and highchairs, feeding, nursing, bath supplies, and everyday consumables, as well as toys, activity centers, and development products. The stores are equipped with private feeding and changing rooms and offer home delivery and setup on everything they sell.

Why Should I Care?

Occasionally a retailer hits on a formula that just works. On the higher end you have Nordstrom's, with its blend of selection, attractive shopping environment, and superior service. At the lower end, you have Wal-Mart, which redefined discount shopping with a clean, well-lit place to buy nearly everything under one roof. Bed Bath & Beyond is not the only player in their niche, and one could argue that it inhabits one of the more crowded segments in the retail space (less so since the departure of Linens 'N Things). What makes BB&B the most attractive player in this segment is the breadth of its selections. It understands that when people are feathering the nest, they enjoy going through as many feathers as possible before selecting just the right one. BB&B stocks more products per category than its competitors and arranges its stores so as to emphasize the broad selection. BB&B also mimics the display styles of specialty stores by presenting related product groups together in vignette form, reinforcing the perception of wide selection and communicating a level of customer service with those specialty stores. It's a well-tested formula that seems to work regardless of store size and location.

The BB&B format has not yet reached saturation levels, and there appears to be room for another 500 stores in the United States and Canada. Still, the company's move into other formats, buybuy BABY in particular, comes along at just the right time, as BB&B is generating more than enough cash to fund its own expansion. The company plans to take CTS and buybuy BABY nationwide and looks to be able to fund the expansion with free cash flow (with $1.4 billion in cash and zero debt, growth prospects are promising). We like the buybuy BABY concept (though we're not crazy about the name) and feel it has terrific expansion prospects. This is a high-margin segment serviced by few large specialists. It has an abundant, low-cost supply chain, is making strong contributions to the bottom line, and is growing faster than the company's other segments.

How's Business?

Comparable store sales were up 7 percent last year, putting the lie to the claim that the segment is too closely tied to the housing market. Forecasts are for an additional 12–15 percent increase in EPS growth through 2010, driven largely by expansion and an improvement in gross margin. The company should exit calendar 2011 with just over 1,200 stores across all segments.

Upside

- Full offering to nest-building consumers
- Exit of Linens 'N Things as competitor
- Quality image

Downside

- Recession continues for home improvement
- Could saturate market
- Competition from other discounters

Just the Facts

INDUSTRY: **Retail (Specialty)**
BETA COEFFICIENT: **0.9**
5-YEAR COMPOUND EARNINGS-PER-SHARE GROWTH: **9%**

		2006	2007	2008	2009	2010
Revenues (Mil)		6,617	7,049	7,208	7,829	8,630
Net Income (Mil)		611	563	425	600	750
Price:	high	41.7	43.3	34.7	40.2	50.9
	low	30.9	28	16.2	19.1	26.5

Bed Bath & Beyond Inc.
650 Liberty Avenue
Union, NJ 07083
(908) 688-0888
Website: *www.bedbathandbeyond.com*

AGGRESSIVE GROWTH

Best Buy Company

Ticker symbol: BBY (NASDAQ) ❑ S&P rating: BBB- ❑ Value Line financial strength rating: A ❑ Current yield: 1.7%

Who Are They?

Founded in 1966, Best Buy is a multinational retailer of technology and entertainment products and services with 180,000 employees and 3,800 stores in the United States, Canada, Europe, China, Mexico, and Turkey. The company's storefronts include Best Buy, Best Buy Mobile, Audiovisions, the Carphone Warehouse, Future Shop, Geek Squad, Jiangsu Five Star, Magnolia Audio Video, Napster, Pacific Sales, and the Phone House.

The various retailers have up to six different revenue categories each, with U.S. Best Buy and the Canadian Future Shop stores offering the broadest selection of merchandise. Other stores offer a subset of the six categories, which include consumer electronics, home office, entertainment software, appliances, services, and "other." The services revenue category consists primarily of service contracts, extended warranties, computer-related services, product repair, and delivery and installation for home theater, mobile audio, and appliances. Overall, Best Buy's product portfolio is dominated by consumer electronics and home office products, which combine for nearly 75 percent of sales.

Why Should I Care?

Nearly two years after Circuit City's exit from the market in CY2009, Best Buy continues to gather market share. Its share is estimated to have grown 240 basis points in CY2009 and another 100 basis points in CY2010. Sales growth has tracked the overall market, though profitability has suffered a bit in the face of the normal decline in the average selling price of tech products and somewhat swollen inventory levels. A new CEO has initiated changes to address both the sales and the operational issues. Product mix is being adjusted to better leverage higher-margin segments, and the company is closing some of its lower-performing stores, including all of its Best Buy outlets in Turkey and China (with some being re-branded to Five Star).

Sales growth in 2010 and early 2011 has moderated somewhat, in large part due to reduced consumer spending power and confidence, continued softness in the housing market (a major driver of appliance and home entertainment sales), and in part due to a dearth of compelling new tech products. Strong competitors such as Wal-Mart and Amazon have also stepped in to capture market share in the consumer electronics spaces, although BBY's strength in the phone market remains, particularly in international markets. And although the competition can offer competitive pricing in some product areas, Best Buy offers the less tech-savvy consumer a far stronger value proposition with its Geek Squad support business and its better-trained sales force. BBY's stock price has fallen some 20 percent from recent averages and is now trading in the low 30s, but we feel this price is fully "washed-out," with all the bad news and reduced expectations built in, and any upside surprises in the financials will reflect well in share value.

How's Business?

Although sales growth has underperformed, the company's financials are in good shape. Earnings showed continued growth through the financial crisis in spite of declining net margins. Cash flow is strong for a retailer and more than adequate to support its expansion plans and restructuring efforts.

Upside

- Strong market presence
- Solid financials
- Currently undervalued

Downside

- Depressed consumer spending
- Growing presence of competitors
- Absence of compelling new tech products

Just the Facts

INDUSTRY: **Retail (Technology)**
BETA COEFFICIENT: **1.1**
5-YEAR COMPOUND EARNINGS-PER-SHARE GROWTH: **16.5%**

		2006	2007	2008	2009	2010
Revenues (Mil)		35,938	40,023	45,015	49,694	50,200
Net Income (Mil)		1,377	1,407	1,208	1,342	1,370
Price:	high	59.5	53.9	53	45.6	48.8
	low	43.3	41.8	16.4	24.0	30.9

Best Buy Company, Inc.
7601 Penn Avenue South
Richfield, MN 55423
(612) 291-1000
Website: *www.bestbuy.com*

AGGRESSIVE GROWTH

Brookfield Asset Management

Ticker symbol: BAM (NYSE) ❑ S&P rating: NA ❑ Value Line financial strength rating: B+ ❑ Current yield: 1.9%

Who Are They?

Brookfield is a global asset manager focused on real estate, power, and infrastructure assets. Incorporated in Canada in 1912 as Brazilian Traction, Light and Power Company, it now manages eight top-level subsidiaries with 18,000 operating employees and twenty-one private funds. In all, it has more than $120 billion in assets under management. The bulk of these are in the United States and Canada, with additional interests in Europe and South America.

The company's real estate holdings include 192 properties in the United States, Canada, Australia, the United Kingdom, and Brazil, with 126 office properties and the rest split between development and retail space. Its power assets are all renewable energy technologies (hydro, wind, and thermal) located in the United States and Canada, with hydro being by far the predominant asset type. The portfolio has a total generating capacity of 4,325 megawatts. Its infrastructure assets are broadly diversified, both geographically and functionally, with holdings in electrical transmission, natural gas pipelines, sea cargo terminals, railroads, and timberlands, among others. These three segments constitute the focus of the business, with the company's funds accounting for the remaining 9 percent of 2010 revenue.

Why Should I Care?

Okay, you caught us. This is not the aggressive stock you're looking for. We can't help it, though—we like what the company has been able to do over the past few years and, we really like its base of assets going forward. Probably the most conservative stock in the book, it is nonetheless positioned well for recovery in the economically sensitive renewable energy and real estate segments, and infrastructure investment has already begun to grow. The value of the company's infrastructure-based fund was up over 17 percent in 2010. Can it be viewed as an aggressive stock on that basis? Probably not, but in 2010 it traded at an average forty-four multiple and this year finds them in the mid-thirties, so market optimism is high for what is almost by definition a value stock, currently trading for a little over book value.

A strong downturn in the real estate market is tailor-made for a company like Brookfield, which has a long-term view and access to significant levels of inexpensive capital. Many of the assets in its current lineup were acquired in the past few years at distressed valuations, particularly in the United States. The acquisitions were broad-based, including shopping malls, apartment buildings, office properties, and wind power projects. At very attractive terms, Brookfield was able to increase its holdings of General Growth Properties from 30 percent to 40 percent; GGP holds 180 regional shopping malls in the United States.

Still, half of the company's capital assets are deployed in Australia, Brazil, and Canada, where it benefits from export-oriented economies, especially as it applies to China.

How's Business?

Savings realized from a recent restructuring should give earnings a nice bump in 2011, with moderating growth in 2012. The company carries just over $30 billion in debt, but should generate $1.5 billion in cash flow in 2012.

Upside

- Steady income to fund cap structure
- The worst appears to be over in commercial real estate
- Improved asset base and corporate structure

Downside

- Somewhat less than attractive share price
- Hydro rates depressed
- United States still lagging

Just the Facts

INDUSTRY: **Investment Services**

BETA COEFFICIENT: **1.3**

5-YEAR COMPOUND EARNINGS-PER-SHARE GROWTH: **34%**

		2006	2007	2008	2009	2010
Revenues (Mil)		6,897	9,434	12,868	12,082	13,623
Net Income (Mil)		1,316	787	649	454	356
Price:	high	33.4	43.8	37.2	24.3	33.5
	low	21.2	29.3	11.6	11.2	20.0

Brookfield Asset Management
Suite 300, Brookfield Place, Box 762
181 Bay Street, Toronto, Ontario M5J 2T3, Canada
(416) 363-9491
Website: *www.brookfield.com*

AGGRESSIVE GROWTH

Brooks Automation, Inc.

Ticker symbol: BRKS (NASDAQ) ❑ S&P rating: NA ❑ Value Line financial strength rating: C++ ❑ Current yield: Nil

Who Are They?

When we think of semiconductor equipment manufacturing, we tend to think of the very large and very expensive machines from the likes of Applied Materials and Lam Research. But there are also many smaller pieces of gear that require specialized expertise as well, and Brooks is one of those companies with the skills and experience that have kept it in business since 1978, supplying equipment such as automated wafer handlers, cryogenic refrigeration systems, and work-in-progress tracking tools. The company's customer base includes semiconductor manufacturers such as Intel and TSMC, and system integrators that assemble solutions and then sell to manufacturers.

The company reports in three segments: the Critical Solutions Group, which produces the bulk of the company's mainline products; the Systems Solutions Group, which provides a range of engineering and manufacturing services, mainly for the purpose of developing custom solutions for a particular application of customer; and Global Customer Operations, the company's training and support services operation. The company typically derives about half of its revenue from outside the United States.

Why Should I Care?

If you wanted a case study for the boom/bust cycles in the semiconductor business, you could do worse than look at Brooks. It's generally feast or famine with all of the smaller players in this industry and with many of the big ones as well. Fortunately for Brooks and investment guide writers, we're in the middle of a boom cycle. Normally this would not be the best time to hop on the bandwagon in Chelmsford, as by now most of the investors will have bid the stock way up beyond the point where a late arriver could expect a decent return. But we like the recent news from Brooks and its efforts at diversifying its customer base. We think there's a bit more growth in the up cycle and a bit less contraction in the down cycle than there's been in the past. The cycles have traditionally had two main drivers: consumer spending and technology shifts. Now, however, we're seeing some smoothing effects coming from the solar panel and LED production. These two products are on their own schedules and are driving significant volumes of wafers. Just last year, twenty-four new LED fabs started up, and another half a dozen are expected to start this year. Brooks is moving aggressively into those markets, as well as the MEMS (micro-electrical mechanical systems) market.

Intel, TSMC, and Global Foundries plan to place orders for more than $22 billion in new equipment in 2011 alone. The entire semiconductor sector should be up 9 percent in 2011 and another 6 percent annually through 2015. If these numbers hold up, then companies like Lam Research, one of Brooks's biggest customers, will be very busy.

The company recently placed a dozen new design wins, two of which displaced competitors and eight of which were for lateral markets where they were not competing previously. Geographically, Brooks is expanding its markets in both Japan and China.

How's Business?

In 2010, the Systems Solution group experienced a 310 percent increase in revenue. The Extended Factory business, which is an operation providing critical manufacturing support for semiconductor OEMs, was responsible for the bulk of that growth. This bodes well for future revenue growth.

Upside

- The harvest is in
- Brooks is in good shape, despite a horrific 2009
- Still trading fairly cheap (9.0 P/E)

Downside

- Shares require adult supervision
- Unreliable earnings
- Much speculative interest

Just the Facts

INDUSTRY: **Semiconductors**
BETA COEFFICIENT: **1.60**
5-YEAR COMPOUND EARNINGS-PER-SHARE GROWTH: **NM**

	2006	2007	2008	2009	2010
Revenues (Mil)	693	743	526	219	593
Net Income (Mil)	36.2	54.3	(-25.8)	(-129.2)	50.1
Price: high	17.8	20.1	13.4	9.1	10.8
low	10.6	11.7	2.5	3.3	5.5

Brooks Automation, Inc.
15 Elizabeth Drive
Chelmsford, MA 01824
(978) 262-2400
Website: *www.brooks.com*

AGGRESSIVE GROWTH

Callaway Golf Company

Ticker symbol: ELY (NYSE) ❑ S&P rating: NA ❑ Value Line financial strength rating: B+ ❑ Current yield: 0.5%

Who Are They?

Callaway Golf designs, manufactures, and sells golf clubs and golf balls, and designs and sells golf accessories for sale through retailers, golf specialty shops, catalogs, and online. Its equipment is designed for all levels of play, from the starting player up to the top ranks of professional golf. Its brands include Callaway, Odyssey, Top-Flite, and Ben Hogan and are sold in more than 100 countries worldwide.

The Callaway brand is in the first group of equipment makers. As such, they compete almost exclusively with Titleist, Taylor Made, Ping, and Nike. Its products command top dollar for their performance and industrial design and are rarely, if ever, discounted. Best known for its clubs, it also sells balls, clothing, and accessories. As a stock, it is one of the best pure golf plays in the clubhouse.

Why Should I Care?

Callaway would not normally be included in anyone's list of aggressive stocks. Prior to the recession, the company had been in a trading range for the better part of ten years, and we don't expect that the recession will turn the company into a growth monster or start it on an acquisition binge. Callaway will recover and resume business as usual. What we do like is its position as one of the best companies in a sector that's understandably in disfavor.

If there's one industry that has yet to rebound from the recession, it's the golf industry. Equipment makers, private clubs and (to a lesser degree) municipal courses, golf destinations, and resorts, all continue to feel the pinch and wait for the recovery. Opportunity knocks for the patient value investor with a tolerance for the occasional errant shot. We like the sector's chances for recovery in 2012 and we think the rising tide is going to lift Callaway's shares back into the $18–$20 range, which would represent a 200-percent increase over its current price. Call this a passive-aggressive pick.

Business is not down everywhere. Although Callaway's sales in the United States, Europe, and Japan were down 2 percent in total, sales in China, Indonesia, and India were up 25 percent versus 2009. If the development of the middle class in these three countries continues, Callaway will benefit. The company is expanding its distribution in both countries.

Callaway is in the midst of a major restructuring to reduce its manufacturing costs. It is transferring significant portions of its club and ball manufacturing capacity from California and Massachusetts to Monterrey, Mexico, to take advantage of lower labor rates there. It expects to complete this transfer by the end of 2011. The company has also taken a number of one-time charges to earnings in 2010, totaling some twenty-four cents per share, and should enter 2012 with a pared-down cost structure and reduced levels of expense.

How's Business?

The company expects 2011 to be mildly profitable, despite the extraordinary costs incurred during the year. Although sales are expected to increase only 3 percent, operating margins should more than double. All the cost-cutting initiatives are internally funded, and the company remains debt free.

Upside

- Best company in a bad sector
- Leaner, meaner for 2012
- Nice story in Asia

Downside

- Beginning of a demographic shift away from golf?
- 23 percent of U.S. courses closed in past two years
- Expect a few bogies on the sales growth card

Just the Facts

INDUSTRY: **Recreational Products**
BETA COEFFICIENT: **1.05**
5-YEAR COMPOUND EARNINGS-PER-SHARE GROWTH: **-5.5%**

		2006	2007	2008	2009	2010
Revenues (Mil)		1,018	1,125	1,117	951	968
Net Income (Mil)		28.8	53.9	59.2	(-17.1)	(-17.9)
Price:	high	17.4	19.5	18.2	10.3	10.2
	low	11.5	13.8	7.6	4.7	5.8

Callaway Golf Company
2285 Rutherford Road
Carlsbad, CA 92008-8815
(760) 931-1771
Website: *www.callawaygolf.com*

AGGRESSIVE GROWTH

Calumet Specialty Products Partners, L.P.

Ticker symbol: CLMT (NASDAQ) ❑ S&P rating: NA ❑ Value Line financial strength rating: NA ❑ Current yield: 9.27%

Who Are They?

Calumet Specialty Products Partners (CLMT) is a petroleum refiner and processor of specialty hydrocarbons. In addition to producing basic fuels such as gasoline, diesel, and jet fuels, it also produces a broad line of special-use compounds, including over a hundred different types of waxes, solvents, paraffins, gels, and oils. It claims to have the most diverse specialty hydrocarbon capability in the world, and in fact, the specialty hydrocarbons line is the mainstay of the company, generating 65 percent of revenues and 95 percent of gross profits in FY2010.

Although the company can trace its roots back to 1918, its stock has only traded as CLMT since early 2006 following a Chapter 11 filing and reorganization in 2005. Since then, the company has had financial success with a solid product line and loyal customer base.

The company has five production facilities in Louisiana, Texas, and Pennsylvania, and a storage facility and terminal in Illinois. Specialty products are distributed worldwide, while fuel products are sold domestically and distributed by rail.

Why Should I Care?

CLMT gets more out of a barrel of oil than any of the volume fuel refiners. With feedstock at $75/per barrel, CLMT is still making about $25/per barrel, where at that price most fuel refiners wouldn't be unhappy with 2 percent after fixed costs. The company is able to pass through feedstock cost increases to its specialty products customers and engages in short-term hedging of petroleum for those products. The fuel products line, where competition effectively limits pass-throughs, employs longer-term hedging. The purpose of the hedging is, of course, to stabilize costs, but they've been so good at it that in some periods they make more money hedging than they do running the plants. In any case, the hedging costs them about seventy-eight cents/per barrel, which is cheap insurance when the news from the oil producing areas is what it is these days.

Hedging also helps maintain the steady, consistent cash flows needed to support CLMT's ongoing R&D efforts. The development of a custom compound for a client is a complex process, and it can take up to a year before production quantities are available. The good news is once CLMT has the product, the customer is unlikely to change suppliers throughout its product's life. In many cases, no other supplier can meet the process or volume requirements at all. In the end, CLMT has carved out a very nice business for itself with smaller, more flexible refineries and the processing expertise required for the production of these custom compounds.

How's Business?

The past year (FY2010) was a tale of two halves for CLMT, with volumes in the first six months still in recovery. The first half of the year saw cash flow generation of only $42 million, while the second half generated nearly $92 million. Also in the second half of 2010, specialty sales were up 22 percent over the second half of 2009, and gross margins were up 370 basis points over the same period.

The partnership is offering an additional 4.5 million common units in the second half of 2011 at $21.45 per unit in order to repay debt under its revolving credit plan. The offering has been very well subscribed and the underwriters plan to exercise an option for an additional 675,000 units.

Upside

- Good size and market cap for a "specialty" supplier
- Customers tend not to change a qualified supplier
- Nice dividend

Downside

- Continued volatility in price of feedstock
- Earnings history somewhat uncertain
- Fuel segment just marginally profitable

Just the Facts

INDUSTRY: **Oil & Gas Operations**
BETA COEFFICIENT: **1.05**
5-YEAR COMPOUND EARNINGS-PER-SHARE GROWTH: **NA**

		2006	**2007**	**2008**	**2009**	**2010**
Revenues (Mil)		1,641	1,637	2,489	1,846	2,191
Net Income (Mil)		95.6	82.9	44.4	61.8	16.7
Price:	high	42	53.7	36	19.4	23.3
	low	22.2	33.8	6.9	8.8	17

Calumet Specialty Products Partners, L.P.
2780 Waterfront Parkway, East Drive, Suite 200
Indianapolis, IN 46214
(317) 328-5660
Website: *www.calumetspecialty.com*

AGGRESSIVE GROWTH

CarMax, Inc.

Ticker symbol: KMX (NYSE) ❑ S&P rating: NA ❑ Value Line financial strength rating: B+ ❑ Current yield: Nil

Who Are They?

CarMax is a nationwide chain of used vehicle stores/superstores, offering customers a new big-box retail-like model for buying cars. CarMax buys, reconditions, and sells cars and light trucks at 100 retail centers in forty-six metropolitan markets, mainly in the Southeast and Midwest. The company specializes in selling cars that are under six years old with less than 60,000 miles in a no-haggle environment; the price is the price. The company emphasizes the condition of the vehicles and a helpful and friendly sales and transaction process. Sales representatives are compensated for cars they sell, but not in such a way that drives them to push the wrong car on a customer. The company sold 357,129 used vehicles in FY2009 and most reports suggest it is gaining market share in the markets it serves with a high degree of customer satisfaction.

CarMax also has service operations and customer tools designed to make the car selection, buying, and ownership experience easier. The CarMax process is unique in the industry, and most think that any potential competitor would have a long way to go to catch up.

Why Should I Care?

CarMax offers a completely new and different approach to used car sales and is a stock you buy if you believe, as we do, that the traditional dealer model is broken. We also believe people who see value in late model used vehicles but who are repelled by traditional used-car markets will welcome the CarMax approach.

On the operations side, CarMax brings the latest in business intelligence and analytic models to the car marketing process, in procurement, merchandising, pricing, and selling the vehicles. Regional preferences for brands and models figure prominently; do green Jeep Commanders sell well in Southern California? Then find some, put them on the lot there, and set a market-based price. KMX is well ahead of the industry in making analysis-based supply and selling decisions.

In addition, its view of the bigger picture and its more sophisticated analytic tools allow CarMax to adjust inventories to business conditions quickly; in the recent downturn such inventory was reduced by tens of thousands of vehicles. As the recovery has progressed, those inventory levels have risen in support of increased demand. CarMax is one of the biggest players in the used auction market, and it is already the largest used car buyer in the world.

There are close to 70,000 new and used car dealerships in the United States, and that number is going to shrink dramatically over the next few years, leaving a clear field for CarMax. With many of its competitors for quality used cars out of business, CarMax should benefit both from opportunities for improved market presence and a reduced cost of goods sold. In fact, operating margin nearly doubled year over year.

How's Business?

The disastrous calendar 2008 is barely visible in the rear-view mirror. Results for FY2010 will show a 19 percent increase in sales and a very healthy 33 percent bump in earnings. This is on top of a spectacular rebound in 2009 in which earnings rose 370 percent to a then-record $282 million. The financing arm has completely turned its business around over the same period and should continue to benefit from very favorable spreads going forward.

Upside

- Growing acceptance of retail model
- Return of financing profits
- Strong untapped geographic markets, such as Denver, New England, and the Pacific Northwest

Downside

- Automotive market volatility
- Stock trading near all-time high
- Availability of good inventory

Just the Facts

INDUSTRY: **Retail (Specialty)**
BETA COEFFICIENT: **1.1**
5-YEAR COMPOUND EARNINGS-PER-SHARE GROWTH: **16.5%**

		2006	2007	2008	2009	2010
Revenues (Mil)		7,466	8,200	6,974	7,470	8,830
Net Income (Mil)		198.6	182	59.2	282	375
Price:	high	27.6	29.4	23	24.8	36
	low	13.8	18.6	5.8	6.9	18.6

CarMax, Inc.
12800 Tuckahoe Creek Parkway
Richmond, VA 23238
(804) 747-0422
Website: *www.carmax.com*

AGGRESSIVE GROWTH

Celestica, Inc.

Ticker symbol: CLS (NYSE) ❑ S&P rating: BB ❑ Value Line financial strength rating: B ❑ Current yield: Nil

Who Are They?

Celestica is an electronics manufacturing services (EMS) operation. If you're a company such as Apple, Sun, IBM, etc., then you most likely use Celestica and several other third parties to build the hardware that goes into your products. You also might use Celestica to design, manufacture, deliver, and support the entire product throughout its lifecycle. Celestica provides many levels of service and support, including design, assembly, test, quality assurance, agency certification, and supply-chain management with facilities in dozens of countries around the world.

Celestica is one of the "mid-tier" players in the EMS game. There's only one player in the top tier, and that's Foxconn, with a market cap approximately sixty times that of Celestica. Flextronics and Jabil Circuits are about twice the size of CLS, and there are many companies smaller than CLS.

Why Should I Care?

Celestica, Foxconn, Flextronics . . . these guys are the lunch buckets of the global electronics business. They build the products that most of us use many times throughout the day. The PC you work on, the radio you listen to, the television you watch, and all the servers you connect to while browsing the web. All of them, whatever the brand on the outside of the product, were built entirely or in part by one or more of these companies, and that business is not going away anytime soon.

The EMS business is not a glamorous business. Margins, even for some of the most successful of them, are *desperately* thin. In its very best year, Celestica generated 5.7 percent operating margin. Their average year is closer to 4 percent, and that's operating margin. Pay the R&D, SG&A, marketing, and taxes, and you're looking at an average net margin in the 2 percent range. You won't find another company in this book that does $8 billion in sales and makes this little money. So you might be asking yourself at this point, "What kind of an endorsement is this?"

As it turns out, Celestica has made some changes recently that should accelerate bottom-line growth even if revenues do not grow as quickly as expected in the economic recovery. The company has reduced its fixed costs over the past five years and is now sized appropriately for the level of anticipated business. They've eliminated their long-term debt entirely and in 2010 retired 7 percent of their shares. Even with revenues at just 75 percent of their peak, the company is turning in record net margins. The company is now in great financial shape for the anticipated turnaround in the EMS business, which is expected to grow to $400 billion in revenues in 2014 (from $270 billion), with operating margins expected to more than double for the sector.

How's Business?

Businesses like Celestica always have volume upsides built into their production contracts. Recognizing the added cost in securing unplanned inventory and labor, these upsides build in significantly higher per-unit marginal revenue for the manufacturer. Perhaps reflective of this, the company announced first-quarter 2011 earnings per share of thirteen cents, which beat the consensus estimate by four cents, or 44 percent.

Upside

- Rising tide, with more business coming from Apple
- Inexpensive—trading at a ten multiple
- Company is much leaner than even three years ago

Downside

- Inventory prices will rise during growth cycle
- Recent Sanmina EPS warning
- Business concentrated in fairly small customer base

Just the Facts

INDUSTRY: **Electronic Instruments & Controls**
BETA COEFFICIENT: **1.25**
5-YEAR COMPOUND EARNINGS-PER-SHARE GROWTH: **21.5%**

		2006	2007	2008	2009	2010
Revenues (Mil)		8,812	8,070	7,678	6,092	6,526
Net Income (Mil)		94.8	52.8	188	142	196
Price:	high	12.2	8.1	9.9	10.1	11.3
	low	7.4	5.2	3.2	2.6	7.4

Celestica, Inc.
844 Don Mills Road
Toronto, Ontario, Canada M3C 1V7
(416) 448-5800
Website: *www.celestica.com*

AGGRESSIVE GROWTH

Celgene Corporation

Ticker symbol: CELG (NASDAQ) ❑ S&P rating: BBB+ ❑ Value Line financial strength rating: A+ ❑ Current yield: Nil

Who Are They?

Celgene is an integrated biopharmaceutical company focused on the development and marketing of treatments for cancers and immune-related diseases. It was spun off from Celanese Corporation in 1986 and was initially focused on developing chemical processes for the chemical and biotech industries, but through a series of acquisitions beginning in 2000, it gained access to both revenue-generating pharmaceutical products and biopharmaceutical research capability. Eleven years later, Celgene's biopharmaceuticals have become the company's main revenue generators and supported its advanced production capabilities.

The company's current revenue-producing drugs include: Revlamid, an oral immunomodulatory used in the treatment of multiple myeloma and some cases of transfusion-dependent anemia; Thalomid, also used in the treatment of multiple myeloma as well as ENL, a complication of Hansen's disease (commonly known as leprosy); Ritalin family of drugs, for the treatment of ADHD and certain oncology-related disorders; and others.

Why Should I Care?

The company has developed an impressive portfolio of work with regard to several different anti-inflammatory and oncological treatment paths. Its IMiDs compounds modulate the immune system through multiple processes and are covered by an extensive body of patents. The company has high expectations for this line. Other lines in development include kinase inhibitors, cellular therapies, activin inhibitors, and oral anti-inflammatories.

Celgene's recent record of success in getting products through clinical trials and into a revenue-generating phase is encouraging, particularly in light of Celgene's current pipeline. The company has fourteen candidates either in Phase II/III trials or about to enter Phase II. The targeted diseases for these candidates include multiple myeloma, psoriasis, arthritis, lupus, lung cancer, Crohn's disease, and multiple sclerosis.

Critical to the success of any pharmaceutical business is a healthy pipeline and patent protection. Celgene's pipeline appears solid, and there are no major revenue contributors coming off patent until Vidaza in 2018 (Europe). Revlimid's revenue contribution (currently 63 percent of sales) should continue to grow through 2011 as acceptance grows in newer markets (Japan, for one) and the drug receives approval for reimbursement in Russia.

The biotech sector is one of the more closely followed markets and, not surprisingly, Celgene has been getting its due share of attention. Of the thirty-one analysts who follow the stock most closely, twenty-four have issued a "buy" recommendation (at the current price of $58 per share) with the remaining seven recommending a "hold." The consensus target price for 2011 year-end was just under $69 per share.

How's Business?

Is there anything prettier than the financials of a pharmaceutical company that's been on a successful run? My goodness, where to start? No debt, $3.5 billion in cash, cash flow five-year compound annual growth rate of 78 percent, average inventory equivalent to just over a week of revenue, and *one-third of every dollar* straight to the bottom line. The company's operating and net margins far exceed those of the (admittedly, much) larger players like Merck, Pfizer, and Johnson & Johnson.

Upside

- Promising pipeline
- Solid track record
- Strong acquisition potential

Downside

- Clinical trials never a sure thing
- Revenue growth moderating
- Would a dividend hurt?

Just the Facts

INDUSTRY: **Biotechnology and Drugs**
BETA COEFFICIENT: **0.8**
5-YEAR COMPOUND EARNINGS-PER-SHARE GROWTH: **90%**

		2006	2007	2008	2009	2010
Revenues (Mil)		899	1,405	2,238	2,690	3,625
Net Income (Mil)		69	226	607	863	1,200
Price:	high	60.1	75.4	77.4	58.1	65.8
	low	31.5	41.3	45.4	36.9	48.0

Celgene Corporation
86 Morris Avenue
Summit, NJ 07901
(908) 673-9000
Website: ***www.celgene.com***

AGGRESSIVE GROWTH

Chico's FAS

Ticker symbol: CHS (NYSE) ❑ S&P rating: NA ❑ Value Line financial strength rating: B+ ❑ Current yield: 1.3%

Who Are They?

Chico's FAS, founded in 1983 on Sanibel Island in Florida, is, according to its annual report, a national specialty retailer of "private branded, sophisticated, casual-to-dressy clothing, intimates, complementary accessories, and other non-clothing gift items" under the Chico's, White House | Black Market, and Soma Intimates brand names. We at *100 Best* are not as well informed on the subject of women's clothing as we could be, so we'll let that description stand as is. As of January 2011, the company operated 1,151 stores across the United States and operated e-commerce websites for each of its brands.

The company's brands target slightly different demographics. Chico's market is thirty-five and older and looking for casual, but current and fashionable clothing, while WH | BM customers are a bit younger and are looking to make more of a statement with their clothes. The Soma line consists "primarily of exclusively designed private branded sensual and luxurious lingerie, loungewear and beauty products." All of the brands are targeted at women with a moderate- to high-income level.

The company's growth strategy for 2011 and beyond includes building the store base, improving store productivity levels, and growing the direct-to-consumer channels (catalog and Internet sales). Growth in the store base will primarily affect the WH | BM and Soma boutiques.

Why Should I Care?

Retail took the brunt of the recession in 2008–2009 and has still not fully recovered. A number of retail chains are building up momentum, however, and Chico's is one of them. The company has been successful in pulling folks into the stores and onto their websites, although inventory apparently grew faster than sales in the most recent quarter. Even so, the operating margin is climbing steadily, although it may never reach its pre-2006 levels in the 23–25 percent range.

The retailer stumbled a bit prior to the recession when it failed to differentiate its merchandise from that of its competitors. Earnings fell by 60 percent in two years, and then the recession hit. The company has since brought in some new management with a focus on operations and a reinterpretation of its styles that are "polished but not fussy." Many loyal customers remain, and the new WH | BM and Soma brands have become quite popular.

Less than 10 percent of Chico's revenue is currently derived from online sales. This is very low compared with most of its peers. Substantial room for growth in this low-cost channel will do wonders for margins. Chico's has spiffed up its website recently in an effort to capture more eyeballs.

Chico's does not carry a broad line of goods and is very much a niche retailer. The good news is niche retailers have done well, by and large, through the recovery, while some larger retailers (including Wal-Mart) are actually seeing declining sales. Buying patterns seem to be very strong for products with top-of-the-line quality and positive brand identity, traits that Chico's promotes.

How's Business?

Growth in the direct-to-customer channel was nearly 40 percent in 2010. The company plans to invest further here to increase sales penetration while also dedicating another online channel for closeout and sale merchandise. The goal is to maintain higher margins at its outlet stores, which currently serve as the market for this lower-margin product.

Upside

- Well-regarded brands
- Healthy sales per square foot at retail
- Potential acquisition candidate

Downside

- High expectations
- Chinese labor costs pushing work to India
- Cotton and other commodity prices continue to rise

Just the Facts

INDUSTRY: **Retail (Apparel)**
BETA COEFFICIENT: **1.25**
5-YEAR COMPOUND EARNINGS-PER-SHARE GROWTH: **-15%**

		2006	2007	2008	2009	2010
Revenues (Mil)		1,647	1,714	1,582	1,713	1,905
Net Income (Mil)		167	86.8	(-19.1)	69.7	115
Price:	high	49.4	27.9	10.9	15.4	16.6
	low	17.3	9.0	1.7	3.4	8.2

Chico's FAS, Inc.
11215 Metro Parkway
Ft. Myers, FL 33966
(239) 277-6200
Website: ***www.chicos.com***

AGGRESSIVE GROWTH

Chipotle Mexican Grill

Ticker symbol: CMG (NYSE) ❑ S&P rating: NA ❑ Value Line financial strength rating: A ❑ Current yield: Nil

Who Are They?

Chipotle Mexican Grill develops and operates Mexican-inspired fast-food restaurants. Founded in 1993, it started 2011 with 1,084 restaurants and plans to open another 140 through 2011. McDonald's Corporation held a 91 percent stake in the company until January 2006, when the company had its IPO. The company sold 7.77 million shares for $22 each, and four months later sold another 4.2 million shares for $61.50 each. McDonald's completed its divestiture in October of 2006.

The concept for the stores is "fast-casual," with fresh ingredients carefully prepared and served quickly in an attractive and modern environment. In general, Chipotle offers better ingredients than those found in most fast-food chains, albeit with a much smaller menu. Instead of rice, beans, and an entrée served in the scores of combinations that you find in the typical Mexican restaurant, Chipotle offers a burrito, a bowl (basically a burrito without the tortilla wrap), and recently, soft tacos. The customer can choose among different ingredients for those three dishes, but there are no other options for entrées. Salads, chips, and guacamole round out the menu.

Sixteen years after their founding, Chipotle is still in the top ten fastest-growing restaurant chains in the United States. The stores tend to be located in urban/suburban areas with strong residential and daytime population. Chipotle's preferred traffic generators include residential, office, retail, university, and hospitals. The company makes a point of using ingredients that are sustainably grown and naturally raised. Its motto is "Food with Integrity," and Chipotle is already the largest restaurant seller of naturally raised meat and the largest restaurant buyer of locally grown produce in the United States. Chipotle supplies its restaurants through twenty-two independently owned and operated distribution centers.

Why Should I Care?

Chipotle occupies a niche in the fast-food market that has very little competition, and what competition there is stems mostly from regional players (Una Mas, Pollo Loco). Chili's touts its "Fresh Mex" cuisine, but the menu is mainly there to sell margaritas. Conversely, Chipotle's design and menu are attractive to those who come for the freshly prepared and rather wholesome food; there are no deep fryers in a Chipotle.

The company continues to gain mindshare nationwide. Given its menu, its success in western and southwestern states is not at all surprising. Even the "message" that comes with the food seems tailored to the left-coast social zeitgeist (not a criticism, just an observation). As it turns out, however, after California, the state with the greatest concentration of Chipotle restaurants is Ohio. And we think if Chipotle can make it there, as they say, they can make it anywhere. Over the past two years, incremental revenue has been driven entirely by improved comps and new store openings. Chipotle's prices remained flat for the second year running, in spite of significant movement in commodities pricing. We expect earnings gains from the new stores to be even stronger in 2011 due to a reduced-cost store design that has proved nearly equal to the larger designs in revenue generation.

And finally, Chipotle is encouraged by its reception in international markets and will be accelerating development there.

How's Business?

The company continues to estimate growth very conservatively and continues to exceed expectations. The bean counters at CMG apparently like to surprise on the upside, a practice that we at *100 Best* approve of. Comps in 2010 were up 9.4 percent (nearly double the company's estimate), and earnings were up 41 percent.

Upside

- Timely concept
- Excellent demographics
- Attractive international growth potential

Downside

- Restaurant "trendiness" risk
- Trading at a very high multiple (40)
- Continued margin pressure from rising commodity costs

Just the Facts

INDUSTRY: **Restaurants**

BETA COEFFICIENT: **1.0**

5-YEAR COMPOUND EARNINGS-PER-SHARE GROWTH: **25.5%**

		2006	2007	2008	2009	2010
Revenues (Mil)		823	1,086	1,332	1,518	1,836
Net Income (Mil)		41.4	70.6	78.2	127	179
Price:	high	67.8	155.5	150	98.7	262.8
	low	40.9	54.6	36.9	46.5	86.0

Chipotle Mexican Grill
1401 Wynkoop Street, Suite 500
Denver, CO 80202
(303) 595-4000
Website: *www.chipotle.com*

AGGRESSIVE GROWTH

Cirrus Logic, Inc.

Ticker symbol: CRUS (NASDAQ) ❑ S&P rating: B ❑ Value Line financial strength rating: C++ ❑ Current yield: Nil

Who Are They?

Cirrus Logic is a designer and marketer of semiconductors targeted at the audio and energy markets. It is one of the largest suppliers in the audio semiconductor market, providing solutions for applications throughout the audio chain to manufacturers such as Apple, Sony, and most (if not all) of the largest players in the business. Its top-of-the-line products are considered to be among the best available. The "energy" products are a bit more broadly defined and include power management circuits, ADCs and DACs, linear amplifiers, seismic applications, and power amplifier modules. The bulk of Cirrus's some 700 products are proprietary, but the catalog includes many industry-standard designs as well. The revenues in 2010 were split 70/30 between audio and energy.

It does not own a fabrication facility, but has broad expertise in the various semiconductor processes required to build their products. Fab capacity has not been an issue for the company in the past and would not appear to be so going forward.

Why Should I Care?

The electronic product markets that have seen the largest growth in the last twenty years have without a doubt been those associated with the computer (PC and server) market. The advancement of the technology in the processor and memory fields are well known and closely followed as bellwethers of the health of the overall semiconductor market. This focus on the core suppliers of digital functionality for the PC and server tends to remove specialty players like Cirrus from the center of attention, but in many ways its position gets more and more attractive even as Intel and AMD gobble up the bulk of the system value-add.

The concentration of digital functionality in three parts—the CPU, the north bridge, and memory—has led to the decline of the margin players like SiS, Cyrix, and many others. Cirrus and other suppliers of analog and mixed-signal parts, on the other hand, are relatively safe from the encroachment of the digital giants. Their business relies on the fact that many digital processing streams either begin or end with an analog signal; Cirrus specializes in the conversion of the signal between the two domains and in the specialized processing of analog signals as a "front-end" to the general-purpose CPU.

Its recent growth is due mainly to its focus on the special applications of portable audio. Every portable music player and smartphone on the planet, regardless of generation or the underlying CPU or OS, is a potential seat for Cirrus silicon. Cirrus has capitalized by reducing both the chip count and footprint of not only its parts but the associated passive components as well. Cirrus's expertise is not just in product design but also in the chip manufacturing process. This expertise is vital in getting the performance from analog parts—unlike in the digital world, performance in analog does not always improve as geometries shrink, and knowing how to optimize a supplier's manufacturing process is a big advantage when optimizing functionality.

How's Business?

The close association with Apple has Cirrus whistling a happy tune. Cirrus provides the core audio silicon for both the iPad2 and the iPhone4, which, as you may know, are fairly popular products. Both operating margin and net margin doubled in 2010. The company has no debt and is well capitalized; we would not be surprised to see Cirrus pick up one or two smaller players during the year.

Upside

- Strong relationship with Apple
- Good product direction
- Strong finances

Downside

- Not much rockin' in pro audio market
- Revenue growth flattening
- Capacity/costs bear watching

Just the Facts

INDUSTRY: **Semiconductors**
BETA COEFFICIENT: **1.0**
5-YEAR COMPOUND EARNINGS-PER-SHARE GROWTH: **34.1%**

		2006	2007	2008	2009	2010
Revenues (Mil)		182	182	175	221	360
Net Income (Mil)		35.9	24.1	17.9	28.6	90.0
Price:	high	10.5	9.4	7.6	6.9	21.2
	low	5.9	4.5	2.3	2.2	6.2

Cirrus Logic, Inc.
2901 Via Fortuna
Austin, TX 78746
(512) 851-4000
Website: ***www.cirrus.com***

AGGRESSIVE GROWTH

Coherent, Inc.

Ticker symbol: COHR (NASDAQ) ❑ S&P rating: NA ❑ Value Line financial strength rating: B+ ❑ Current yield: Nil

Who Are They?

Coherent is one of the world's leading suppliers of lasers for commercial, industrial, and scientific applications. They also supply tools for laser measurement and control, and accessories for use with lasers in laboratory and production environments. In addition to stand-alone lasers, the company also supplies fully integrated shop-floor laser machining cells and workcells customized for the solar panel industry.

Why Should I Care?

Photonics has come into its own. The technology base has been growing steadily over the past few decades, supported mainly by industrial and military users, and there are now tools and applications that hadn't even been dreamed of as little as thirty years ago. The unique properties of laser light, which had made lasers irreplaceable as laboratory tools, now make them equally valuable in commercial products as mundane as a $5 laser pointer and as exotic as the excimer laser used to perform eye surgery (a procedure which, to show how far the technology has come, is now also considered fairly mundane).

Coherent supports the broad commercialization of the technology with a product line that covers all existing laser technologies and most high-value applications. Applications in the microelectronics and semiconductor industries have been growing rapidly as device geometries are shrinking beyond the point where standard wide-band optical techniques operate effectively. A monochromatic, coherent light source is ideal for detection of sub-micron faults in silicon wafers and in the semiconductor device itself, for example. Lasers are also used in the wafer cutting and die separation processes, leading to higher yield and fewer defects when compared to traditional diamond saw methods. Lasers are also used to produce many of the fine geometries in special materials employed in LCD and plasma flat panel displays, and lasers are the only tool capable of creating the inner-layer connections in the tiny circuit boards used in densely packed handheld devices like cell phones and music players. Finally, lasers have found new applications recently in the processing of raw silicon and the production of LEDs, which yield significant improvements in brightness and efficiency, two properties of very high value to flat panel display manufacturers.

How's Business?

With the advent of some high-volume, cutting-edge applications Coherent has been recognized as a growth opportunity, and the shares have been bid up accordingly. Still the company is trading at just over two times book value, in part due to its rather bleak operating margins (roughly 8 percent in 2011). With a high-mix, low-volume production model, ten separate R&D facilities, thirteen separate manufacturing facilities, and expensive/exotic raw material, it's not surprising that COGS is a high 57 percent. This is a problem that is partially mitigated by higher volumes, but Coherent will be saddled with these costs for some time. The company plans to buy back $75 million in stock. While we wish there were higher-leverage opportunities for the cash, it does represent nearly 5 percent of the outstanding shares, which is not bad for comps going forward.

Upside

- Momentum with higher volume customers
- Intriguing new applications
- Market share leader

Downside

- Poor cost structure
- Shares won't be cheap
- Perhaps better as a longer-term play

Just the Facts

INDUSTRY: **Semiconductors**

BETA COEFFICIENT: **0.9**

5-YEAR COMPOUND EARNINGS-PER-SHARE GROWTH: **4.5%**

		2006	2007	2008	2009	2010
Revenues (Mil)		585	601	599	436	605
Net Income (Mil)		49.2	16.2	34.3	(-16.0)	36.9
Price:	high	38.1	33.4	38.5	30.2	47.3
	low	28.6	24.6	20.0	14.3	25.9

Coherent, Inc.
5100 Patrick Henry Drive
Santa Clara, CA 95054
(408) 764-4000
Website: *www.coherent.com*

AGGRESSIVE GROWTH

Coinstar, Inc.

Ticker symbol: CSTR (NASDAQ) ❑ S&P rating: BB+ ❑ Value Line financial strength rating: B+ ❑ Current yield: Nil

Who Are They?

Coinstar owns and operates the familiar Coinstar coin-counting and Redbox movie rental kiosks, as well as global money transfer and e-payment services. The coin-counting network of 19,000 kiosks processes some 50 billion coins per year in the United States, Canada, Puerto Rico, the United Kingdom, and Ireland, accounting for 23 percent of the company's total revenue. In 2009 Coinstar, already the majority shareholder in Redbox, acquired the remaining outstanding shares. In 2009, its 22,400 Redbox kiosks processed over 1 billion rentals, accounting for 67 percent of revenue. All of the company's kiosks and other services are typically co-located in high-traffic locations in existing retail establishments such as supermarkets, drugstores, shopping malls, and convenience stores. Kiosks located at Wal-Mart, Walgreen's, and McDonald's together accounted for approximately 40 percent of 2009 revenue, for example.

Why Should I Care?

Movies and coins have been successful for Coinstar so far, and though there have been no announcements as yet, we fully expect the company to move into other high-volume product sectors, as the company has built considerable expertise in the delivery of retail products on demand. Possible targets would include health and beauty (specialized, high-value, high-mix, boutique appeal) and coffee (how about a machine that makes *good* coffee?).

Although it's not part of their current box-in-a-box model, the company has already announced that they will move into the video-on-demand business, competing directly with Netflix, though an infrastructure partner has not yet been announced. Wal-Mart, perhaps?

And in our favorite customer-centric move of 2011, Coinstar has dropped their counting fee for coins. That's right—no more 10 percent off the top of your hard-earned nickels. The catch? You have to accept payment not in cash, but in retail gift cards from places like Amazon, Starbucks, Lowe's, and others. That's fine with us. There's a lot to like about that bargain for all involved, and we think it's a smart play that anticipates the capture of far more than the 10 percent counting fee.

Many people are downplaying the future of Redbox, making the argument that digital content delivery will put DVDs out of business. This argument ignores many key issues with the Netflix model. First, not everyone has access to or can afford a high-speed Internet connection. According to the International Telecommunications Union, in 2010 fewer than 30 percent of Internet users had a broadband connection capable of streaming video content. Second, the advent of Blu-Ray content further limits the number of households capable of receiving content via the Internet. Displaying Blu-Ray content requires an average video transfer speed far higher than that available to all but a small percentage of the Internet users in the United States, meaning that if you have a nice high-definition screen and want to see movies in all their glory, chances are a disk is your only real option, and will be for many years to come.

How's Business?

After an earnings warning in January 2011, the stock has been trending upward on the momentum of somewhat favorable Q4 comps. Inventory management issues and a change in the rental-delay policy, however, had left the kiosks overstocked and undersold, a condition the company is working quickly to address.

Upside

- Appears to be plenty of margin in the Netflix model
- EPS up fivefold since 2008
- Mechanized retail model may play well for other kinds of products

Downside

- Inventory management always an issue with movies
- Threats from video on demand and Blockbuster resurrection
- Short interest close to 40 percent of float at $46 per share

Just the Facts

INDUSTRY: **Recreational Products**
BETA COEFFICIENT: **0.85**
5-YEAR COMPOUND EARNINGS-PER-SHARE GROWTH: **-7.5%**

		2006	2007	2008	2009	2010
Revenues (Mil)		534	546	912	1,145	1,436
Net Income (Mil)		18.6	44.8	16.1	27.8	65.9
Price:	high	34.4	35.0	38.9	38.3	67.6
	low	21.6	24.7	15.7	18.8	25.4

Coinstar, Inc.
1800 114th Avenue SE
Bellevue, WA 98004
(425) 943-8000
Website: *www.coinstar.com*

AGGRESSIVE GROWTH

Constant Contact, Inc.

Ticker symbol: CTCT (NASDAQ) ❑ S&P rating: NA ❑ Value Line financial strength rating: NA ❑ Current yield: Nil

Who Are They?

Constant Contact is a marketing services solution provider. Its primary products include software for the management of on-demand e-mail marketing, event marketing, and online surveys for market intelligence. It also provides product training and outsourcing services for customers who prefer to have Constant Contact manage the marketing process.

Constant Contact's products offer customizable templates for e-mail creation, tools to manage contact lists, and tracking/reporting tools to allow the clients to understand what's happening to their mail after it's been sent. The customer's goal is to create, execute, and manage an effective marketing campaign, and that's Constant Contact's primary product focus.

Why Should I Care?

Small businesses, nonprofits, and other organizations are always looking for ways to make their relatively small marketing budgets go farther. The Internet provides a made-to-order infrastructure for contact-based marketing programs, but as anyone with an e-mail address can attest, e-mail marketing is not always useful, welcome, or even legal. Constant Contact, on the other hand, provides professional tools and services to help its clients connect to and maintain contact with customers, clients, and members. Even the smallest organizations can get access to marketing expertise that has been proven to work for their specific needs.

Traditional advertising methods, such as television and radio broadcasting, have always been some of the most expensive methods available, but had the benefit of reach. Year after year the television and radio networks could lay claim to the largest audiences of current and potential customers. Those days may not be over, but there are real alternatives available. E-mail has the potential for far greater reach, and has the enormous advantage of interactivity and self-identification.

Internet and e-mail–based marketing, despite what your inbox may tell you every morning, is still in its infancy. Companies such as Constant Contact are still learning what works and what doesn't with regard to the management of customers and clients. It's a bit like the exploration of the Wild West, and the map is not fully drawn in. What seems clear is the enormous potential of the electronic channels, given their tremendous leverage in cost per contact, their timeliness, and their potential for rich content. Television advertising took some time to find its stride, and many thought it could not compete with print advertising given the limits of the technology at the time. We think that's where Internet and e-mail–based marketing is now, and companies such as Constant Contact are going to grow with the medium. We like Constant Contact because it chooses to focus on the small players who have traditionally been left out of the game when it came to smart, focused marketing. It has got a market with unmet needs and a product that fits the budget; at some point it just becomes a matter of critical mass. With thirteen years of experience and over 430,000 clients, we like CTCT's chances.

How's Business?

The company recorded its first profitable year in 2010 since going public in late 2006. They added 185,000 new unique paying customers with a monthly retention rate of nearly 98 percent. Average monthly revenue per customer was up 4 percent year-to-year, while the cost of acquiring new customers held steady. Projections for 2011 are for revenue of $218 million and earnings of $7 million.

Upside

- Medium fish, large pond
- Path to profitability found
- Solid strategic acquisitions

Downside

- Very competitive market
- Stratospheric price/earnings
- Profit/growth tradeoff could scare away share buyers

Just the Facts

INDUSTRY: **Computer Services**
BETA COEFFICIENT: **1.06**
5-YEAR COMPOUND EARNINGS-PER-SHARE GROWTH: **Not Meaningful**

	2006	2007	2008	2009	2010
Revenues (Mil)	27.6	50.5	87.3	129	174
Net Income (Mil)	(-7.8)	(-8.3)	(-2.1)	(-1.3)	2.91
Price: high	—	29.5	22.8	22.6	16.8
low	—	17.7	11.6	13.3	31.4

Constant Contact, Inc.
1601 Trapelo Road
Waltham, MA 02451
(781) 472-8100
Website: ***www.constantcontact.com***

AGGRESSIVE GROWTH

Costco Wholesale

Ticker symbol: COST (NASDAQ) ❑ S&P rating: A+ ❑ Value Line financial strength rating: A+ ❑ Current yield: 1.2%

Who Are They?

Costco Wholesale Corporation operates a multinational chain of membership warehouses, mainly under the Costco Wholesale name, that carry brand-name merchandise at substantially lower prices than are typically found at conventional wholesale or retail sources. The warehouses are designed to help small to medium-sized businesses reduce costs in purchasing for resale and for everyday business use, but as most know, the individual consumer has been their big growth driver. The company capitalizes on size and operational efficiencies, like "cross-docking" shipments directly from manufacturers to stores, to achieve attractive pricing to its customers. Costco is the largest membership warehouse club chain in the world based on sales volume and is the fifth-largest general retailer in the United States.

Costco carries a broad line of product categories, including groceries, appliances, television and media, automotive supplies, toys, hardware, sporting goods, jewelry, cameras, books, housewares, apparel, health and beauty aids, tobacco, furniture, office supplies, and office equipment. The company also operates self-service gasoline stations at a number of its United States and Canadian locations. Approximately 56 percent of sales come from food, beverages, alcohol, sundries, and snacks, the rest from an assortment of hard and soft lines.

Costco is open only to members of its tiered membership plan. As of August 2010 Costco has 566 locations, 521 of them in North America, Mexico, and Puerto Rico.

Why Should I Care?

Costco occupies an enviable spot in the retail landscape—a low-cost outlet with outstanding customer demographics. An $800 watch sells thirty feet from a seventy-nine cent eat-it-now hot dog. Why sell one pen when you can sell a package of twenty for just five times as much? Drop by to pick up a gallon of milk and some bread and leave with two bottles of high-end Scotch and a sixty-inch plasma television. Costco, with generally low prices and a "cash-and-carry" shopping experience, has made it easy for people to feel good about impulse purchases.

The international stores have done extremely well in FY2011, with comps up 14 percent for the nine months ended May 2011. Even adjusting for inflation in the price of gasoline sales, the international growth rate was more than double that of the U.S.-based stores. This is important for Costco, as they have begun to scale back their new store openings in the United States.

The company recently announced that it likes itself so much that it's going to buy back $4 billion of its own stock. At current prices, this represents roughly 12 percent of its outstanding shares. We call this "free EPS," and we like it a lot more than a bump to the dividend.

How's Business?

Early 2011 comps are very encouraging. February was up 4 percent, March was up 7, and April up a whopping 12 percent, over three points higher than expectations. For the year, Costco expects a revenue increase of 11.4 percent and EPS growth of 13.3 percent.

Upside

- Death, taxes, and 12.5 percent gross margins at Costco
- Visits up 4 percent in 2011
- Membership renewal rate is 89 percent

Downside

- Food as a loss-leader has competition at Target and Wal-Mart
- North American saturation in sight?
- Shares not far from fully valued

Just the Facts

INDUSTRY: **Retail (Warehouse Club)**
BETA COEFFICIENT: **0.75**
5-YEAR COMPOUND EARNINGS-PER-SHARE GROWTH: **9.0%**

		2006	2007	2008	2009	2010
Revenues (Mil)		60,151	64,400	72,483	71,422	77,946
Net Income (Mil)		1,103	1,083	1,283	1,086	1,307
Price:	high	57.9	72.7	75.2	61.3	73.2
	low	46	51.5	43.9	38.2	53.4

Costco Wholesale Corporation
999 Lake Drive
Issaquah, WA 98027
(425) 313-8203
Website: *www.costco.com*

AGGRESSIVE GROWTH

Cree, Inc.

Ticker symbol: CREE (NASDAQ) ❑ S&P rating: NA ❑ Value Line financial strength rating: B+ ❑ Current yield: Nil

Who Are They?

Cree, Inc., is a manufacturer of semiconductor devices and materials. Founded in 1987 in Durham, North Carolina, the company has grown to 4,300 employees and more than $850 million in revenue, with manufacturing facilities in North Carolina and China. The bulk of its revenues are derived from products based on light-emitting diode (LED) technology. Recently it has also developed a new line of power-switching products based on their silicon carbide process expertise. Cree is also one of the largest providers of gallium nitride semiconductor devices, used primarily in low- to medium-power LEDs.

Why Should I Care?

Cree is the leader in the development of light-emitting diodes based on silicon carbide processes. Both silicon carbide and gallium nitride provide specific benefits when compared to the more common doped silicon semiconductors that have been used since the early 1960s in nearly every electronic product in the world. These benefits are leveraged primarily for applications requiring the efficient production of light and efficient, high-speed switching of power devices. The company's ability to leverage these formerly rather niche technologies into a near-$1 billion business is the story of the LED and Haitz's Law.

When they were first introduced in 1962, LEDs were not very bright, limited to one color (red), and horribly expensive. Since the mid-1960s, however, LED brightness has improved by a factor of two every three years or so, a trend that has come to be known as Haitz's Law (similar to Moore's Law for computing devices). The result is that now we have LEDs that can produce over 200 lumens per watt, or nearly fifteen times the specific output of an incandescent bulb. Cree's business is about leveraging these improvements into product applications as they become practical and producing the device to enable it. Some of the more easily identifiable applications include automotive lighting, household lighting, and flashlights. Others include fiber-optic sources, signage, and telecommunications.

Further progress along the Haitz trend line will bring into play even more applications and lower costs for existing uses. Next in line will be automotive headlamps, cost-effective interior lighting, and the elimination of all but a few specialty uses for incandescent and fluorescent lamps. Cree is out in front on all these uses, with product designs that ease the conversion from older technology to LEDs that it supplies.

The company also recently introduced a new class of devices, a MOSFET based on silicon carbide technology that enables a dramatically more efficient mode of operation for power-switching equipment. The device's function may be the most ubiquitous technology you've never heard of; the company claims the market for this single device is close to $4 billion today, and we have no reason to doubt it. If it can produce this device in quantity with reliability, the company can charge a healthy premium for it, as it's a potential game changer.

How's Business?

Cree lit all the lights last year, with profits nearly as high as the previous four years combined. This is the classic semiconductor model, where the marginal income curve gets very steep as volumes rise above critical levels. FY2011 looks equally solid, though without the dramatic year-over-year growth. The company carries no debt and is sitting on over a billion in cash. Acquisitions or a stock buyback would not be out of the question.

Upside

- Solid core business
- Well-funded R&D
- Enormous displacement potential

Downside

- Somewhat speculative
- Better tech is always possible
- Slow adoption from traditional industries

Just the Facts

INDUSTRY: **Semiconductors**
BETA COEFFICIENT: **1.20**
5-YEAR COMPOUND EARNINGS-PER-SHARE GROWTH: **2.5%**

		2006	2007	2008	2009	2010
Revenues (Mil)		423	394	493	567	867
Net Income (Mil)		80	26.3	31.8	59.3	179.2
Price:	high	35.3	34.9	35.5	57.3	83.4
	low	15.3	15.3	12.6	15.6	47.3

Cree, Inc.
4600 Silicon Drive
Durham, NC 27703
(919) 313-5300
Website: ***www.cree.com***

AGGRESSIVE GROWTH

Deckers Outdoor Corp.

Ticker symbol: DECK (NASDAQ) ❑ S&P rating: NA ❑ Value Line financial strength rating: B++ ❑ Current yield: Nil

Who Are They?

Deckers Outdoor designs, produces, and markets footwear for men, women, and children looking for innovative, high-quality products for casual and outdoor wear. They were founded in 1973 by a student at a California university to produce sandals for beachgoers and surfers. Although the sandals are no longer made, Deckers were so successful in the seventies and eighties that the founder was able to acquire a license to produce and distribute the Teva brand sandal, a design made for whitewater rafters but used almost universally in water sports for its durability and comfort. The Teva brand proved very successful and soon Deckers acquired several other brands, including UGG Holdings in 1995.

At the time, UGG Holdings's sales were approximately $17 million. In 2010, sales of UGG brand footwear exceeded $800 million, making them one of the biggest success stories in the shoe business in decades.

Why Should I Care?

Clothing retailers have come back in a big way during the recovery. Deckers is one of the top performers in the category, with its iconic UGG boots and popular Teva outdoor footwear.

A big part of the appeal of Deckers as a brand holder is the breadth of products available. Although it does not make formal footwear, dedicated sports equipment, or couture, it makes just about everything else. A family of four can be outfitted in nothing but Deckers products and have 90 percent of their shoe needs met. Special use footwear, for outdoor recreation such as hiking and climbing, is also available, and these are often repurposed for everyday casual use.

We also like Deckers's position with regard to its two biggest brands, Teva and UGG. These two lines are near the top of the industry in terms of customer awareness, acceptance, and loyalty. Deckers's growth will be based in large part on the successful expansion of those brands, and we feel good about their chances here. The brand concepts for each are broad enough to accommodate dozens of uses and styles—UGG, focused on an outdoor luxury/comfort concept primarily for women, and Teva, the outdoor performance/casual brand. These two brands have matched up well with young, modern athletic lifestyles for over twenty years, and we don't see the appeal fading going forward.

It needs to be said, however, that nearly three-quarters of the company's revenue is derived from one line of footwear, the UGG boot. Made from sheepskins, this design has been popular for over a decade and has been counterfeited for nearly as long. When the bloom is off of that particular rose, we hope that Deckers will be ready with a replacement or several of us will be wishing we'd given this one the boot earlier.

How's Business?

The company's 2010 was its first-ever $1 billion year. Per share earnings rose 36 percent to $4.03, well above estimates. International sales were very strong, growing 42 percent to $237 million. The company's reworking of its international sales from a distribution model to a wholesaler model is generating higher profits as it now sells directly to the retailers.

Upside

- Bags and outerwear hitting stores in fall 2011
- Expansion of men's casual footwear
- Greater emphasis on European expansion

Downside

- It's still the fashion world
- Three-quarters of revenue tied to UGG boot
- Counterfeiting, particularly of UGG brand

Just the Facts

INDUSTRY: **Footwear**

BETA COEFFICIENT: **1.45**

5-YEAR COMPOUND EARNINGS-PER-SHARE GROWTH: **46%**

		2006	2007	2008	2009	2010
Revenues (Mil)		304.4	449	689	813	1,001
Net Income (Mil)		41.5	66.4	96.0	117	145
Price:	high	20.2	55.5	52.3	34.8	87.9
	low	9.0	18.7	15.4	12.4	31.1

Deckers Outdoor Corporation
495-A South Fairview Avenue
Goleta, CA 93117
(805) 967-7611
Website: *www.deckers.com*

AGGRESSIVE GROWTH

Dell, Inc.

Ticker symbol: DELL (NASDAQ) □ S&P rating: A- □ Value Line financial strength rating: A □ Current yield: Nil

Who Are They?

Dell is one of the largest computing equipment and services suppliers in the world. It designs, manufactures, and markets personal computers, servers, networking equipment, storage subsystems, and computer peripherals. Its consumer division also resells Dell-branded and third-party equipment and accessories such as televisions, printers, monitors, memory, and storage. The company markets through its direct sales teams to corporate and institutional customers and sells direct via catalog, retail outlets, and the Internet.

Dell's biggest impact on the PC market may have been its original direct-to-the-consumer order fulfillment model. Rather than being forced to choose among prebundled configurations, Dell customers were able to configure systems as they liked. In the process, Dell was able to capture the retail markup while still offering products at a competitive price. HP, IBM, Sony, and others had nothing like this and were forced to rely on the retail channel for the bulk of their sales.

Why Should I Care?

Dell, which many would say characterized the bullish 1990s perhaps more than any other company, may look like the most boring stock in this book. Most view the company as a "me too" seller of consumer-grade personal computers, a low-margin business that IBM had the good sense to depart when it sold its PC division to Lenovo in 2004. As it turned out, IBM's timing couldn't have been better; Dell's stock peaked in late 2004 and has been on a pretty steady decline ever since.

In reality, though, Dell's consumer business represents only 20 percent of revenue, while PCs overall account for only 55 percent. In 2010 its enterprise business brought in 30 percent of revenue at record margin levels. And even though the consumer segment revenue fell 8 percent in 2010, the company nearly doubled its earnings overall, as the server and storage businesses averaged 21 percent growth year-over-year. Dell is clearly not driven by the consumer PC business and certainly isn't the company that most people think it is.

Dell was famous in its heyday for its supply-chain management. Because it was so efficient at turning inventory (for several years they averaged fifty-four inventory turns per year), it was essentially running with negative inventory cost; it got paid on a Monday for products whose parts it wasn't planning to buy until Friday. Given the "value rot" aspect of computer inventory, this expertise is priceless. And Dell has not lost their touch; in 2009 it was still carrying less than eight days of inventory and were ranked only behind Apple in the overall quality of its supply chain management.

How's Business?

Talk about a rebound year. Dell's 2010 pulled them out of the recession with significant advances in margins, particularly in the final quarter. Dell's fourth quarter produced fifty-three cents per share in earnings, against a consensus expectation of thirty-seven cents, and gross margins of 21.5 percent versus a consensus of 18.7 percent. Sales to small, medium, and large businesses were all up 12 percent, with the bulk of the gains coming in storage and services.

Upside

- No longer reliant on the PC business
- Retail presence fills a void
- Still managing the basics well

Downside

- A bit late to the services party
- PCs have to figure out how to make money
- Direct model no longer a big advantage

Just the Facts

INDUSTRY: **Computer Hardware**
BETA COEFFICIENT: **0.95**
5-YEAR COMPOUND EARNINGS-PER-SHARE GROWTH: **-3.0%**

		2006	2007	2008	2009	2010
Revenues (Bil)		57.4	61.1	61.1	52.9	61.5
Net Income (Bil)		2.58	2.95	2.48	1.43	2.64
Price:	high	32.2	30.8	26.0	17.3	17.5
	low	19.0	21.6	8.7	7.8	11.3

Dell, Inc.
One Dell Way
Round Rock, TX 78682
(512) 338-4400
Website: *www.dell.com*

AGGRESSIVE GROWTH

Digi International, Inc.

Ticker symbol: DGII (NASDAQ) ❑ S&P rating: NA ❑ Value Line financial strength rating: NA ❑ Current yield: Nil

Who Are They?

Digi is one of a number of companies supplying "smart" devices to, among others, operators of alternative energy systems and traditional electric utilities. These devices are designed primarily to monitor and communicate the status of a device's energy consumption, but are also used for monitoring the operation of mobile equipment such as truck fleets, agricultural equipment, and public safety vehicles. The company's products are also used for remote monitoring of large storage tanks for temperature, capacity, and other valuable data.

The company's strategy is to target the value of the communication link between the device and the grid, rather than the monitor/sensor itself. Digi launched its "Drop-in Networking" four years ago and plans to focus on this core capability going forward. Drop-in Networking is designed to make nearly any device with any basic data port a wired/wireless Internet Protocol device with specific, customized monitoring features. Digi's belief is that the Internet is a far more robust and flexible communications network than any proprietary network could be (we agree). Its product line is split roughly 50/50 on a revenue basis between embedded devices (designed into the customer's product) and stand-alone, external products.

The company also provides "cloud" services (basically, they own the data center) and supplies software tools to integrate desktop and mobile applications that interface with the customer's data.

Why Should I Care?

"You manage what you measure" is an axiom used in many fields. The ability to monitor electricity consumption at the customer's level in real time has profound implications not just for the generating utility but for the individual user as well. A consumer who can see the positive monetary effect of a single change in how he uses electricity is a consumer who's about to change his behavior. This is the thinking behind a number of the incentives the U.S. government is proposing in its vision for a "smart grid," whereby conservation will become easier and more effective. The Electric Power Research Institute estimates the implementation of current smart grid tools will save between 4 and 5 percent of all electric use by 2030 (about $20 billion per year in 2012 dollars).

You're driving down a little-used road late at night, and as you make your way the streetlights turn on ahead of your arrival and turn off after you pass by. This is similar in concept to the motion-detection lighting in modern buildings, but it's how approximately 10,000 streetlights work in a Digi-based lighting network in Norway. The system also allows for multiple users to be billed for power consumed by multiple lights attached to the same standard, and for partial dimming in Norway's unique environmental conditions. This particular pilot program has shown nearly a 66 percent reduction in energy usage.

How's Business?

The company had a good turnaround in 2010 in both revenue and earnings, with earnings acceleration in 2010 versus the prior three years. The company recently introduced the industry's first devices that comply with a new data security specification, FIPS 14-2. This new spec is particularly important to users of wireless IP devices and is a requirement for most federal contracts. This is an important certification, assuming the federal government has any money left with which to buy communications hardware.

Upside

- Government incentives of $4 billion to grid industry
- No debt, very good cash flow
- Established technology, new market

Downside

- Trading at a high multiple
- Some negative-earnings surprises recently
- Bumpy ride; volume trading by large financials

Just the Facts

INDUSTRY: **Computer Hardware**
BETA COEFFICIENT: **0.77**
5-YEAR COMPOUND EARNINGS-PER-SHARE GROWTH: **NM**

		2006	2007	2008	2009	2010
Revenues (Mil)		145	173	185	166	183
Net Income (Mil)		11.1	19.8	12.4	4.1	8.94
Price:	high	14.1	16.5	7.8	10.6	11.8
	low	10.9	14.7	13.1	6.8	7.6

Digi International, Inc.
11001 Bren Road East
Minnetonka, MN 55343
(952) 912-3444
Website: *www.digi.com*

AGGRESSIVE GROWTH

Discover Financial

Ticker symbol: DFS (NYSE) ❑ S&P rating: BBB- ❑ Value Line financial strength rating: B+ ❑ Current yield: 0.4%

Who Are They?

Discover Financial Services is a direct banking and payment services company. Operating as a bank and financial holding company, Discover offers its own branded credit cards, student loans, personal loans, and deposits through its Discover Bank as part of its Direct Banking segment. Other services provided through Direct Banking include prepaid cards and consumer lending. The other operating segment of the company, Payment Services, includes the PULSE ATM/debit network, Diners Club International, and Discover's third-party issuing business, which provides credit, debit, and prepaid cards issued by third parties operating on the Discover Network. And beginning in calendar 2011, the company operates the Student Loan Corporation as a wholly owned subsidiary of Discover Bank.

Discover's PULSE network links cardholders of more than 4,400 financial institutions with ATMs and point-of-sale terminals located throughout the United States. PULSE also provides cash at over 750,000 ATMs in more than eighty countries. PULSE's primary source of revenue is transaction fees charged through the use of debit cards issued by participating financial institutions.

The company's direct banking products compete with many of the largest banks in the country, although Discover maintains very few actual brick-and-mortar banks. The company's payment services products compete mainly with other card-issuing institutions and network operators, such as American Express, STAR, Capital One, MasterCard, and Visa.

Why Should I Care?

Over the past few years, billions of dollars in credit card debt has been written off by the card issuers and the underwriting banks as debts simply became uncollectable. The top six card issuers, including Discover, had $75 billion worth of defaults, for a "charge-off" rate that peaked at nearly 11 percent in the second quarter of 2010. As a result, issuers are becoming more selective about who gets credit cards and are more conservative in their terms of use. The previous year's write-offs and the more conservative approach to credit issuance are expected to lead to a far lower charge-off percentage in 2011. Moody's Investor Services, a major market analyst, estimates that the six top card issuers will see their default rates drop to below an annualized 4 percent. The effect of reduced provisions for bad debt has a dramatic effect on the financial performance of the company—a 0.5 percent change can lead to a 10 percent swing in the price of the stock.

This would be a good sign in and of itself, but it gets especially interesting when you look at the company's 2010 annual report, which shows that Discover had set aside $3.2 billion in credit loss provisions in 2010, even in the face of a declining default rate, which for the year meant that $1.7 billion of that provision was used. This had a dramatic negative effect on reported earnings, although the company was actually far healthier than it appeared. If the 2011 default rate drops to the predicted levels, Discover will be able to put these funds back into circulation and generate significant income.

How's Business?

Analyst David Trainer ranks DFS as the top performer among consumer finance companies in terms of return on invested capital (an important benchmark), with an ROIC of 22.5 percent. Two of Discover's competitors, Capital One and Bank of America, have ROICs of 6.2 percent and 1.6 percent, respectively.

Upside

- E-commerce transactions on the rise
- Worldwide acceptance and growing use of credit
- Clean balance sheet

Downside

- Slower credit growth compared to past
- Unemployment rate still high
- Fees under regulatory pressure

Just the Facts

INDUSTRY: **Consumer Financial Services**

BETA COEFFICIENT: **1.40**

5-YEAR COMPOUND EARNINGS-PER-SHARE GROWTH: **NM**

		2006	2007	2008	2009	2010
Total Assets (Mil)		29,067	37,376	39,892	46,021	60,785
Net Income (Mil)		1,077	838	528	54.0	668
Price:	high	—	32.2	19.9	17.4	19.5
	low	—	14.8	6.6	4.7	12.1

Discover Financial Services
2500 Lake Cook Road
Riverwoods, IL 60015
(224) 405-0900
Website: ***www.discoverfinancial.com***

AGGRESSIVE GROWTH

Eastman Chemical Company

Ticker symbol: EMN (NYSE) ❑ S&P rating: BBB ❑ Value Line financial strength rating: B++ ❑ Current yield: 2.1%

Who Are They?

If you're old enough to be reading this book, you might remember the original Eastman Kodak. That company's cameras and especially its process for creating roll film made Kodak (a name invented in 1888 by George Eastman) the world's leading photography brand. The chemicals used in the production of that film were made by Eastman Chemical. In 1993, Eastman Chemical was spun off from Kodak and became a separate company engaged in the business of manufacturing plastics, chemicals, and fiber products. That company now has a market cap of about ten times that of its old parent Kodak, and by the time this goes to print, Kodak itself may be on the auction block.

Please excuse the trip down memory lane—we're both photographers who started out shooting Kodak Tri-X black-and-white film.

Back on topic, Eastman Chemical is not only no longer tied to the photography business, they're not tied to any particular business. It is pretty much everywhere. Its broad product line includes basic materials like yarns, water treatment, adhesives, wood preservatives, inks, polymers, paints, resins, acetate fiber . . . the list goes on and on. Its products are used extensively in packaging, medical equipment and supplies, agriculture, industrial goods, apparel, consumer and durable goods, and even consumables like, yes, photographic film.

Why Should I Care?

Eastman Chemical produces many of the basic ingredients of industry. Its products are key raw materials, integrated directly into other products or used as part of the production process. When industry grows, Eastman grows and is one of the first companies to get paid. Not surprisingly, it has been getting paid a lot as of late. Its top line is not yet back to prerecession levels, but the recovery has been very good to sales so far and the company looks to be well positioned for further growth. It's sold off an underperforming plastics operation and added significant capacity in its high-margin olefins feedstock unit. Debt is quite low and there's adequate cash on hand for acquisitions.

The real story of the past year, however, has been the growth in the bottom line. It has been beating earnings estimates in each of the last four quarters. Over the past two years, earnings have more than doubled. Cash flow is up over 60 percent over the same period. Earnings estimates for 2012 keep rising, but as of right now they're at $8.82, which would predict a share price in the $140–$150 range at recent multiples. Rising cigarette sales, particularly in the Far East, has given Eastman's fibers unit a big boost. The company has a new acetate operation in South Korea and plans to build another in China in 2013 to further serve this market.

How's Business?

Eastman had a monster 2010, as we mentioned. Even with the rise in petroleum prices, operating margins increased significantly. This bodes extremely well for performance over the next few years, given the recent political uncertainty and the speculative nature of that market.

Upside

- Good production capacity
- Innovative company
- Fair amount of pricing power

Downside

- Shares could get pricey in a hurry
- Petroleum a major feedstock
- Foreign currency exposure in largest segments

Just the Facts

INDUSTRY: **Chemicals—Plastics & Rubber**
BETA COEFFICIENT: **1.2**
5-YEAR COMPOUND EARNINGS-PER-SHARE GROWTH: **33%**

		2006	2007	2008	2009	2010
Revenues (Mil)		7,450	6,830	6,726	4,396	5,842
Net Income (Mil)		416	423	342	266	514
Price:	high	61.3	72.4	78.3	61.9	84.6
	low	47.3	57.5	25.9	17.8	51.1

Eastman Chemical Company
200 South Wilcox Drive
Kingsport, TN 37662
(423) 229-2000
Website: ***www.eastman.com***

AGGRESSIVE GROWTH

Entropic Communications, Inc.

Ticker symbol: ENTR (NASDAQ) ❑ S&P rating: NA ❑ Value Line financial strength rating: NA ❑ Current yield: Nil

Who Are They?

Entropic is a fabless semiconductor company located in San Diego, an area that seems to spawn communications companies the way Silicon Valley used to spawn computer makers. Perhaps it's the ghost of Motorola's set-top box operation moving over the land. In any case, Entropic operates in four markets: home networking, digital broadcast satellite, "silicon tuners," and broadband access.

The home networking business is based on a proprietary chip design that provides the ability to record and access digital video simultaneously in every room in a typical home via a standard Internet Protocol network. Gaming access is also supported, as is the sharing of any type of file. The digital broadcast satellite business is built around a family of chips that can support the transfer of up to twelve simultaneous channels through a single downlink. Up to four LNBs (dishes) can be connected to a single coaxial cable, greatly simplifying installation in multi-room homes and apartment buildings. The silicon tuners are basically solid-state RF tuning equipment for digital televisions, and the broadband access solutions are hardware and software for the last 500 meters—the span from a fiber drop to customer premises.

Why Should I Care?

What's especially appealing about Entropic's product plan is that it has a solution for any and all of the current media delivery scenarios. DBS providers can use the BTS/CSS products to a single co-ax drop point, rather than having to run as many as three cables to each room with a set-top box. Cable TV providers can create standard IP-based home networking packages that utilize the same co-ax backbone used to distribute media content and still maintain interoperability. Home PCs can connect to the network through a media adapter and have access content on all other networked devices. It's a pretty compelling story, made more so because of the MoCA (media over co-ax alliance) standards body and the dozens of MoCA-certified devices already on the market from companies like Samsung, Netgear, and DirecTV.

The advent of "smart" TVs with support for streaming and DVR capability built in paves the way for the elimination of the set-top box altogether (finally!), and the Entropic network chipset provides the streaming capability that such a set would need in the scenario envisioned by the TV makers.

The company introduced the first MoCA 2.0–compliant parts at the Consumer Electronics Show in January 2011. The 2.0 spec parts offer enhanced reliability, better security, new power-management features, and higher speed (up to 1Gbps), while maintaining backward compatibility with the older spec.

How's Business?

Revenues in 2010 climbed above Entropic's break-even point for the first time in the company's ten-year history. Despite the long track record of losses, the company's finances are in good shape, with adequate cash reserves and minimal debt. Its R&D, which stood at 40 percent of revenue in 2009 and 24 percent in 2010, is likely to remain relatively high, as the company expands the MoCA software portfolio.

Upside

- Good set of strategic partnerships
- The streaming trend is their friend
- Nothing like a breakout year to motivate the troops

Downside

- The competition includes Broadcom
- Costly R&D
- Relatively high volatility

Just the Facts

INDUSTRY: **Semiconductors**
BETA COEFFICIENT: **2.5**
5-YEAR COMPOUND EARNINGS-PER-SHARE GROWTH: **NM**

		2006	2007	2008	2009	2010
Revenues (Mil)		41.5	122	146	116	210
Net Income (Mil)		(-7.05)	(-32.0)	(-136)	(-13.2)	64.7
Price:	high	—	7.4	7.2	3.5	12.1
	low	—	6.3	0.6	0.5	3.2

Entropic Communications, Inc.
6290 Sequence Drive
San Diego, CA 92121
(858) 768-3600
Website: *www.entropic.com*

AGGRESSIVE GROWTH

Exact Sciences Corporation

Ticker symbol: EXAS (NASDAQ) ❑ S&P rating: NA ❑ Value Line financial strength rating: NA ❑ Current yield: Nil

Who Are They?

Exact Sciences is a biotechnology company engaged in the development of a methodology for the early detection of human colorectal cancer. Its approach is somewhat unique in that it employs non-invasive, DNA-based stool screening and so can be handled without an office visit or other more expensive procedures. The process is also designed to detect precancerous bodies and can provide earlier screening horizons than most other processes. No special preparations or diet are required, nor are any radioactive materials employed.

Exact Sciences has licensed certain core aspects of the process from the Mayo Clinic and Dr. David Ahlquist. The company will make royalty payments to both parties and will retain the exclusive rights to commercialize additional development that may derive from the license or the collaboration.

Why Should I Care?

Other screening methods for colorectal cancer utilize the examination of stool samples, but none is as specific as that proposed and tested by Exact Science. Its method seeks to detect minute traces of DNA that have undergone mutations, correlating these DNA fragments with known markers for precancerous polyp formations in the colon. Other stool sampling approaches require the presence of blood secreted by these precancerous polyps or by active tumors in order to make a positive diagnosis, but these tissues do not secrete blood at all times, reducing the odds of detection. On the other hand, the polyps do shed surface cells on a continual basis, and a percentage of these cells will have DNA that can be detected as cancerous or precancerous in nature. In the largest clinical trial of the approach to date, the Exact Science Cologard method was 64 percent effective at detecting precancerous tissues, while the three current competitive non-visual screening methods were 22 percent, 20 percent, and 12 percent effective. The current "gold standard" screening method, colonoscopy, was 95 percent effective in the same test, but the cost of a colonoscopy is between three and thirteen times the projected cost of Cologard and requires a significant level of training to perform and interpret results in order to achieve that level of effectiveness. The Cologard process, compared to existing stool-based methods, is more sensitive and specific, and appears to be easily automated.

In short, Cologard looks to be a very good candidate to replace all of the current or projected screening methods for colorectal cancer. Since colorectal cancer is far easier to treat when detected early, and since colorectal cancer is the second most deadly form of cancer in the United States, the argument for widespread screening is compelling. The American Cancer Society recommends annual screening for colorectal cancer for everyone over the age of fifty (over 90 million people in the United States) and Exact Sciences estimates the potential market value of its screening process at $1.2 billion annually.

How's Business?

Exact Sciences is not yet profitable, but the prospects are very encouraging. Its burn rate is manageable and it has sufficient capital to see the company through at least 2013, which is when it expects Cologard to be in general availability. It already has over a thousand LabCorp sales reps promoting their current ColoSure product.

Upside

- Solid trial data
- Compelling mortality argument
- Excellent demographics

Downside

- Obvious buyout candidate (not always a bad thing)
- Potential regulatory obstacles
- May require an additional stock offering to complete trials

Just the Facts

INDUSTRY: **Biotechnology and Drugs**
BETA COEFFICIENT: **1.05**
5-YEAR COMPOUND EARNINGS-PER-SHARE GROWTH: **NM**

		2006	2007	2008	2009	2010
Revenues (Mil)		4.75	2.94	(-0.87)	4.76	5.34
Net Income (Mil)		(-12.9)	(-12.0)	(-9.74)	(-9.13)	(-11.6)
Price:	high	4.2	5.4	3.3	4.0	8.8
	low	1.7	2.4	0.4	0.6	3.4

Exact Sciences, Inc.
441 Charmany Drive
Madison, WI 53719
(608) 284-5700
Website: *www.exactsciences.com*

AGGRESSIVE GROWTH

Fair Isaac

Ticker symbol: FICO (NYSE) ❑ S&P rating: NA ❑ Value Line financial strength rating: B++ ❑ Current yield: 0.3%

Who Are They?

Fair Isaac Corporation provides decision support analytics, software, and solutions to help businesses improve and automate decision making and risk management. The most well-known and best example of these solutions is the "FICO score," an analytic single-figure estimate of a consumer's creditworthiness used in the credit industry and for other purposes such as employment and insurance.

FICO provides its analytic solutions and services to a variety of financial and other service organizations, including banks, credit reporting agencies, credit card processing agencies, insurers, retailers, marketers, and health-care organizations. It operates in three segments: Applications, Scores, and Tools. The Applications segment provides decision and risk management tools, market targeting products, and fraud detection tools. The Scores segment includes the business-to-business scoring solutions and myFICO solutions, which delivers FICO scores for consumers. The Tools segment provides software products and consulting services to help organizations build their own analytic tools.

About 75 percent of the company's revenues are derived from transaction and unit-priced products, such as the access and sale of a FICO score, with about 70 percent of sales to the consumer credit, financial services, and insurance industries.

Why Should I Care?

Fair Isaac is a stock we've liked for a while as a provider of services primarily to the retail and financial sectors. And although retail has come back in a big way, the financial sector is still walking off a couple of pretty deep thigh bruises. This is not great for Fair Isaac, but it's a good opportunity for investors to pick up a quality issue at a still-discounted price. FICO is trading near its record-low multiple, even though cash flow is strong and earnings growth for 2011 will exceed growth in the top line by 400 percent.

Although revenues for FY2010 were down 4 percent overall, international revenues were actually up 5 percent in adjusted dollars. This is another encouraging sign, as the company has placed particular emphasis on international sales. Fair Isaac's client list includes over half of the 100 largest banks in the world.

The expertise that Fair Isaac has developed in modeling financial risks and consumer behaviors could very well be applied to the modeling of other activities in the economy. Longer term, this could lead to products that might benefit governmental bodies, large non-profit organizations, educational institutions, etc. The company has made no statements regarding this kind of initiative, but we here at *100 Best* are always willing to talk, should they be interested.

The company is taking restructuring charges throughout 2011 and should enter 2012 with a fairly clean slate. If it appears that the market is still taking a wait-and-see approach to FICO shares at the start of 2012, it would be prudent to move early.

How's Business?

Financials for the second quarter of 2011 came in slightly above expectations. Applications and Tools revenues were up 10 and 11 percent, respectively, while Scores revenues were off 4 percent compared to last year. New services bookings were up 6 percent overall. In all, a good showing with no trouble on the horizon, other than the likely continued slow pace of recovery for the transaction-based revenues.

Upside

- No credibility issues here
- New regulations means new product opportunities
- Solid financials

Downside

- Bulk of revenue still transaction-based
- Expect slower recovery than most
- Long-term damage to financial industry margins?

Just the Facts

INDUSTRY: **Software and Programming**
BETA COEFFICIENT: **1.1**
5-YEAR COMPOUND EARNINGS-PER-SHARE GROWTH: **-1.5%**

		2006	2007	2008	2009	2010
Revenues (Mil)		825.4	822.2	744.8	630.7	605.6
Net Income (Mil)		103.5	104.7	81.2	65.1	64.5
Price:	high	47.8	41.8	32.2	24.5	27.0
	low	32.5	32.1	10.4	9.8	19.5

Fair Isaac Corporation
901 Marquette Avenue, Suite 3200
Minneapolis, MN 55402-3232
(612) 758-5200
Website: ***www.fairisaac.com***

AGGRESSIVE GROWTH

Faro Technologies, Inc.

Ticker symbol: FARO (NASDAQ) ❑ S&P rating: NA ❑ Value Line financial strength rating: B+ ❑ Current yield: Nil

Who Are They?

Faro designs, manufactures, and markets 3D measurement and imaging systems used in manufacturing, construction, industrial, and forensic applications. The six basic systems, which consist of a measurement device, their CAM2 imaging software, and a host computer, provide users with a fast and accurate method of dimensioning an object with features as small as five millionths of a meter or the inside of a warehouse 400 feet long. Its systems are used for in-process inspections, reverse engineering, incoming inspection, process characterization, quality monitoring, and many other common industrial requirements. As a measure of the breadth of the applications for Faro's equipment, consider that they have been sold to over 11,000 different customers, from small machine shops to large companies including Boeing, Lockheed, GM, Honda, and General Electric.

Why Should I Care?

There are few things more fundamental to the manufacturing process than measurement. Every object created in a factory is measured in some way before it's shipped off to a customer. In order to measure mechanical dimensions you need tools, an operator (or robot), and a reference. The operator applies the tool to the object, takes a measurement, and based on the comparison of the measurement to the reference, takes some action. This can happen hundreds of times for each object, adding time and labor and in the process, increasing the cost of the product. Most of Faro's products are used to significantly reduce the time needed to perform these inspections. Its unique use profile (portable, handheld, multi-axis) sets it apart from its competitor's products, as the products can be quickly moved and re-tasked with no tooling changes other than a download of the design files for the part to be inspected.

Faro's tools are also invaluable in the design process. Prototype fabrication is accelerated and first articles are quickly verified. Custom tooling needs are minimized, saving significant time and money, and complete dimensioning of hand-built parts can be accomplished in minutes.

There's still a place for quick and easy measurements to be taken with hand tools such as calipers, hole gauges, micrometers, etc., but these tools do not lend themselves to the measurement of anything even as complex as a simple curve. They cannot automatically record and report process variation data, nor are they capable of automatically updating their inspection criteria to reflect the latest process changes. Faro's tools do all of these things. They're capable of replacing all but the very most precise measurement tools available, and they allow even small, low-volume shops to quickly and reliably produce complex, dimensionally accurate products.

How's Business?

Like most of the suppliers of industrial goods, Faro took a beating in 2009 but turned things around in 2010 as orders returned. A revenue up-tick of 30 percent brought them back to profitability, and 2012 looks very promising. Production tooling in general is in demand again, and Faro has just one competitor across most of its product lines.

Upside

- Enormous customer base and product appeal
- Global manufacturing
- Powerful IP protection

Downside

- Faro products can be expensive, limiting demand
- Shares may be pricey
- Margins still pretty spotty

Just the Facts

INDUSTRY: **Scientific & Technical Instruments**
BETA COEFFICIENT: **1.10**
5-YEAR COMPOUND EARNINGS-PER-SHARE GROWTH: **NM**

		2006	2007	2008	2009	2010
Revenues (Mil)		152	192	209	148	192
Net Income (Mil)		8.2	21.4	14.0	(-8.0)	11.0
Price:	high	24.8	50.3	36.2	22.1	33.5
	low	11.7	23.7	10.6	10.8	16.8

Faro Technologies, Inc.
250 Technology Park
Lake Mary, FL 32746
(407) 333-9911
Website: ***www.faro.com***

AGGRESSIVE GROWTH

First Solar, Inc.

Ticker symbol: FSLR (NASDAQ) ❑ S&P rating: NA ❑ Value Line financial strength rating: A ❑ Current yield: Nil

Who Are They?

First Solar is the world's largest manufacturer of thin-film solar panels. It produces panels for sale to integrators, developers, and directly to end users for large-scale programs. The panels produced are typically installed in commercial installations ranging in size from 10 kilowatts up to utility-scale projects, the largest of which so far is 80 megawatts on over a thousand acres.

There are many producers of photovoltaic solar panels, but First Solar's process is a bit different from most others. It does not use wafer silicon and classic semiconductor technologies to produce its products. Instead, it uses standard glass coated on one side with vapor-deposited amorphous silicon and a thin film of cadmium telluride as the collecting material. These panels are much less expensive to manufacture than traditional wafer-based panels and are lighter and more durable, making for a simpler, cheaper, and faster installation process.

The company was founded in 1999 and began production in 2002. Its production capacity in 2012 is expected to be 2.3 gigawatts, or the equivalent of two to three modern, full-scale nuclear generation facilities.

Why Should I Care?

The promise of solar energy—nearly free electricity—has been around for a long time, but the economics had been snared in a Catch-22 for decades. The cost of the photovoltaic device had always been comparatively high on a dollars-per-watt basis, and making them less expensive required much R&D and volume manufacturing techniques that could not be economically justified without committed customers. Customers, on the other hand, were unwilling to commit until cost-effective devices were proven and tested in the field. The tipping point came when a number of industrialized countries threw tax incentives at the problem, spurring the development of advanced PV designs and creating a class of customers for PV-generated electricity in the bargain.

China, Inc., has decided to own the market for traditional wafer silicon panels, which have higher conversion efficiency but higher manufacturing costs, while the thin-film business has fallen largely to First Solar and a few smaller players.

GE recently announced its plans to build the country's largest thin-film panel manufacturing plant somewhere in the United States by 2013. While this means that First Solar now has one of the world's largest diversified manufacturers as a competitor, it's also good news in that it will likely expand the market for both company's products. The entry to the market of an industrial bellwether such as GE will draw significant attention and should help to advance the acceptance of solar as a mainstream technology.

How's Business?

The recent rapid growth of the PV industry was due in part to the tax incentives offered by the governments of Germany and France, and those incentives have an uncertain future. Germany has started to scale back, but other initiatives based on carbon footprint reduction may effectively take their place. In any case, we see First Solar running at capacity for several years to meet existing demand.

Upside

- Technological lead
- Cost advantage
- Robust cash flow

Downside

- GE's entry is a concern
- Margins fading somewhat
- Tellurium supply may be constrained

Just the Facts

INDUSTRY: **Semiconductors**
BETA COEFFICIENT: **1.45**
5-YEAR COMPOUND EARNINGS-PER-SHARE GROWTH: **NM**

		2006	2007	2008	2009	2010
Revenues (Mil)		135	504	1,246	2,066	2,564
Net Income (Mil)		4.0	112	348	640	664
Price:	high	30	283	317	207.5	153.3
	low	23.5	27.5	85.3	100.9	98.7

First Solar, Inc.
350 West Washington Street, Suite 600
Tempe, AZ 85281
(602) 414-9300
Website: *www.firstsolar.com*

AGGRESSIVE GROWTH

Flow International Corp.

Ticker symbol: FLOW (NASDAQ) ❑ S&P rating: NA ❑ Value Line financial strength rating: C ❑ Current yield: Nil

Who Are They?

Ever find yourself staring at a 200-pound block of aluminum, wondering how best to sculpt it into a flying pig for your sister's birthday? No? Well, actually, neither have we, but if we had we'd know the tool to use is a water jet cutter. These clever machines are capable of accurately cutting almost any material using nothing but a high-pressure stream of water. Flow International is the pioneer and market leader in the commercial use of high-pressure water jet cutting tools and has delivered over 10,000 systems since 1974. The company also makes high-pressure surface cleaning systems, but the bulk of its sales are from cutting tools.

Why Should I Care?

Both the company and the market have a number of attractive features. The company is the technology leader in the field, having developed the initial concept and then nearly all of the subsequent commercial refinements. Flow has the broadest and deepest product line and the most advanced integration with articulation robotics and 3D modeling software. And although all of the manufacturers took a hit to the top line during the recession, Flow has the largest installed base, the largest number of service contracts, and the largest recovery potential; it is currently trading at less than half of its prerecession average.

The market itself, currently at about $500 million, is estimated to be worth more than $1 billion with further upside when global markets are more fully developed. The technology favors the new production model of rapid prototyping and displaces several other alternative cutting/milling technologies. At the high end, these tools are not inexpensive, but smaller systems are affordable and yet still versatile. Some continuous-process manufacturers (such as paper mills) use water jets exclusively for their cutting operations, as they create no waste, run year-round with little downtime, and can be easily reconfigured or repurposed, unlike most hard tooling. Textile and plastic extrusion manufacturers would be large potential markets.

Although the company is relatively small, it maintains an Advanced Systems business, which works with select accounts to develop custom, integrated solutions for specific production problems. The company recently worked with Airbus to develop custom tooling for its wing production, for example. These quasi-partnerships are valuable to both companies, and Flow's maintenance of its Advanced Systems operation will pay benefits down the road.

How's Business?

Although revenues were reasonably steady through the 2008–2009 recession, the company took a number of hits to the bottom line due to some extraordinary charges. It found itself in a bit of a cash flow bind and so had a period of mandated salary and benefit reductions, as well as a round of layoffs. The company also added a second distribution channel, which spiked SG&A 30 percent in 2009, closed a manufacturing facility, and introduced two major new products. In total, a number of one-time charges followed by a slow sales year in 2010 has led to consecutive years of losses, but the company is well positioned for growth, with a leaner organization, attractive new products to sell, and a much larger sales channel to put them in.

Upside

- Revitalized customer base
- Growing acceptance of technology
- New, impressive 3D functionality

Downside

- Nearly eighty competitors
- Cash flow is still lean
- High price still a problem on some capital budgets

Just the Facts

INDUSTRY: **Misc. Capital Goods**
BETA COEFFICIENT: **2.05**
5-YEAR COMPOUND EARNINGS-PER-SHARE GROWTH: **NM**

		2006	**2007**	**2008**	**2009**	**2010**
Revenues (Mil)		202	213	244	210	174
Net Income (Mil)		6.7	3.8	22.4	(-23.8)	(-8.5)
Price:	high	14.7	13.1	10.5	3.1	4.2
	low	8.9	7.6	1.4	1.4	2.1

Flow International Corporation
23500 64th Avenue South
Kent, WA 98032
(253) 850-3500
Website: ***www.flowwaterjet.com***

AGGRESSIVE GROWTH

General Electric Co.

Ticker symbol: GE (NYSE) ❑ S&P rating: AA+ ❑ Value Line financial strength rating: B++ ❑ Current yield: 2.8%

Who Are They?

General Electric is the second-largest company (after ExxonMobil) in the United States, and among the largest and most diversified industrial companies in the world. It makes jet engines and clothes dryers, microwave ovens and nuclear reactors, railroad locomotives, and nasal probes. So be careful when filling out your order form.

We can't really start to describe all the products it makes, but the company's businesses are grouped into four segments: Energy Infrastructure, Technology Infrastructure, GE Capital, and Home and Business Solutions. The company also retains a 49 percent share of the former NBC Universal following its sale in January 2011 to Comcast. Interestingly, the product for which it might be best known—light bulbs—it no longer manufactures, and the segment that does no manufacturing, GE Capital, is its largest by revenue.

Why Should I Care?

General Electric and General Motors, both in a book devoted to a review of "aggressive" stocks: Who saw that coming? We wouldn't have thought it likely at all prior to 2011, but here we are, after the worst recession in many decades, with a very fresh perspective on large U.S.-based manufacturers. During the go-go period leading up to the recession, most of these companies barely kept pace with the broader indexes, as concerns over pension obligations, international competition, and reduced spending on infrastructure damped share prices across the board. Following the recession, many of these same companies are still wondering when the rebound will start to affect stock prices—GE's shares are still trading at less than half of their 2007 average share price.

In the early months of 2011, however, companies such as GE, United Technologies, Honeywell, and Danaher have reported first-quarter earnings that have significantly exceeded analyst's expectations. With its fourth consecutive quarter of strong earnings growth, GE came in nearly 20 percent higher than expected, but the reaction from the market has been a big ho-hum. Much attention was given to the slower-growth energy segment, as energy has significant mindshare in the market right now, but ignored were the tripling of profits in the Capital segment and the 8 percent increase in revenues in the Technology segment.

The company has grown its R&D over 50 percent since 2008 and claims, as a result, to have the strongest product pipeline in its history. Initiatives in energy, aircraft engines, and lighting are some of GE's bigger bets. The company has also created a number of energy and transportation ventures in China that target its rapidly growing infrastructure.

Will the market change its view on GE, GM, and the rest of the large industrials that are turning in good, if not spectacular numbers? Hopefully not before you get a chance to buy in on these still relatively inexpensive stocks.

How's Business?

GE's margins, which had taken a beating during the recession, are well on their way to returning to the 13 percent net they achieved in 2007. The 2011 net should come in a full percentage point ahead of 2010's 8.4 percent, and 2012 projects to come in at 11.6 percent.

Upside

- NBC was a distraction, good riddance
- Boeing shipments . . . soon, please
- Infrastructure, infrastructure, infrastructure

Downside

- Military business likely to suffer a bit
- Total debt nearly one-half trillion dollars
- Ten billion shares outstanding

Just the Facts

INDUSTRY: **Consumer Financial Services**
BETA COEFFICIENT: **1.20**
5-YEAR COMPOUND EARNINGS-PER-SHARE GROWTH: **-4.0%**

		2006	2007	2008	2009	2010
Revenues (Bil)		163	173	183	157	150
Net Income (Bil)		20.7	22.5	18.1	11.4	12.6
Price:	high	38.5	42.2	38.5	17.5	19.7
	low	32.1	33.9	12.6	5.7	13.8

General Electric Company
3135 Easton Turnpike
Fairfield, CT 06828
(203) 373-2211
Website: ***www.ge.com***

AGGRESSIVE GROWTH

General Motors Company

Ticker symbol: GM (NYSE) ❑ S&P rating: BB- ❑ Value Line financial strength rating: B+ ❑ Current yield: Nil

Who Are They?

Here's a little IPO you may have heard of. It makes cars. It used to be quite profitable but ran into some problems and had to go through a bankruptcy proceeding. In 2005, it was roughly the size of Ireland, New Zealand, and Hungary, combined. Now its market cap has dwindled to the size of Idaho's 2010 GDP, or about one-quarter the size of Google. Hard times.

In the biggest IPO in American history, GM was (financially) reborn amidst hoopla, doubt, recriminations, informed optimism, blind faith, and more than a few crossed fingers. They claim to have the right products and the right business, but can they convince the rest of world?

Why Should I Care?

If you're familiar with the expression "getting in on the ground floor," then the new GM might appeal to you in a big way. The underwriters seem to have positioned the stock very well, as the IPO price of $33 has held fairly steady even in the light of questions about oil supplies, availability of parts from Japan, and continued uncertainty about the price of commodities such as steel and aluminum. If the initial investors had doubts about the validity of that pricing, the recent global news (which has not been what one would traditionally call "good" for automakers) would seem to provide enough of a reason to sell, but downward pressure on the shares has been minimal. In fact, a number of players have bought in recently, including George Soros (very surprising) and the Goldman Sachs Group, which in December 2010 took a $300 million long position.

On the other hand, the $33 IPO price point had perhaps more to do with the cancellation of a great deal of debt than it did the long-term prospects for a company that's been promising a turnaround for the past ten years. We suspect that despite the innate optimism of the American investor, it's going to take several strong quarters before confidence in GM can be fully restored.

Projections are for an 18 percent growth in revenues through 2012, with net margins up 300 basis points to 6.6 percent, and market share rising to 22.5 percent from its current level of 19.9 percent. Most analysts feel good about the company's cost structure and the reviews for its newer designs (including the all-electric Volt) have been universally positive. And if that isn't enough, Buick is still the most popular luxury car brand in China. Go figure.

How's Business?

Without even a year's worth of history to examine, it's difficult to say what kind of shape they're really in. The first two quarters of operation have been encouraging, with March 2010 sales up nearly 10 percent and the first quarter up 24 percent year to year. All four of the company's brands—Chevrolet, Buick, Cadillac, and GMC (in case you've lost track)—gained retail and total market share during the quarter, but still fell behind Ford, which had an even stronger quarter.

Upside

- The most familiar car brand in the most car-loving country in history
- Lean-ish, mean-ish, and a clean-ish slate
- The full faith and credit of the U.S. government

Downside

- Toyota, Honda, Ford . . .
- The UAW pension fund
- The burden of proof

Just the Facts

INDUSTRY: **Auto & Truck Manufacturers**
BETA COEFFICIENT: **NA**
5-YEAR COMPOUND EARNINGS-PER-SHARE GROWTH: **NM**

		2006	2007	2008	2009	2010
Revenues (Mil)		—	—	—	—	—
Net Income (Mil)		—	—	—	—	—
Price:	high	—	—	—	36.9	39.0
	low	—	—	—	33.2	30.7

General Motors Company
300 Renaissance Center
Detroit, MI 48265
(313) 556-5000
Website: ***www.gm.com***

AGGRESSIVE GROWTH

Globe Specialty Metals, Inc.

Ticker symbol: GSM (NASDAQ) ❑ S&P rating: NA ❑ Value Line financial strength rating: NA ❑ Current yield: 0.69%

Who Are They?

Globe is one of the world's largest producers of chemical and metallurgical grade silicon metal. These silicon metal materials (about 98.5 percent pure silicon) are used primarily in the production of alloy steels and silicon-based compounds used in the manufacturing of silicone rubber, urethane foam, adhesives and sealants, food additives (mmm . . . silicon), coatings, polishes, and cosmetics. Silicon metal is also the first stage of a refining process that ends with the production of monocrystalline silicon, the raw material used as the platform for all integrated circuits. Globe does not produce these extremely high purity grades (99.9999 percent pure silicon), but does make an "upgraded metallurgical-grade silicon" as an alternative to solar-cell-grade amorphous silicon.

Globe also owns a China-based producer of the graphite rods used as electrodes in its submerged arc furnaces. Critical to the production of silicon metal, these rods are also sold into the aluminum, steel, and chemical industries.

Globe's customers include the major aluminum and steel manufacturers, silicone chemical producers, silicon ingot and chip manufacturers, and concrete producers, among others. The company has four production facilities in the United States and one each in Argentina and mainland China. Due to the high power requirements of the refining process, the facilities are typically located near electrical generation facilities, rather than near material sources.

Why Should I Care?

The silicon refining process is similar to that of aluminum—mix up a big pot of stuff, plop in two inert electrodes, and blast current through it until everything melts. The price you pay for electricity and the efficiency of your furnaces are a big part of the success or failure of your business. The metals industry research firm has found Globe's plants to be among the most efficient and lowest cost facilities in the industry.

Globe has a significant market share of the ferrosilicon materials critical to the production of what is called "ductile" iron, which is a cast material that, unlike traditional cast iron, is tough, very resistant to cracking, and casts easily into finely detailed parts. As such, ductile iron has found broad acceptance as a replacement for expensive cast and forged steels in applications such as automotive crankshafts and cams, exhaust manifolds, and steering gear, as well as machine frames and commercial water pipe. Ductile iron, first commercialized in the late 1950s, is seeing a rapid growth in applications recently and the market for the material is expected to outgrow the economy at large for the next decade.

Globe recently announced its plans to build a new silicon metal plant in Iceland, which it expects will be the lowest-cost producer in Europe and one of the lowest-cost producers in the world. The 40-megaton facility will increase Globe's current silicon metal output by approximately 20 percent and will provide additional buffer during maintenance periods at other facilities. Significantly, all energy in Iceland is from renewable sources only, and Globe has signed fixed-cost contracts for eighteen years of supply at competitive rates.

How's Business?

As of the first quarter 2011, all of Globe's production furnaces are running at full capacity, with average selling prices up 10 percent from the prior quarter. The company announced that it "anticipates meaningfully increased" EBITDA and EPS starting with the third quarter of 2011. Specifically, analysts expect a third quarter EPS of twenty-six cents, versus EPS of forty-six cents for the entire 2010.

Upside

- Pricing power due to shortage of global capacity
- New applications accelerating demand
- No raw material constraints

Downside

- Energy intensive
- Process has significant downtime
- Business has low barriers to entry (China)

Just the Facts

INDUSTRY: **Construction Supplies & Fixtures**
BETA COEFFICIENT: **1.15**
5-YEAR COMPOUND EARNINGS-PER-SHARE GROWTH: **NA**

	2006	2007	2008	2009	2010
Revenues (Mil)	—	222	453	426	473
Net Income (Mil)	—	12.6	36.5	(-42.0)	34.1
Price: high	—	—	—	9.8	17.9
low	—	—	—	7.2	9.3

Globe Specialty Metals, Inc.
1 Penn Plaza, Suite 4125
New York, NY 10119
(212) 798-8122
Website: ***www.glbsm.com***

AGGRESSIVE GROWTH

Google, Inc.

Ticker symbol: GOOG (NASDAQ) ❑ S&P rating: AA- ❑ Value Line financial strength rating: A++ ❑ Current yield: Nil

Who Are They?

Google owns and operates the world's leading Internet search engine. The vast majority of its income (97 percent in 2010) is derived from the delivery of targeted advertising through its Google AdWords and Google AdSense products. The licensing of its search technology (Google Search Appliance) to other companies generates the remainder of its revenue.

The revenue model is pretty simple. Google's AdWords scans the HTML code that's displayed on a user's screen, searching for keywords. When keywords are found, ads relevant to the keywords are displayed on the page as well. Advertisers select their own target keywords and pay when customers click on their ads. Google and the advertiser are notified of every click, and other tracking information relevant to the click is transmitted as well.

Advertisers get targeted ads without a great deal of up-front cost and the ads appear on pages from Google's large roster of partners, from AOL to the *Washington Post*. Partners in turn receive a share of the advertising revenue when ads on their pages are clicked.

Why Should I Care?

If you track Google's average annual price-to-earnings ratio you can get a sense of the market's expectations for this stock: In 2004, average P/E was 100; 2005, 53; 2007, 40; 2010, 20. Google's current 20 is a typical P/E ratio for a mildly speculative tech stock and just above the median for the stocks in this book. Based on what the market seems to be saying with their money, then, Google is no longer the growth darling it once was. Or is it?

While it's true that Google's share price hasn't changed materially since the beginning of 2010, its earnings per share, revenue, margins, and cash position have all grown substantially over the same period. And while it's true the company's revenue model hasn't changed, Google's (free) browser and (free) smartphone OS have made significant advances in their respective market shares. With $35 billion in the bank and a dominant position in search, the path forward with these assets seems pretty clear: Develop technologies to aid in the growth of mobile search, acquire promising companies working in those fields, and dominate those markets as well. While their core ad-placement business continues to spin off mountains of cash, Google knows the business it is in is the information business—knowing who its users are, where they are, and what they're interested in as *they* go about *their* business. Google's non–revenue generating businesses generate market intelligence, and the intelligence is what Google uses to monetize its core. New revenue-generating opportunities will arise; we look for Google, through acquisition in those markets, to position itself for significant growth.

We feel Google is simply undervalued in the current market. The shares are not inexpensive, but represent real value when compared to even a fine company like Amazon. Amazon is currently trading at 70 times earnings, while Google is trading at a 20 multiple. That's an easy choice for us.

How's Business?

Google's $6 billion offer for Groupon was rebuffed, but it has made thirty other strategic acquisitions since mid-April 2010, most of them targeted at the online retail and cloud computing spaces. Even so, Google puts nearly $1 billion per month in the bank.

Upside

- Undervalued
- Mobile search and ads just starting to take off
- One enormous wallet with which to defend AdSense

Downside

- The average investor may not commit to $600 shares
- China will be a tough nut
- Speculative push appears to have faded

Just the Facts

INDUSTRY: **Computer Services**
BETA COEFFICIENT: **0.90**
5-YEAR COMPOUND EARNINGS-PER-SHARE GROWTH: **98%**

		2006	2007	2008	2009	2010
Revenues (Bil)		10.6	16.6	21.8	23.7	29.3
Net Income (Bil)		2.94	4.20	5.30	6.52	8.50
Price:	high	513.0	747.2	697.4	626.0	630.8
	low	331.5	437.0	247.3	282.8	433.6

Google Inc.
1600 Amphitheatre Parkway
Mountain View, CA 94043
(650) 253-0000
Website: ***www.google.com***

AGGRESSIVE GROWTH

GT Solar International, Inc.

Ticker symbol: SOLR (NYSE) ❑ S&P rating: NA ❑ Value Line financial strength rating: B ❑ Current yield: Nil

Who Are They?

GT Solar is one of the larger providers of polysilicon production technology for the solar industry. Its customers include several of the world's largest producers of solar cells and solar panels, as well as companies in the chemical industry. Its primary products are chemical vapor deposition (CVD) reactors, which are used to produce raw polysilicon, and directional solidification systems (DSS), which take polysilicon as an input and produce very large multicrystalline silicon ingots. These ingots are then cut into wafers, which are the platforms for individual solar cells.

The company typically sells multiple CVD and DSS units to larger customers. Unit sales figures are closely held, but it would not be unusual to find a single customer with hundreds of furnaces operating around the clock. Growing silicon takes time; three days for a 600kg ingot.

Why Should I Care?

GT Solar occupies a fairly unique position in the broader solar industry. Many of the more well-known players occupy niches built around either a single product or a single process. The big refiners make ingots, the huge panel assemblers build finished, installable product, and the integrated facilities do a lot of everything on their custom lines. GT Solar produces nothing that goes into the end product, but instead supplies the larger producers with the materials, tools, and support they need to do their jobs. If the solar energy boom is a gold rush, then GT Solar is selling the picks and shovels.

The company has demonstrated some significant advances in the operating efficiency of polysilicon in solar cell applications. The crystalline silicon used in solar panels is typically either monocrystalline (each cell is one contiguous crystal lattice) or polycrystalline (each cell has more than one crystal) in form. Monocrystalline cells have higher efficiency, but their cost is substantially higher. GT Solar has built polycrystalline-based panels with efficiencies equivalent to some of the best production-quality monocrystalline devices. This combination of low production cost and high operating efficiency will be very attractive to equipment buyers.

The company's sapphire production technology (obtained in the August 2010 acquisition of Crystal Systems) is used to make large sections of pure sapphire for later processing. This type of sapphire has extremely high transmissibility across a broad spectrum of light and stands up to intense heat. It's been used in military and high-power laser applications for decades, and is now finding wide acceptance as a component of high-brightness LEDs. The company has aggressive growth plans for this very complementary segment and looks for accretive earnings in mid-2012.

How's Business?

The company's plan for aggressive expansion of the acquired sapphire business got a very nice tailwind as we went to press. The original acquisition costs of Crystal Systems penciled out to around $75 million; GT Solar just released news of a $220 million order from a Chinese supplier to the LED market. The order, which includes furnaces and other equipment used in the production of sapphire, will be incremental to the company's FY2012 revenue. Combined with earlier orders this year, the unit has added more than $300 million in backlog in just eight months of sales under GT Solar. The company had set the revenue target at less than $100 million.

Upside

- Good representation in China
- Leading technology
- Pricing power from high demand

Downside

- Outside sourcing—production capacity a question
- One customer accounts for 19 percent of revenue
- Some open programs showing signs of weakening

Just the Facts

INDUSTRY: **Semiconductors**
BETA COEFFICIENT: **1.65**
5-YEAR COMPOUND EARNINGS-PER-SHARE GROWTH: **NM**

		2006	2007	2008	2009	2010
Revenues (Mil)		60.1	244	541	544	850
Net Income (Mil)		(-18.4)	36.1	88.0	87.3	163
Price:	high	—	—	17.0	9.0	10.0
	low	—	—	1.6	2.8	4.9

GT Solar International, Inc.
243 Daniel Webster Highway
Merrimack, NH 03054
(603) 883-5200
Website: ***www.gtsolar.com***

AGGRESSIVE GROWTH

HealthStream, Inc.

Ticker symbol: HSTM (NASDAQ) ❑ S&P rating: NA ❑ Value Line financial strength rating: C ❑ Current yield: Nil

Who Are They?

Founded in 1990, HealthStream, Inc., provides Internet-based learning and research products to meet the education and information needs of the health care industry. The company's learning products provide training and assessment tools, while its research products provide the organization with feedback from patients, employees, and the community served by the organization. HealthStream's customers include service providers, pharmaceutical and medical device companies, and other participants in the health care industry. Its customer base across both learning and research business units includes over 2,500 health care organizations throughout the United States (predominately acute-care facilities). Its courses are delivered to customers through the company's flagship learning product, the HealthStream Learning Center (HLC), a proprietary, Internet-based learning platform. As of December 31, 2010, HLC had nearly 2.5 million contracted subscribers, up from 2.1 million the year before.

Why Should I Care?

All of the 5.6 million hospital-based health care professionals in the United States are required by federal mandates and accrediting bodies to complete training in a number of areas. Hospital staffing issues and personnel shortages also create a need for on-site development tools and competency-based training. HealthStream provides products to meet both of these needs as well as assist in career development via continuing education. The federal government also requires that hospitals submit data for certain quality measures in order to receive full reimbursement for services, and HealthStream's products are certified for this purpose.

Lastly, HealthStream's training products are quite a bit less expensive than the alternative of on-site live training or off-site classes. Licenses are priced locally on a per-seat basis and can be adjusted for local conditions. This typically makes HealthStream's products more affordable and, as a consequence, more available to a larger number of people at the facility. HealthStream's HLC platform is standardized and the content is server-based at HealthStream facilities, simplifying delivery and ensuring that content is updated system-wide at once.

By focusing on standardization of a core set of content, HealthStream can sell its subscription as a practical, low-cost solution for meeting state and federally mandated policies. Once the subscription is in place, HealthStream can then up-sell the additional training as part of a custom development program for each potential seat at a facility. It's a formula that works well in a number of service industries, and health care, with its byzantine set of constantly changing regulations, is a natural target for this approach.

Spending in the health care industry reached approximately $2.3 trillion in 2008, or 16.2 percent of the gross domestic product. Hospital care expenditures accounted for approximately 32 percent of this $2.3 trillion. Approximately 14.3 million professionals are employed in the health care segment, with approximately 5.6 million employed in HealthStream's target markets, meaning HealthStream already has subscription contracts with approximately 40 percent of its potential customers. A business could stay healthy with those kinds of numbers.

How's Business?

The company recently stated that it expects 2011 revenues to grow 15–19 percent over the prior year, with operating income tracking closely. The company has approximately $2.5 million in cash, an unused $15 million credit line, and no long-term debt. Note that net income for 2009 and 2010 in the table below reflects the effects of some tax adjustments—EBITDA for the two years are $10.9 million and $12.6 million, respectively.

Upside

- Economies of scale on core business
- Up-sell opportunities
- Uncle Thomas Frist, Chairman of HCA

Downside

- Competitive market
- Closer federal scrutiny of health care costs
- Small fish, massive pond

Just the Facts

INDUSTRY: **Computer Services**

BETA COEFFICIENT: **1.1**

5-YEAR COMPOUND EARNINGS-PER-SHARE GROWTH: **NM**

		2006	2007	2008	2009	2010
Revenues (Mil)		31.8	43.9	51.6	57.4	65.8
Net Income (Mil)		2.5	4.1	2.9	14.0	4.2
Price:	high	5.0	4.6	3.3	4.8	8.0
	low	2.4	2.6	2.1	1.7	3.7

HealthStream, Inc.
209 10th Avenue South
Nashville, TN 37203
(615) 301-3237
Website: ***www.healthstream.com***

AGGRESSIVE GROWTH

Hecla Mining Company

Ticker symbol: HL (NYSE) ❑ S&P rating: NA ❑ Value Line financial strength rating: NA ❑ Current yield: Nil

Who Are They?

Founded in 1891 in northern Idaho, Hecla Mining Company is the oldest U.S.-based precious metals mining company in North America and the largest silver producer in the United States. Hecla has two mines currently producing (primarily) silver: Greens Creek (one of the ten largest silver mines in the world) and Lucky Friday, which in 2010 produced 7.2 million and 3.4 million ounces respectively.

The company also has interests in two properties currently under exploration: San Juan in Colorado and San Sebastian near Durango, Mexico. The San Sebastian property was formerly a producing gold vein, but is now an exploratory program only. The San Juan property is located in a historically rich production area not far from Silverton, Colorado. Hecla has a right to as much as a 70 percent interest in the claim, on which 48 million ounces have already been identified with the potential for "considerably" more through targeted exploration.

Why Should I Care?

The 10.6 million ounce output from the two mines was close to Hecla's record silver production of 10.9 million ounces (produced from the same two mines in 2009). In both mines, lead and zinc are produced as by-product. Greens Creek also produces gold as a by-product, with the gold yield being approximately 1 percent of the silver weight, or approximately one-third of the silver value. The company estimates the total weight output for 2011 will be somewhat lower than the 2010 production for both mines, due to lower-grade ores being mined as consequence of normal mine sequencing procedures. The ores to be mined in 2012 are expected to be of a higher grade, which, if metals prices hold, would give Hecla four consecutive years of near-record production.

Silver is not just about jewelry, coins, and investments. The price of silver has been rising fairly steadily since 2005, and with good reason. In 2006, the United States (and several other countries) adopted RoHS (reduction of hazardous substances) guidelines as they apply to electronic equipment. Prior to those guidelines going into effect, the solder that attached nearly every component to nearly every circuit board manufactured was made of a tin/lead eutectic. With the elimination of lead as an allowed component of most all solders, new formulations were developed, nearly all of which employ up to 2 percent silver content where silver had been used only rarely beforehand.

The company is optimistic about the potential for large reserves in the San Juan formation. The terrain and vein configuration is of a type that favors Hecla's particular expertise, and they feel confident they can develop several extensions of the vein that have so far yielded very high grade ore. The potential for an additional 100 million ounces is a strong possibility. Where are our shovels!?

How's Business?

Early in 2011 the company took an accrual of $193.2 million against fourth quarter 2010 earnings as part of a lawsuit tied to the remediation of old mining territories. The suit, brought in part by the federal government, stems from practices employed by several mining companies along the Coeur d'Alene river basin prior to 1968. The total bill for the remediation, which involves the removal of toxic heavy metals, will come to $2.2 billion. Hecla expects to limit its liability in the matter to $262 million, with the balance of approximately $70 million applied against future earnings.

Upside

- Gold and silver remain at historically high prices
- Production cost of silver at Greens Creek in 2010 was thirty-five cents per ounce
- It's a mining stock

Downside

- Remediation losses could impact funding for exploration
- Share volatility partly a function of monetary policy
- It's a mining stock

Just the Facts

INDUSTRY: **Gold and Silver**
BETA COEFFICIENT: **2.15**
5-YEAR COMPOUND EARNINGS-PER-SHARE GROWTH: **NM**

		2006	2007	2008	2009	2010
Revenues (Mil)		126	223	193	313	419
Net Income (Mil)		69.1	53.2	(-54.5)	67.8	49.0
Price:	high	7.7	12.1	12.7	6.8	11.3
	low	4.1	6.6	1.3	1.3	4.6

Hecla Mining Company
6500 North Mineral Drive, Suite 200
Coeur d'Alene, ID 83815
(208) 769-4100
Website: ***www.hecla-mining.com***

AGGRESSIVE GROWTH

Insight Enterprises

Ticker symbol: NSIT (NASDAQ) □ S&P rating: NA □ Value Line financial strength rating: B+ □ Current yield: Nil

Who Are They?

Here at *100 Best* we strive to provide insight, and so we present Insight Enterprises. Seriously, this retailer of computer hardware and software was an easy choice for our list. The world's largest software reseller, Insight focuses on the small business, education, and governmental customer base. It has operations in twenty-one countries and customers in 191 countries (fun fact: there are 195 countries in the world). It buys hardware and software directly from manufacturers such as HP, Apple, Cisco, Oracle, and IBM, and resells it via catalog, phone, and online sales. It provides more than 250,000 products and services, from computer accessories up to planning services for an entire IT infrastructure.

Why Should I Care?

As a value-added reseller, Insight provides services over and above simply stocking and selling name-brand merchandise. After all, in many cases it is competing directly with the company that sold Insight the product in the first place. In order to be successful selling HP products against HP, it has to offer the customer a fairly compelling set of reasons to buy. Insight is able to compete with its suppliers by providing product bundling and pricing incentives that may simply be unavailable from the manufacturer. It also offers installation, financing terms, warranty options, service plans, integration, and support packages that may be a better fit for the customer than the (often) fairly limited plans offered by the manufacturer. Finally, as a one-stop source, it can offer large buyers the opportunity to completely configure hundreds or even thousands of units with components from different suppliers, and have all of them covered under a single purchasing and support plan.

Since we're talking about insight, this might be a good place to talk about PEG ratio. PEG is one of the ratios we at *100 Best* use as a filter when we're looking for potential stocks. The PEG ratio is a valuation measure that takes into account price, earnings, and predicted annual earnings-per-share growth rate (P/E/G or simply PEG). Since a stock's price is a bet on the company's future earnings, a price/earnings/growth ratio would yield a PEG of 1.0 for a company that is currently priced fairly. If a company's predicted earnings growth is greater than its P/E ratio, then the PEG would be less than 1.0 and the company's shares would be viewed as undervalued. As of May 2011, Insight's shares have a PEG of 0.72, which is considered low for a company with its size and earnings history. PEG is certainly not the only measure we use to rate a stock for its growth potential, but it can be a handy place to start your due diligence as a value investor.

How's Business?

A nice earnings surprise early in the year sent Insight's share price up over 20 percent in one day. Share price grew another 8 percent the following day, indicating there was even more good news once people started looking closely at the earnings report. As the company continues to focus on cost controls, we expect more earnings surprises from this conservatively run, quality retailer as the year goes on and into 2012.

Upside

- Businesses are starting to update hardware again
- Stock is undervalued at its current price of $16.50
- Small share base

Downside

- Very little pricing power
- Lackluster sales growth in EMEA (Europe, the Middle East, Africa)
- Receivables at 90+ days, worth keeping an eye on

Just the Facts

INDUSTRY: **Computer Hardware**

BETA COEFFICIENT: **1.30**

5-YEAR COMPOUND EARNINGS-PER-SHARE GROWTH: **1.5%**

		2006	**2007**	**2008**	**2009**	**2010**
Revenues (Mil)		3,817	4,800	4,826	4,137	4,810
Net Income (Mil)		65.7	72.0	48.2	30.8	75.5
Price:	high	22.9	28.4	20.3	14.1	16.9
	low	16.1	17.3	3.3	2.0	11.2

Insight Enterprises, Inc.
6820 South Harl Avenue
Tempe, AZ 85283
(480) 902-1001
Website: *www.insight.com*

AGGRESSIVE GROWTH

Intuit, Inc.

Ticker symbol: INTU (NASDAQ) ❑ S&P rating: BBB ❑ Value Line financial strength rating: A ❑ Current yield: Nil

Who Are They?

Most of us know Intuit primarily as the producer of TurboTax, a software package that helps us get through April without doing violence to innocent state and federal forms. The company is also well known for its Quicken family of personal finance products, which help many of us stay out of trouble. The rest of Intuit is probably more familiar to owners of small businesses and others in the accounting profession.

Intuit serves the small business community with a family of software products known as the QuickBooks series. The functionality (and price) of QuickBooks grows with the level of features and requirements, but all are targeted at users needing an integrated package that handles billing, inventory, payroll, banking, payments, and other tasks normally handled by a dedicated finance staff. The company also produces training and support software for professional accountants, point-of-sale software, and supplies such as checks, forms, and other documents used in the day-to-day of accountancy.

Why Should I Care?

People like to talk about "killer apps"; software that's so indispensable you don't think twice about buying it and maybe the underlying hardware as well just so you can run the software. For us, those earliest killer apps were a word processor (because editing is fun), a spreadsheet (because math is tedious), and TurboTax. Those three programs embodied what computers did best: freeing up the mind by taking the drudgery out of the task, saving time, and eliminating errors.

This, it seems to us, is what has driven Intuit's product development ever since—providing the average person with tools that offer real value by doing the nasty, boring, humdrum work quickly and reliably. We also think this is why Intuit has posted record revenues for each of the past twelve years, including through two recessions. The relative revenue contribution from each of its top five business segments hasn't varied more than 1 percent over the last four years, even though overall revenue is up 30 percent. The products it sells are the staples of most people's financial world; you don't buy more of it when times are good, but you don't dare do without it when times are bad.

So how does producing staples make for an aggressive stock? Fair question. Leveraging its broad appeal among small businesses, Intuit has released a set of website development and hosting tools with which businesses can quickly and easily establish a presence on the Internet. Included in this platform are purchasing and payment methods that link to Intuit's accounting software. The company also mentions that more apps of a mobile variety are under development, and wouldn't it be handy to be able to check inventory levels via your iPhone? In 2010 Intuit Health acquired Medfusion, Inc., which provides online patient-to-provider communication solutions.

Services are delivered through a standard Web browser on a subscription basis and include features such as appointment scheduling, patient preregistration, prescription renewal, and electronic bill payment.

We think somewhere in there is a killer app.

How's Business?

Steady as she goes. The company's net margin has been between 17 and 20 percent for each of the last ten years.

Upside

- Reliable earnings
- Some interesting new initiatives
- Good execution

Downside

- Large share base (310 million)
- H&R Block looks strong in the segment
- Aggressive enough?

Just the Facts

INDUSTRY: **Software and Programming**
BETA COEFFICIENT: **0.85**
5-YEAR COMPOUND EARNINGS-PER-SHARE GROWTH: **17%**

		2006	2007	2008	2009	2010
Revenues (Mil)		2,342	2,673	3,071	3,183	3,455
Net Income (Mil)		441	507	542	601	685
Price:	high	36.0	33.1	32.0	31.3	50.3
	low	24.0	26.1	20.2	21.1	29.0

Intuit, Inc.
2700 Coast Avenue
Mountain View, CA 94043
(650) 944-6000
Website: ***www.intuit.com***

AGGRESSIVE GROWTH

Itron, Inc.

Ticker symbol: ITRI (NASDAQ) ❑ S&P rating: BB- ❑ Value Line financial strength rating: B+ ❑ Current yield: Nil

Who Are They?

Itron is the world's largest provider of "intelligent" metering systems for residential and commercial gas, electric, and water usage. Intelligent meters, in addition to tracking raw usage over a period of time, can also measure at the point of use operating parameters such as pressure, temperature, voltage, phase, etc. This information can be extremely valuable to the supplying utility but in the past has been difficult and expensive to obtain. Itron supplies a range of products from basic meters that are read manually to meters that act as network devices and transmit their data in real time to the managing utility. Itron also sells a range of software platforms for the management of the installed base and the analysis and optimization of usage.

The company was founded in 1977 and in 2004 acquired the electric meter operations of Schlumberger, which at the time was the largest global supplier of this equipment.

Why Should I Care?

The push for a more intelligent infrastructure has been a getting a lot of press recently, but Itron has been in the business of supplying products and services to utilities for over thirty years. Itron is the biggest player in the business, with an enormous installed base and Rolodex of over 8,000 utility customers in 130 countries.

The case for the implementation of these systems can be very strong. In a typical scenario, a utility might require 100,000 meter reads for water, gas, and electric usage. Only half of these will be done per month, as the cost of reading all would be prohibitive. Of the meters that are read, only 80 percent are actually correct, with the other 20 percent requiring adjustments on the next billing cycle. In any given month, then, 60 percent of the readings are actually estimates. Doubling the number of meter readers would only reduce the number of inaccurate billings to 20 percent.

In the case of a utility in Ohio, the implementation of an automatic meter reading (AMR) system improved the accuracy of the meter readings to over 99.85 percent, with every reading taken monthly. Customer billings now line up with actual usage, and all of the customers are given accurate data on which to base their own usage decisions. Meter tampering and theft of service have been reduced, and it has reduced the number of readers from nine to one and cut out many associated costs.

Due to sharply reduced tax revenues and the virtual evaporation of state and federal program matching grants, municipalities across the country are scrambling to come up with ways to save money and reduce pension exposure. And although the up-front costs of a system-wide AMR implementation is a big-budget item, these systems are typically rolled out incrementally over the course of a few years, softening the fiscal impact to any single year's budget. Any municipality with a long-term view is going to look hard at this sort of system; the opportunities at the municipality level to provide a higher level of service at a lower cost are few and far between.

How's Business?

The company reported record sales and earnings in 2011 and should do so again in 2012. Fewer than 10 percent of utilities in the United States are currently using smart metering, so the potential for growth is encouraging, particularly given the success stories from early adopters in the European market.

Upside

- Compelling product benefits
- Low-cost sourcing
- Solid financing

Downside

- Rollout may lag, given municipal budgets
- Management tempered guidance for 2011
- Share base has doubled in seven years

Just the Facts

INDUSTRY: **Electronic Instruments & Controls**
BETA COEFFICIENT: **1.10**
5-YEAR COMPOUND EARNINGS-PER-SHARE GROWTH: **20%**

		2006	2007	2008	2009	2010
Revenues (Mil)		644	1,464	1,910	1,687	2,259
Net Income (Mil)		56.4	87.3	117	44.3	130
Price:	high	73.7	112.9	106.3	69.5	81.9
	low	39.4	51.2	34.3	40.1	52.0

Itron, Inc.
2111 North Molter Road
Liberty Lake, WA 99019
(509) 924-9900
Website: *www.itron.com*

AGGRESSIVE GROWTH

JetBlue Airways Corp.

Ticker symbol: JBLU (NASDAQ) ❑ S&P rating: B- ❑ Value Line financial strength rating: C++ ❑ Current yield: Nil

Who Are They?

JetBlue is one of the newer regional passenger airlines operating in the United States. JetBlue began operations in February 2000 with New York's JFK airport as its base. Just over a year later, it began operations out of Long Beach airport, near Los Angeles. It provides primarily point-to-point service to sixty locations in twenty states, Puerto Rico, Mexico, Latin America, and the Caribbean with a fleet of 150 short-medium-haul narrow-body aircraft from Airbus and Embraer.

Based on passenger revenue miles, JetBlue is the sixth largest passenger carrier in the United States. In 2010, they averaged 650 flights per day, with most traffic originating or terminating in Boston, Fort Lauderdale, Los Angeles/Long Beach, New York/JFK, or Orlando.

Rather than adopting the classification of a "discount" carrier, it refers to itself as a "value airline." It doesn't buy older, hand-me-down aircraft, but rather has the youngest fleet among U.S. carriers. It offers free movies and television service on all flights, leather seating in coach, roomy cabins, and (what used to be) the standard free drinks and snacks.

JetBlue also owns LiveTV, a service that provides DirecTV video service, XM radio, and text messaging services to passengers in flight. LiveTV service is offered on JetBlue flights and on several competing domestic and international carriers.

Why Should I Care?

JetBlue's approach to building the brand lies with providing a superior customer experience; it has a number of amenities available as standard or premium offerings not available on other carriers, and its terminal facilities are, on average, better-regarded than its competitors.

It can offer a superior customer experience in part due to the age of its fleet (by far the youngest among U.S. carriers at 5.4 years) and the efficiency of its operations. All of its tickets are distributed electronically, and its aircraft consume less fuel per passenger mile, require less maintenance, and are flying on average 11.6 hours per day (the highest in the industry). JetBlue also has the lowest CASM (cost per available seat mile, an important break-even measure) in the industry of 9.92 cents. With all of these cost factors working in its favor, we feel JetBlue is in very good shape to capitalize in its markets, as long as the travelers are actually traveling.

We've heard a great deal about a rebound in the travel and entertainment industries due to an improved economic outlook. It started in mid-2010 and appears to be gaining momentum in 2011, although rising fuel costs are a problem. JetBlue has about 30 percent of its fuel requirements hedged to below market levels, but jet fuel is up almost 40 percent over 2010's prices. Adding to the fuel cost woes was a dreadful holiday flight season on the east coast of the United States, with blizzard conditions causing airport shutdowns and thousands of canceled flights.

How's Business?

JetBlue anticipates top-line growth of 18–20 percent in 2011 and an additional 10 percent in 2012. Earnings in 2011 should increase nearly 50 percent over 2010, and another 35 percent in 2012. After a number of very bad years for the industry, the near term is looking very good, and we see this stock trading near $10 before the end of 2012.

Upside

- Vacations seem to be back in the plans
- Recent fare increases are holding
- Low cost structure

Downside

- Reliance on New York and Boston for 60 percent of flights
- Margins still quite thin
- Despite successful hedging, fuel cost volatility worries

Just the Facts

INDUSTRY: **Airline**

BETA COEFFICIENT: **1.25**

5-YEAR COMPOUND EARNINGS-PER-SHARE GROWTH: **18.1%**

		2006	**2007**	**2008**	**2009**	**2010**
Revenues (Mil)		2,363	2,842	3,388	3,286	3,779
Net Income (Mil)		(-7.0)	18.0	(-23.0)	57.0	97.0
Price:	high	15.8	17.0	7.3	7.7	7.6
	low	8.9	5.9	3.0	2.8	4.6

JetBlue Airways Corporation
118-29 Queens Boulevard
Forest Hills, NY 11375
(718) 286-7900
Website: ***www.jetblue.com***

AGGRESSIVE GROWTH

Johnson Controls

Ticker symbol: JCI (NYSE) ❑ S&P rating: BBB+ ❑ Value Line financial strength rating: A ❑ Current yield: 1.6%

Who Are They?

Johnson Controls is a large manufacturer of automotive, HVAC controls, and energy controls and products. Its products are found in over 200 million vehicles, 12 million homes, and 1 million commercial buildings. Its business operates in three segments: Automotive Experience, Building Efficiency, and Power Solutions.

The Automotive Experience business is one of the world's largest automotive suppliers, providing seating and overhead systems, door systems, floor consoles, instrument panels, cockpits, and integrated electronics. Customers include virtually every major automaker in the world. The business produces automotive interior systems for original equipment manufacturers (OEMs) and operates in twenty-nine countries worldwide, with partial ownership of affiliates in Asia, Europe, North America, and South America.

Building Efficiency produces integrated control systems, mechanical equipment, services, and solutions designed to improve the comfort, safety, and energy efficiency of non-residential buildings and residential properties with operations in more than 125 countries. Revenues come from facilities management, technical services, and the replacement and upgrade of controls and HVAC mechanical equipment in the existing buildings market.

The Power Solutions business produces lead-acid batteries, serving both automotive, light truck, and utility vehicle OEMs and the general vehicle battery aftermarket. It also offers absorbent glass mat (AGM), nickel-metal-hydride, and lithium-ion battery technologies to power hybrid vehicles.

Why Should I Care?

Over the past several years, Johnson has taken a number of steps to improve its competitiveness on the worldwide stage. The efforts are starting to bear fruit with big increases in operating margin and overall profitability. The 2012 calendar year is looking like a very strong period for this company, so closely tied to the health of the worldwide automotive sector.

Looking to leverage on the rebound in the industry, Johnson recently acquired the European manufacturers Hammerstein and Keiper/Recaro, makers of premium automotive seating. The acquisitions are expected to be income neutral in 2011 and strongly accretive in 2012.

It's hard to know what to believe with regard to the Chinese market in batteries and vehicles. Nearly every company with a stake in the game is making strong claims of future growth for their particular product or technology. Compounding the fear, uncertainty, and doubt is the Chinese government's penchant for saying one thing and doing another. What we do know is that Johnson plans to increase its production capacity of batteries in that country from 4 million units today to 30 million units in 2015. The company also announced contracts between its joint venture Johnson-Saft and two Chinese automotive manufacturers to supply lithium batteries for their electric car production of up to 150,000 units beginning in 2012.

How's Business?

The results for the first half of 2011 are in and they're pretty good. Income from the business segments is up 18 percent year over year on a similar increase in sales. The second quarter showed much improved momentum, however, with increases of 30 percent in income and 22 percent in revenues. The company increased revenue guidance for the year from $38.5 billion to $39.5 billion based on higher growth expectations for the Building Efficiency segment.

Upside

- Leaner organization than two years ago
- Available capacity meets increasing demand
- Good margins on lithium technology

Downside

- Shares have been bid up recently
- No consensus leader in automotive green-tech
- Lithium sourcing still unsettled

Just the Facts

INDUSTRY: **Auto & Truck Parts**

BETA COEFFICIENT: **1.3**

5-YEAR COMPOUND EARNINGS-PER-SHARE GROWTH: **6.0%**

		2006	**2007**	**2008**	**2009**	**2010**
Revenues (Mil)		32,235	34,624	38,062	28,497	34,305
Net Income (Mil)		1,028	1,252	1,400	281	1,361
Price:	high	30	44.5	36.5	28.3	40.2
	low	22.1	28.1	13.6	8.4	25.6

Johnson Controls, Inc.
P. O. Box 591
Milwaukee, WI 53201-0591
(414) 524-2375
Website: ***www.johnsoncontrols.com***

AGGRESSIVE GROWTH

Layne Christensen Company

Ticker symbol: LAYN (NASDAQ) ❑ S&P rating: NA ❑ Value Line financial strength rating: B++ ❑ Current yield: Nil

Who Are They?

Normally when a drilling company finishes a job, it brings the same number of workers out of a hole as they put down it. In October of last year, though, Layne Christensen drilled a hole in Chile and closed the job thirty-three miners ahead of the game. Yes, these are those guys.

When they're not fishing Chileans out the ground, they're providing equipment and services for a broad variety of activities in water infrastructure and minerals exploration. The company, founded in 1882, began as a well-drilling service, providing water for farmers in the Dakotas and Kansas. It still drills a lot of water wells, but it also designs and builds complete freshwater treatment facilities, wastewater treatment facilities, and perform pipeline installation and rehabilitation. Its minerals exploration business provides mining operations with drilling services for geological assessment, in-situ mining, and mineral exploration with over 150 drilling rigs worldwide. In North and South America, these services are used primarily by major gold and copper producers and to a lesser extent, iron ore producers. In 1991, the company commenced mineral exploration drilling operations in Mexico and now has foreign affiliates operating in South America, Australia, Asia, and Africa as well.

Why Should I Care?

Layne's two big segments, Water and Minerals, both look promising. Water projects are up as the construction sector starts to recover, and the company's extensive stable of gear is in top condition. Water quality and locating new water sources are becoming national concerns as global population growth accelerates. The company's backlog of water infrastructure work is up 6 percent over last year and represents nearly nine months of current revenues.

Precious metals prices continue their run of all-time highs, creating strong demand in Layne's minerals exploration business. Revenues in the Minerals Exploration segment increased 70 percent year over year in 2010, with particular strength in the latter part of the year. This business has some legs—gold and silver prices appear to have strong support at record levels.

What's especially attractive about these two businesses from Layne is their degree of vertical integration. Layne makes most, if not all of the equipment used in its operations, including the pumps, pipe, drills, even the filtration materials. In times of high demand, Layne will not miss out on opportunities for lack of third-party resources or because a competitor has a lock on rigging or other infrastructure.

Layne Energy, the company's energy play, is a wholly owned subsidiary specializing in unconventional coal bed methane and shale gas plays in the Cherokee Basin. Earnings from this business are down a bit due to the current low prices for natural gas. Growth in gas production is exceeding the growth in wellhead count, however, as the company is gaining expertise and finding higher-quality sources. Layne is one of the few companies operating in this area, and its advantages in the technical aspects of this unique process could well pay off handsomely down the road.

How's Business?

The quarter ending June of 2011 brought a big jump in operating and net margins, both up 65 percent over the prior four quarters' average. Earnings for the quarter doubled over the prior year, due largely to strength in the minerals exploration segment. The share price is all the more attractive as business conditions improve, as it remains at less than half of its prerecession peak.

Upside

- Water infrastructure getting its due in the recovery
- Gold/silver prices re-invigorating exploration
- Recent surprises in top/bottom line growth

Downside

- No apparent respite from gloomy gas pricing
- Growing exposure to foreign competition
- Some attention from the Foreign Corrupt Practices folks

Just the Facts

INDUSTRY: **Construction Services**

BETA COEFFICIENT: **1.40**

5-YEAR COMPOUND EARNINGS-PER-SHARE GROWTH: **32.0%**

	2006	**2007**	**2008**	**2009**	**2010**
Revenues (Mil)	723	868	1,008	866	1,026
Net Income (Mil)	26.3	37.3	42.6	17.4	30.0
Price: high	36.5	59.2	58.3	35.1	36.9
low	24.4	30.2	10.4	14.1	23.0

Layne Christensen Company
1900 Shawnee Mission Parkway
Mission Woods, KS 66205
(913) 362-0510
Website: ***www.laynechristensen.com***

AGGRESSIVE GROWTH

Lufkin Industries, Inc.

Ticker symbol: LUFK (NASDAQ) ❑ S&P rating: NA ❑ Value Line financial strength rating: NA ❑ Current yield: 0.6%

Who Are They?

Lufkin business falls under the very broad heading of oilfield equipment, but it basically has three product lines: pumps, transmissions, and foundry services. Its pumps are used to provide lift in producing wells that for one reason or another have insufficient pressure to raise the petroleum to the collecting apparatus at the surface. These pumps are a familiar sight on most oilfields, and in fact, Lufkin's reciprocating design is the industry standard. The pumps are fabricated at Lufkin's facilities out of materials formed at Lufkin's own foundries, primarily steel plate, steel rod, and iron castings. Its power transmissions are used mainly in support of oilfield needs for oil and gas transmission, and are also used in power generation and in processing applications, such as extrusion, milling, and mining. Its foundry operations service many of the company's own needs for large castings as well as the demands of the OEM market. It produces low to medium volumes of ductile and gray iron castings of up to twenty tons each and a full range of engineering services in support.

Why Should I Care?

Lufkin's energy and petroleum-based business cycle follows that of the economy at large—and as the oil business goes, so goes Lufkin Industries. The next eighteen months (through 2012) should be a solid growth period for Lufkin for a number of reasons. First is the overall strength of the economic recovery, which has energy suppliers looking forward to (and in many cases, already enjoying) very strong revenue gains. Second is the recent tsunami in Japan which has dealt a blow to most, if not all, of the nuclear generation facilities currently under construction and, by extension, given a boost to natural gas for electrical generation and to shale plays in Canada and the Rockies, where rig count has increased fourfold since late 2009. Finally, offshore leases in the United States are still being delayed in the aftermath of the BP rig explosion in the Gulf of Mexico. This is good news for all primarily onshore producers, and particularly for those equipment suppliers like Lufkin that specialize in extending the productive life of marginal fields.

As it turns out, Lufkin is located in the heart of a region with a number of very large wind farm installations. Lufkin's power transmission operation, then, has recently moved into the business of repair and maintenance of wind turbine gearboxes—an interesting development for a company traditionally tied to fossil fuels.

How's Business?

The company recently announced that it expects revenues for FY2011 to be in the range of $800–$850 million, with earnings in the range of $2.50–$3.00 per share. This announcement, however, was made prior to the recent unrest in the oil-producing regions of the Middle East. Petroleum has since been trading at more than $100 per barrel and there is no clear end in sight to the political turmoil in Libya, Bahrain, Yemen, and other states in and around the Persian Gulf. Elevated oil prices create the possibility of earnings surprises for oilfield suppliers, and Lufkin is in a good position to capitalize, with its vertical integration and a solid cash position.

Upside

- Upward mobility in oil price
- Strong exploration cycle
- Found business in wind turbines

Downside

- No decline in iron or steel pricing
- Share price recently bid up significantly
- Margins are below sector average and trending down

Just the Facts

INDUSTRY: **Oil Well Services & Equipment**
BETA COEFFICIENT: **1.3**
5-YEAR COMPOUND EARNINGS-PER-SHARE GROWTH: **-1.1%**

		2006	2007	2008	2009	2010
Revenues (Mil)		606	597	741	521	646
Net Income (Mil)		73.0	74.2	88.2	22.0	43.8
Price:	high	33.9	34.0	46.4	37.0	62.4
	low	25.0	26.0	16.5	16.0	30.6

Lufkin Industries, Inc.
601 South Raguet
Lufkin, TX 75902-0849
(936) 634-2211
Website: *www.lufkin.com*

AGGRESSIVE GROWTH

McKesson Corporation

Ticker symbol: MCK (NYSE) ❑ S&P rating: A- ❑ Value Line financial strength rating: A+ ❑ Current yield: 0.9%

Who Are They?

McKesson is the largest health care company in the world. Now you know. The bulk of its revenue (95 percent) is derived from the North American pharmaceutical distribution business, a $250 billion pie it shares with two other companies—Cardinal Health and Amerisource Bergen. Its customer base in this business includes retail pharmacies, hospitals, clinics, and homecare providers.

McKesson also operates a medical supplies distribution business focused on the "alternate-site" health care providers (physician's offices, clinics, long-term care facilities) where margins are quite a bit higher than the 1–2 percent seen in the drug distribution business. McKesson's other business is called Provider Technologies, which supplies a range of software and IT services for health care organizations including clinical management, payroll services, and document imaging. Provider Technologies is its smallest segment in terms of revenue but has by far the highest operating margins.

Why Should I Care?

Around 2005 the pharmaceutical distribution business switched from a buy-and-hold model to a fee-for-service (FFS) model. Under the old system, distributors like McKesson would buy and maintain large inventories of drugs for later resale to customers, counting on what had become a systemic drug price inflation to boost margins. This model had a number of significant drawbacks tied mainly to the speculative nature of the distributor's buying decisions, and so, with some reluctance from the manufacturers, a fee-for-service system was instituted industry-wide. Under fee-for-service, the distributors own far smaller levels of inventory and derive new revenues from the manufacturers in the form of fees, with potential discounts for meeting certain performance metrics. This new model has cut down on the effect of price inflation, but since not every product fits the FFS model, some are still managed using the traditional distributorship approach, and price inflation still accounts for about 25 percent of McKesson's margins.

The key to FFS for the distributors is that their revenues are now tied largely to volume, rather than guessing right on stocking levels and successfully gaming the availability process. And for McKesson, volume is just what the doctor ordered. Beginning with the introduction of FFS in 2005, McKesson's margins and share price grew steadily, doubling just before the onset of the recession in early 2008. Now, with the recovery under way, McKesson's fundamentals are in great shape and the share price line has regained its upward slope, passed its prerecession levels, and is approaching an all-time high. What's McKesson's real valuation under the new revenue model? Hard to say, but as earnings continue to accelerate, it's pretty clear we've got a way to go before we find out.

McKesson still plays buy-low, sell-high with many generics, and there are approximately $70 billion worth of branded drugs coming off patent in the next five years, creating significant potential cost reductions.

How's Business?

Given the strong competition, the distribution business will always be a battlefield. The company is well capitalized and has outstanding cash flow; this may be the best time in quite a while to go shopping, and McKesson has plenty of room for the right fit.

Upside

- Aging demographics in their favor
- Well positioned for strategic acquisitions
- Health care software has real potential in fragmented market

Downside

- More regulatory churn could eat away at earnings
- Strong competition
- Recent oncology clinic purchase could be expensive defensive move

Just the Facts

INDUSTRY: **Biotechnology and Drugs**
BETA COEFFICIENT: **0.75**
5-YEAR COMPOUND EARNINGS-PER-SHARE GROWTH: **14%**

	2006	2007	2008	2009	2010
Revenues (Bil)	93.0	101.7	106.6	108.7	111.5
Net Income (Mil)	881	1,021	1,194	1,251	1,300
Price: high	55.1	68.4	68.4	65.0	71.5
low	44.6	50.8	28.3	33.1	57.2

McKesson Corporation
One Post Street
San Francisco, CA 94104
(415) 983-8300
Website: *www.mckesson.com*

AGGRESSIVE GROWTH

Mentor Graphics

Ticker symbol: MENT (NASDAQ) ❑ S&P rating: NA ❑ Value Line financial strength rating: B ❑ Current yield: Nil

Who Are They?

Mentor Graphics is one of the leading electronic design automation (EDA) suppliers. Although it got its start in logic design, its software is now used to assist in the design and verification of many different types of products, not just integrated circuits and printed circuit boards. Diversification of its customer base reduces its exposure to economic downturns in any one area, providing benefits over and above the incremental revenue.

The company is one of the originators of the EDA market, and its products are some of the most respected and trusted anywhere. Mentor's products are tools that many companies have come to rely on heavily. Converting to another tool base (from one of Mentor's competitors, for instance) is a tricky and lengthy process, and for that reason is seldom done. Once an EDA firm is ingrained and established in another company's design process, the account is guarded and protected and the relationship becomes very much akin to a partnership. Software license contracts have typical durations of three to four years, with large enterprise-scale customers accounting for over half of Mentor's total revenue.

Why Should I Care?

Designing and manufacturing a complex integrated circuit is an expensive and risky process. It's a bit like building a mid-sized American city—buildings, roads, subways, sewers, power distribution, everything—in a few months or more and having it work perfectly right away. Well, that's the goal, anyway. What usually happens is the first parts come out of the Easy-Bake and go straight to a test environment where each part gets poked and probed to determine how much of it actually works as intended. Once these first parts are characterized, it's back to the drawing board for a second pass, fixing the errors and adding in some features that may not have made it into the first parts. This iterative process continues for as long as it takes, and it can take a long time and a lot of money. Companies have gone out of business trying to perfect their implementations in silicon.

EDA software attempts to minimize the number of iterations required to produce working silicon. It does this by modeling the physics of the underlying structures in the circuit, simulating their behaviors given every possible range of inputs and environmental conditions. Mentor then supplies a rules-based system to the designer that virtually guarantees a highly functional first part, as long as it has passed Mentor's simulations of its behavior.

As parts get more complex and product cycles compress further and further, the need for sophisticated modeling tools increases. As a client gains expertise with its own technology and becomes more proficient with the Mentor toolset, it is able to design more complex parts with higher levels of functionality, which often leads in turn to more software sales for Mentor. This is the "win/win" scenario that tool companies like to sell and that has worked well for Mentor in the IC and PCB design markets. Mentor has branched out and is supplying design tools for many other high-demand applications, such as mechanical analysis, wire harness design, EMI simulations, and most recently, software simulation.

How's Business?

After two years of losing money, Mentor is back in the black with greatly improved prospects for the rest of 2011 and well into 2012. Pent-up demand in the automotive and consumer electronics industries should lead to healthy improvements in earnings and cash flow. The service and support contracts that follow the new licenses will provide further momentum to the financials in 2012.

Upside

- Fairly stable revenue
- Good international growth
- Robust return to profitability

Downside

- Margin/cash flow volatility
- Increasing share base
- Likely to be a relatively high buy in

Just the Facts

INDUSTRY: **Software and Programming**

BETA COEFFICIENT: **1.05**

5-YEAR COMPOUND EARNINGS-PER-SHARE GROWTH: **-9.5%**

		2006	**2007**	**2008**	**2009**	**2010**
Revenues (Mil)		792	880	789	802	915
Net Income (Mil)		27.2	28.8	-88.8	(-21.9)	28.6
Price:	high	18.5	19.4	16.0	9.7	12.4
	low	9.5	10.3	3.4	3.3	7.6

Mentor Graphics Corporation
8005 S.W. Boeckman Road
Wilsonville, OR 97070-7777
(503) 685-7000
Website: *www.mentor.com*

AGGRESSIVE GROWTH

MetroPCS Communications, Inc.

Ticker symbol: PCS (NYSE) ▫ S&P rating: B+ ▫ Value Line financial strength rating: B ▫ Current yield: Nil

Who Are They?

A relative newcomer to the mobile communications market, this Texas-based company offers its services in a popular no-long-term contract, paid-in-advance basis. Beginning operations in 2002 (and reorganized/renamed in 2004), the company has seen its subscriber base grow to over 8 million. The company has licenses for spectrum in areas with a total population of 142 million, and with the roaming agreements currently in place, it can offer service to its customers in an area covering over 280 million in total population.

In 2007, Metro made a bid for Leap Wireless priced at $75 per share, but was turned down. Leap is now trading at $16 per share with a market cap of $1.3 billion. There are thinly veiled references to an acquisition strategy in Metro's most recent 10-K, and we wouldn't be at all surprised to see Metro make another play for Leap in the near future.

Why Should I Care?

Metro's rate plans are proving to be very popular with their targeted metropolitan markets. The majority of its plans are unlimited use, with all fees and taxes included in the bundled price. Its plans start at a flat rate of $40, which includes unlimited local and long distance, unlimited text and photo messaging, and Internet access through Metro's portal. That's a pretty compelling bundle—we know several people who would have saved a fortune on their first bill if only their teenagers had had unlimited texting.

The popularity of its offerings is underscored by its top-line growth, which has quadrupled over the past five years. Earnings on those revenues have been less steady, but the recession and Metro's rollout of 4G phones and equipment have been behind most of that. Margins in 2011 and 2012 are expected to show a very strong recovery.

The U.S. market is something of an anomaly with regard to the use of no-contract plans. In the United States, only 10 percent of subscriptions are no-contract, whereas in France, the United Kingdom, and Italy the numbers are 39, 67, and 88 percent respectively. This may have more to do with network build-out financing models than any usage trend, but the match of Metro's coverage plan to that of the more densely populated areas of Europe seems to work in its favor.

Metro's target markets are lower-income urban populations. The company's focus on densely populated markets pays off in customer acquisition costs. The industry average is $358 per new customer added, while Metro spends only $124 on average for each new subscriber. This has a lot to do with Metro's low operating costs, and its operating margin is the best in the industry (nearly 28 percent in 2010).

How's Business?

Customer adds in 2011 are not expected to match 2010's 1.5 million new subscribers, but something along 1 million is likely. Tiered pricing in simple $5 increments provides an attractive and profitable up-sell for those on smartphone plans. Metro offers four such tiers and has added features to the 4G plans to provide further incentives for hardware up-sells.

Upside

- Real potential to steal market share from the big kids
- Fast 4G rollout
- Reasonable P/E

Downside

- Near-term growth may be "limited" to urban areas
- Still shopping for smaller players
- Not-insignificant debt service

Just the Facts

INDUSTRY: **Communications Services**
BETA COEFFICIENT: **0.85**
5-YEAR COMPOUND EARNINGS-PER-SHARE GROWTH: **23.6%**

		2006	2007	2008	2009	2010
Revenues (Mil)		1,547	2,236	2,752	3,481	4,069
Net Income (Mil)		89.6	198	176	175	257
Price:	high	—	40.9	21.9	19.0	12.9
	low	—	13.8	10.2	5.6	5.5

MetroPCS Communications, Inc.
2250 Lakeside Blvd.
Richardson, TX 75082
(214) 570-5800
Website: ***www.metropcs.com***

AGGRESSIVE GROWTH

Motorola Mobility

Ticker symbol: MMI (NYSE) ❑ S&P rating: NA ❑ Value Line financial strength rating: B++ ❑ Current yield: Nil

Who Are They?

Motorola Mobility is the mobile services business of the former Motorola, Inc., which in January 2011 divested its mobile business and split into MMI and Motorola Solutions (MSI). MMI's revenues in 2010 (retroactive) were about $11.5 billion and should reach $15.5 billion in 2012, while MSI's revenues should grow from $7.9 billion to $8.7 billion over the same period (MMI licenses the Motorola brand name to MSI). MMI's post-split charter is to focus on the consumer with mobile products such as cell phones, accessories, tablet products, navigation systems, and two-way radios. It also designs and manufactures products for the home market, including cable set-top boxes, cable and DSL gateways, wireless networking gear, POTS phones, and IP video interfaces. Many of both the home and mobile products are produced for and branded by the service provider. MMI also produces and markets the backend hardware for large-scale video distribution systems.

The split was motivated in no small part by a long series of legal pressures applied by a very fussy Carl Icahn. Mr. Icahn believed strongly that the company should have been split in 2008, but Motorola's board (who offered Icahn two seats, which he declined) held out for several years before agreeing to the change.

Why Should I Care?

MMI is one of the leading innovators in the marketplace, with very few low-margin, "me-too" offerings. Its new Atrix 4G smartphone, for example, employs a dual-core, 1GHz processor, 1GB of RAM, 16GB of storage and a very high-resolution, high-contrast display. In terms of raw performance, it's the most capable phone on the market, and it includes many other high-end features, including the ability to dock to a large display and function as a desktop. Motorola holds nothing back on this product, and its recent Xoom tablet product is also aggressively featured. Given the apparent bifurcation of the smartphone market (Apple and everybody else), the innovators in the non-Apple camp are the players to watch. Motorola is pretty clearly at the top of this pile, with perhaps only HP (with Web OS) being in a position to upset the non-Apple cart.

The company would probably benefit from further attrition. The networking business has been up against very stiff pricing pressure for years, and the set-top market has been basically flat since 2008. Motorola was looking for buyers for these units prior to the split, but interest was low. MMI may test the waters again in the next few years, unless it can develop a particularly compelling convergence message around the phone/set-top link.

How's Business?

Motorola's Mobility business has been losing money since its inception ($1.2 billion in 2007 alone). It seems ironic then that just as the split is about to take place, MMI turned its first-ever quarterly profit, good for $3 million in the third quarter of 2010. Earnings will continue to be based on narrow margins through 2012, but the revenue and operating margin acceleration is promising.

Upside

- Strong recent product introductions
- Android application base continues to grow
- Debt-free and healthy cash flow

Downside

- Lackluster network business
- Service provider consolidation could impact ASPs
- Competition? Just Apple and HP . . .

Just the Facts

INDUSTRY: **Communications Equipment**
BETA COEFFICIENT: **NA**
5-YEAR COMPOUND EARNINGS-PER-SHARE GROWTH: **NM**

		2006	2007	2008	2009	2010
Revenues (Mil)		—	—	—	11,050	11,460
Net Income (Mil)		—	—	—	(-1,342)	(-86.0)
Price:	high	—	—	—	—	36.5
	low	—	—	—	—	23.0

Motorola Mobility
600 North U.S. Highway 45
Libertyville, IL 60048
(847) 523-5000
Website: *www.motorola.com*

AGGRESSIVE GROWTH

NetApp, Inc.

Ticker symbol: NTAP (NASDAQ) ❑ S&P rating: NA ❑ Value Line financial strength rating: A ❑ Current yield: Nil

Who Are They?

NetApp provides storage and data management solutions designed to reduce the cost of managing and protecting data while at the same time increasing its availability. The company designs and produces systems, software, and services that implement secure backup, archival, and online storage and retrieval of business-critical data across a number of platforms. NetApp's products are designed for large, network-leveraged installations and, as such, the company works with key partners such as Cisco, IBM, Microsoft, SAP, and VMware to develop integrated solutions that optimize final system performance for its applications and infrastructure.

The company operates in three segments defined by sales: Product, which generally means preconfigured hardware and software sold as a bundle or add-on hardware sold for use with a preconfigured system, and integrated accessories; Software entitlements and maintenance, which consists of the initial sale of a software license and the cost (if any) of updates, patches, etc.; and Service, which consists of contractual and non-contractual hardware maintenance, professional services, and training. Over the past three years, growth in Service revenues has exceeded that of both Product and Software revenues. Indirect sales channels (VARs, etc.) accounted for approximately 70 percent of the company's sales in 2010.

Why Should I Care?

You can never be too rich, too thin, or have too much fast, deep, hard-drive space. Massive amounts of space solves a lot of problems in the IT universe, from safety to security to performance, and companies have found out that throwing hard drives at problems is often the fastest and cheapest way to make them go away. Storage is also a massive enabler for many of the new business models that leverage a company's internal data. Drive space can turn out to be very inexpensive when it provides instant access to any and every piece of data in a company's arsenal.

The company's revenue stream had been trending away from hardware prior to the most recent product launch. The new systems have been well received in the marketplace and hardware sales numbers should rise significantly over the next year. This will have the effect of reducing margins somewhat, but the systems will act as platforms for future system and service revenue generation.

NetApp recently closed its biggest-ever acquisition: the External Storage Systems business of LSI. The company paid $480 million for the business, which collected about $700 million in 2010 revenue. The unit is already profitable for LSI and the deal will add to NetApp's 2012 bottom line. The deal also creates cross-selling opportunities for NetApp into ESS's current customer base.

How's Business?

NetApp's first three quarters of FY2011 are in and they are well ahead of last year's results. Revenue is up 31 percent year to year and earnings are up 88 percent. The third quarter's two big product launches, the V3200 and V66200 systems, were so well received that the units went into backorder status, as the company had not built enough overage into the anticipated demand. Oops. Shipments are expected to be on track by the end of the fiscal year. By the way, note that the table below projects NetApp's full-year FY2011, as their fiscal year ends May 31, 2011.

Upside

- Leading technology
- Nice ongoing service revenues
- Application base continues to expand

Downside

- Two customers account for one-third of revenue
- Cyclical business
- Relatively expensive at the moment

Just the Facts

INDUSTRY: **Computer Storage Devices**

BETA COEFFICIENT: **1.10**

5-YEAR COMPOUND EARNINGS-PER-SHARE GROWTH: **12.5%**

		2007	2008	2009	2010	2011
Revenues (Mil)		2,804	3,303	3,406	3,850	5,000
Net Income (Mil)		298	310	87	375	635
Price:	high	40.9	27.5	35.0	58.0	61.0
	low	22.5	10.4	12.4	28.9	44.5

NetApp, Inc.
495 East Java Drive
Sunnyvale, CA 94089
(408) 822-6000
Website: *www.netapp.com*

AGGRESSIVE GROWTH

Netflix, Inc.

Ticker symbol: NFLX (NASDAQ) ❑ S&P rating: NA ❑ Value Line financial strength rating: A ❑ Current yield: Nil

Who Are They?

With 20 million subscribers, Netflix is the world's largest Internet subscription-based provider of television and movie content to the home. Subscribers can also view content on computers and mobile devices, and can also use physical media (DVDs and Blu-Ray discs) delivered to their homes via the U.S. Postal Service. The company licenses content from movie and television studios and other sources through fixed-fee licenses, revenue-sharing agreements, and outright purchase. Most of its operations are outsourced to providers such as Amazon Web Services and Level 3 Communications for content delivery. The company also operates a network of regional shipping centers for the management and delivery of physical media.

Why Should I Care?

Here's a stock for those who might be looking for something a little spicier than Chipotle, more expensive than Titanium, and higher-flying than Cirrus. If you hate a dull ride, you could do worse than Netflix.

To be honest, the needle on our *100 Best* ValueMeter is pointed straight at "Are you kidding me?" This is not the sort of stock we would normally recommend to people, and isn't even the sort of stock we sometimes take a chance on ourselves. The momentum and hoopla surrounding this stock puts it well into uncharted territory for many of us, and normally only those who were lucky enough to get in early might be excused for cheerleading a stock trading at sixty-eight times *projected* twelve months earnings. However. . . .

Netflix has spearheaded the biggest change in the entertainment business since the advent of the VCR. Its name is on almost every DVD player and home theater receiver now sold in the United States—it's even on the remote controls. The Internet address of its servers is hard-coded into every plasma and LCD screen over forty-two inches in size. Its name is practically synonymous with the delivery of movie content into the home, and it is the major reason Carl Icahn may be picking Blockbuster out of the bargain bin in a few months. In short, the company knows its business and appears to be very good at breaking new ground. It is also the first company in memory to do business with Hollywood and not end up under their thumb.

Whether you want to bet on Netflix is up to you, obviously, but unlike the 30 percent short interest out there, we're not betting against it.

How's Business?

For FY2010, year-over-year growth in paid subscribers came in at 54 percent, while growth in revenue came in at 34 percent. The gap between the two is a strong indicator of the trend that Netflix is banking on—new users are opting for lower-cost streaming plans over traditional DVD rentals. If Netflix has played its cards right, the reduced revenue growth will be more than offset in reduced cost of goods sold (COGS) as the subscriber count increases. Streaming content carries no inventory costs and the cost of the content is fixed for the life of the supply contract, meaning an incremental subscriber is a marginal COGS reducer.

Upside

- Large customer base = content purchasing clout
- Hollywood studio model starting to show its age
- It won't be boring

Downside

- At these valuations, you have to be a true believer
- Competition is trailing, but capable
- Will the Postal Service continue to work weekends?

Just the Facts

INDUSTRY: **Broadcasting & Cable TV**
BETA COEFFICIENT: **1.0**
5-YEAR COMPOUND EARNINGS-PER-SHARE GROWTH: **71%**

		2006	2007	2008	2009	2010
Revenues (Mil)		997	1,205	1,365	1,670	2,163
Net Income (Mil)		49.1	63.4	84.2	116	161
Price:	high	33.1	29.1	40.9	61.7	209.2
	low	18.1	15.6	17.9	28.8	48.5

Netflix, Inc.
100 Winchester Circle
Los Gatos, CA 95032
(408) 540-3700
Website: *www.netflix.com*

AGGRESSIVE GROWTH

Nike, Inc.

Ticker symbol: NKE (NYSE) ❑ S&P rating: A+ ❑ Value Line financial strength rating: A++ ❑ Current yield: 1.6%

Who Are They?

Nike's principal business activity is the design, development, and worldwide marketing of footwear, apparel, equipment, and accessory products. Nike is the largest seller of athletic footwear and athletic apparel in the world, but a big part of the story is how it is extending beyond traditional footwear and apparel. Its products are sold to retail accounts, through Nike-owned retail outlets, and through a mix of independent distributors and licensees in over 180 countries around the world. Nike does no manufacturing—virtually all of its footwear and apparel are manufactured by independent contractors outside the United States, while equipment products are made both in the United States and abroad.

Nike has a number of wholly owned subsidiaries, including Cole Haan, Converse, Hurley, and Umbro, which variously design, distribute, and license dress, athletic, and casual footwear, sports apparel, and accessories. In FY2010 these subsidiary brands, together with Nike Golf, accounted for approximately 45 percent of total revenues. About 58 percent of the company's total sales are overseas, and Nike is one of the strongest U.S. consumer brands abroad.

Why Should I Care?

Why buy Nike? In a word, brand. The Nike brand and its corresponding "swoosh" are one of the most recognized—and sought after—brands in the world. It is a lesson in simplicity and image congruence with the product behind it. Nike doesn't sit still with it; rather, it is learning to leverage it into more products outside the traditional athletic wear circuit—golf clubs, golf balls, even a new line of GPS watches and apps. Further, Nike doesn't just limit the brand appeal to athletes: Slogans like "Just Do It" and "If you have a body, you're an athlete" emphasize the appeal and lifestyle across all segments of the population. We think this is drop-dead smart.

Of course, solid brand and brand reputation lead to category leadership and hence, higher profitability, and Nike has finished far ahead of the pack in this area too. The brand and "moat" created by the brand seem to have nowhere to go but forward, and improved manufacturing efficiencies, strong channel relationships, and international exposure all keep the company moving faster in the right direction. Despite its size, the company continues to deliver double-digit earnings, cash flow, and dividend growth even as revenues have matured into the high single-digit range. We like the combination of protected profitability through brand excellence, combined with a clean conservative balance sheet, providing a good combination of safety and growth potential.

In short, if you have aces, you bet them. If you have a swoosh, you fly the brand as far as you can. Yes, Nike is large and very conservative as sports brands go, but it still moves aggressively into new markets and new geographies and brings all its resources to bear when it does.

How's Business?

At the three-quarter mark, Nike's 2011 leads 2010 by a length (horseshoes being one of the few they don't make). Global sales are up 8 percent, with China and emerging markets leading the charge at 19 and 22 percent, respectively. Per share earnings are moving quickly along the rail, up 12 percent.

Upside

- Worldwide growth accelerating
- Pricing power to offset higher input costs
- Golf due for a rebound

Downside

- Finding an attractive buy-in point may be tricky
- May have lost some agility
- Labor issues may linger for some time

Just the Facts

INDUSTRY: **Footwear**
BETA COEFFICIENT: **0.85**
5-YEAR COMPOUND EARNINGS-PER-SHARE GROWTH: **15%**

		2006	2007	2008	2009	2010
Revenues (Mil)		14,955	16,326	18,627	19,176	19,014
Net Income (Mil)		1,392	1,458	1,734	1,727	1,907
Price:	high	50.6	67.9	70.6	66.6	83.4
	low	37.8	47.5	42.7	38.2	60.9

Nike, Inc.
One Bowerman Drive
Beaverton, OR 97005
(503) 671-6453
Website: ***www.nike.com***

AGGRESSIVE GROWTH

Nucor Corporation

Ticker symbol: NUE (NYSE) ❑ S&P rating: A ❑ Value Line financial strength rating: A ❑ Current yield: 3.1%

Who Are They?

Nucor is the fourth-largest global steel producer (by market cap) and the largest U.S.-based producer. It is also the largest recycler in North America, recycling some 13.4 million tons of scrap steel in 2009. Its production model is unique, based on numerous mini-mills and the exclusive use of scrap material as production input. Nucor operates scrap-based steel mills in twenty-two facilities, producing bar, sheet, structural, and plate steel product. Production in 2009 totaled 14 million tons, after a far more robust 20.4 million tons in 2008.

Nucor's steel mills are considered to be among the most modern and efficient in the United States. Recycled scrap steel and other metals are melted in electric arc furnaces and poured into continuous casting systems. Sophisticated rolling mills convert the various types of raw cast material into rebar and basic shapes such as angles, rounds, channels, flats, sheet, beams, plate, and other products.

The company operates in three primary businesses: steel mills, steel products, and raw materials. The steel mills segment produces hot-rolled steel in a variety of shapes and forms, including plate and cold-rolled products. These products are sold to a variety of heavy manufacturing concerns and some construction businesses. The steel products segment produces materials primarily for the commercial construction industry, such as steel joists and girders, steel deck, fasteners, wire, and wire mesh. The raw materials segment gathers and sells ferrous and non-ferrous metals and provides brokerage, transportation, and other handling services.

Why Should I Care?

Steel is getting hammered on both sides it seems. Input prices are up 33 percent year to year due to low volumes of steel scrap and scrap substitutes, and prices for finished product are off due to the continued weakness in the construction market. The cure is improved demand, and infrastructure programs appear to be on the way (politics permitting).

The company believes strongly in better times ahead, and soon. In the past year the company has added capacity in the form of a bar mill in Memphis and a galvanizing line in Decatur, Alabama. It also acquired permits for the construction and operation of two direct reduced iron facilities in St. James Parish,

Louisiana. Nucor broke ground on the first of these facilities in March. In addition to the second DRI plant, plans for the Louisiana location include a coke plant, blast furnace, pellet plant, and steel mill. Partial funding for the facility comes from a $576 million Gulf Opportunity Zone Bond issued in November of 2010.

Nucor is the lowest-cost producer in the world—its gross margin is 40 percent higher than the largest player in the industry. Its capital structure is solid and puts the company in better position than any of its competitors to buy up capacity should others fail to recover quickly. Its large rapid-start capacity positions Nucor well to take advantage of the opportunity as demand turns around, and it is widely acknowledged to be one of the best-run and most innovative players in the industry.

How's Business?

After a dismal 2009–2010 for the industry, nearly any news would be good news, but Nucor's first quarter was even better than expected. Earnings of $160 million topped 2010's first quarter by 416 percent. Per share guidance had been in the thirty to thirty-five cents range, whereas actuals came in at fifty cents per share. These are the best numbers in ten quarters for Nucor, and projections for the 2011–2012 period are for more of the same, and better.

Upside

- Operating margins may double in 2011
- Top line should grow 25 percent
- Very good cash generator

Downside

- One or two quarters may not qualify as "momentum" in big steel
- Massive fixed costs, volume badly needed
- High market expectations

Just the Facts

INDUSTRY: **Iron and Steel**
BETA COEFFICIENT: **1.20**
5-YEAR COMPOUND EARNINGS-PER-SHARE GROWTH: **19%**

		2006	2007	2008	2009	2010
Revenues (Mil)		12,701	14,571	16,593	23,663	11,190
Net Income (Mil)		1,310	1,758	1,472	1,831	(-294)
Price:	high	35.1	67.6	69.9	83.6	51.1
	low	22.8	33.2	41.6	25.3	29.8

Nucor Corporation
1915 Rexford Road
Charlotte, NC 28211
(704) 366-7000
Website: ***www.nucor.com***

AGGRESSIVE GROWTH

OM Group

Ticker symbol: OMG (NYSE) ❑ S&P rating: BB- ❑ Value Line financial strength rating: B+ ❑ Current yield: Nil

Who Are They?

OM Group is a global provider of chemicals, advanced materials, batteries, and other technologies critical to its customers' applications. OM Group believes it is the world's largest refiner of cobalt and producer of cobalt-based specialty products, while at the same time producing over 400 hundred different metal-based specialty chemicals and powders based primarily on cobalt, copper, and nickel chemistries. The company's three operating segments—Advanced Materials, Specialty Chemicals, and Battery Technologies—supply products for more than 4,000 customers in more than fifty industries. Its products are used in applications as diverse as PCB production, semiconductors, lubricants, disk drive media, paints, rechargeable batteries, rubber, steel, fibers, and many more.

The company maintains more than thirty technical facilities in fourteen countries around the world, with manufacturing facilities in North America, Europe, Asia, and Africa.

Why Should I Care?

One of OMG's big hitters is the electroless plating business. Electroless plating puts a very thin layer of nickel onto aluminum in such a way that the resulting surface is atomically smooth. Every platter in every hard disk drive in the world, whether it goes into a PC or a video camera or anything else gets this plating treatment, and hard disk drive shipping volumes will be up nearly 20 percent in 2012. Another technology application where OMG has a significant presence is the photomask business. Photomasks are tools used in the production of integrated circuits—the "template" used to produce the layers of an integrated circuit. OM Group grew its mask business 12 percent in 2010, accounting for $120 million in revenues. The mask business in 2012 should be better still. Finally, OM Group is the market leader in the production of cobalt materials critical for lithium ion and lithium polymer batteries. These batteries are the current state of the art in terms of their power-to-weight ratio, and are used in hundreds of high-value applications including laptops, tablets, smartphones, and hybrid and electric cars.

Overall, though, what we find especially appealing about OMG is not the one or two or three high-volume products but rather the breadth of OMG's lines across a number of very promising industries and applications. Some of these fields, like lithium battery chemistry and photovoltaics, have growth potential that's readily apparent, and some of that potential is already cooked into the price. What's not cooked into the price is the *number* of products the company has in established and nascent technologies with broad applications—powder metallurgy for water filtration, etching and plating chemicals for advanced PCB manufacturing, and ultrapure chemicals for MEMS and nanotechnology. It may not have enormous volumes in all of these areas, but it is plugged into these industries at a very fundamental level, and therein lies opportunity.

How's Business?

The company reported a sales increase of 9 percent in the first quarter of 2011 with good profitability in the Advanced Materials segment. The company closed an underutilized manufacturing facility in its Specialty Chemicals segment and has taken additional steps to improve profitability there.

Upside

- Battery segment could blossom with OMG's healthy finances
- Semiconductor market recovery will help
- Cobalt price spike was brief

Downside

- Most cobalt sourced from Democratic Republic of Congo
- Considerable earnings uncertainty
- Revenue growth unlikely across all product lines

Just the Facts

INDUSTRY: **Chemical Manufacturing**

BETA COEFFICIENT: **1.60**

5-YEAR COMPOUND EARNINGS-PER-SHARE GROWTH: **NM**

	2006	2007	2008	2009	2010
Revenues (Mil)	660	1,022	1,737	872	1,197
Net Income (Mil)	23.6	164	135	(-19.4)	82.6
Price: high	59.7	63.7	66.0	36.0	39.9
low	17.1	36.2	12.2	13.9	22.0

OM Group, Inc.
127 Public Square, 1500 Key Tower
Cleveland, OH 44114-1221
(216) 781-0083
Website: *www.omgi.com*

AGGRESSIVE GROWTH

Oracle Corporation

Ticker symbol: ORCL (NASDAQ) ❑ S&P rating: A ❑ Value Line financial strength rating: A++ ❑ Current yield: 0.6%

Who Are They?

Oracle Corporation supplies the world's most widely used information-management software, the Oracle database. It is also the world's second largest independent software company. In addition to its namesake database, Oracle also develops, manufactures, markets, distributes, and services middleware and applications software that help its customers manage their businesses.

Oracle is organized into three businesses: software, hardware systems, and services, which in the most recent quarter accounted for 68 percent, 19 percent, and 13 percent of revenues respectively. The company's software licenses segment includes the licensing of database and middleware software, which consists of Oracle Database and Oracle Fusion Middleware, as well as applications software.

Oracle's database and middleware software provides a platform for running and managing business applications for mid-size businesses and large global enterprises. Designed for enterprise grid computing, the Oracle Database is available in four editions, scaled to the size of the intended application. Oracle Exadata is a family of storage software and hardware products designed to improve data warehouse query performance.

Oracle Consulting assists customers in deploying its applications and technology products. The company's consulting services include business/IT strategy alignment; business process simplification; solution integration; and product implementation, enhancements, and upgrades. The company provides training to customers, partners, and employees. Oracle offers thousands of courses covering all of its product offerings.

The company has over 370,000 customers in 145 countries around the world, including all of the *Fortune* 100. Worldwide sales in FY2011 thus far are split 53/47, domestic/international.

Why Should I Care?

Oracle's new Exadata integrated systems are the focus of a lot of attention. The Sun acquisition made possible an integrated software/hardware product sold as a unit to run Oracle's database in an OLTP (on line transaction processing) environment. It's designed to be easy to deploy and configure, and provide very high levels of performance due to its use of extremely low-latency (fast response time) storage. By all reports, it has been selling well, but the numbers don't provide a lot of support for the claim—sales of hardware are down 9 percent over the year. However, the company has slashed hardware segment expenses to the tune of 23 percent, yielding an increase in earnings in hardware of about 7 percent. The company has originally forecast early sales of only $100 million per quarter for Exadata systems, so it's still too early to tell if the decline in revenues is due to lagging Exadata demand or simply the natural decline in sales of Sun's older Intel x86-based hardware.

How's Business?

One big question about the Sun acquisition was what sort of synergies, if any, would result from the addition of a hardware segment to Oracle's business. So far, the answer would have to be "not a lot." Other than a moderate bump in Q4 FY2010 (the traditional order pull in), the hardware revenues have not impressed, though software and services revenues have continued to grow at a measured pace. Still, the bleeding at the former Sun organization has been stopped, and the hardware business is now in the capable hands of one Mark Hurd.

Upside

- Almost as much cash as Google
- Earnings predictability
- Passed Recessionville without stopping for gas

Downside

- Three large hardware partners now selling against them
- Five billion shares out there
- Maybe a bit slow to move into some new ventures

Just the Facts

INDUSTRY: **Software and Programming**
BETA COEFFICIENT: **0.95**
5-YEAR COMPOUND EARNINGS-PER-SHARE GROWTH: **22.5%**

		2006	2007	2008	2009	2010
Revenues (Mil)		14,771	18,208	22,609	23,495	27,034
Net Income (Mil)		4,246	5,295	6,799	7,393	8,494
Price:	high	19.8	23.3	23.6	25.1	32.3
	low	12.1	16.0	15.0	13.8	21.2

Oracle Corporation
500 Oracle Parkway
Redwood City, CA 94065
(650) 506-7000
Website: ***www.oracle.com***

AGGRESSIVE GROWTH

Orbotech

Ticker symbol: ORBK (NASDAQ) ❑ S&P rating: NA ❑ Value Line financial strength rating: B ❑ Current yield: Nil

Who Are They?

Orbotech develops and manufactures a number of high-value process tools for the printed circuit board and LCD flat panel display industries. Its product line includes computerized electro-optical systems for the automated inspection and repair of PCBs and displays, as well as laser-based imaging systems for the production of PCBs, IC substrates, flex circuits, and solder masks. It also designs and markets a number of software tools for the preproduction optimization of PCB and panel designs, including simple layout programs and very advanced tools for the parametric analysis of a circuit's electrical properties.

The company, founded thirty years ago, has grown both organically and through a series of strategic acquisitions, including the 2008 acquisition of Photon Dynamics, a Silicon Valley–based company engaged in test and repair solutions for flat panel displays. In 2009, the company established a joint venture with LT Solar for the manufacturing of solar energy photovoltaics.

Why Should I Care?

The printed circuit board and flat panel display manufacturing businesses rely on high yields as much as they do on low-input costs and economic volumes. Just as in IC production, it's not practical to test products as they're being built up layer by layer, and the manufacturer relies on its process to generate functional products. By the time a PCB (or a flat panel display) gets to end-of-process testing, there's already a great deal of material and process costs built into the product, and throwing out a large, complex assembly because of a single defect is a major hit to operating costs. Orbotech's products are designed to reduce these losses to their practical minimum, if not entirely eliminate them. Costly manual inspection and repair processes are replaced with efficient automated processes; in many cases I&R is performed on products that simply can't be handled manually due to the fine-feature size of high-density layouts.

Another advantage of its technology is the flexibility it offers the manufacturer in terms of factory flow. Its laser direct imaging products, while ideally suited for low-volume, high-mix production, can easily be ganged for high-volume production. This sort of repurposing assumes you have extra machines on hand, of course, so the benefits flow to the larger PCB manufacturers, which is exactly where the industry is moving. Smaller, specialty shops that can swing the up-front cost will benefit from the low operating costs and elimination of their dependence on many optical and chemical processes, and high-volume, lower-margin producers will appreciate the yield and throughput improvements. It's no wonder these tools are in high demand and that owners are willing to pay for Orbotech's service programs.

How's Business?

The company's first quarter results came with a nice earnings surprise and updated guidance for FY2011. Revenues were up 34 percent over 2010, with earnings up 200 percent to thirty cents per share. Guidance for the remainder of FY2011 is for 10 percent net margin, or $1.55 per share, up from analysts' consensus of $1.35 per share. The company expects to sell 170 of its direct imaging systems this year, compared to 107 in 2010.

Upside

- Leading disruptive technology
- Very attractive share price
- Aggressive tech company with proven demand

Downside

- Products priced at top of market
- Costly, sole-sourced inputs
- Shares may not be cheap for long

Just the Facts

INDUSTRY: **PCB Manufacturing**

BETA COEFFICIENT: **0.85**

5-YEAR COMPOUND EARNINGS-PER-SHARE GROWTH: **-24%**

		2006	2007	2008	2009	2010
Revenues (Mil)		417	361	430	378	529
Net Income (Mil)		58.1	15.8	12.5	9.9	34.0
Price:	high	27.3	25.7	19.1	12.2	13.4
	low	20.9	15.2	2.9	3.3	8.6

Orbotech Ltd.
Sanhedrin Blvd, North Industrial Zone
Yavne 81101, Israel
972 8-942-3533
Website: ***www.orbotech.com***

AGGRESSIVE GROWTH

Ormat Technologies

Ticker symbol: ORA (NYSE) ❑ S&P rating: NA ❑ Value Line financial strength rating: B ❑ Current yield: 0.8%

Who Are They?

Ormat is the largest geothermal energy pure play in North America. It operates in two segments: it builds, owns, and operates geothermal power plants, selling the electricity; it also sells power plant equipment using its proprietary geothermal technology to geothermal operators and to industrial users for use in remote power generation and recovered energy applications. Its geothermal plants (78 percent of revenue in 2010) top out at about 35 megawatts and are located in approximately forty thermally active locations in the western United States, the Pacific Rim, and the Mediterranean. The power generation products are particularly attractive for harsh, remote locations, as the technology requires very little in the way of management or maintenance. The vast majority of these units are currently sold outside of the United States. The recovered energy units are commonly used in gas pipeline compressor stations, but are suited to any process that generates significant waste heat.

The company owns a large number of patents on its very efficient energy-conversion process. Its products do not require exotic manufacturing processes or materials, and the company builds almost all of its own products at its plants in Nevada.

Why Should I Care?

This is a stock you buy partly on the facts and partly on faith. There's no riskier stock in the book, and while we feel this stock has significant potential, it will have to be watched closely. There's a great deal of speculative interest in this issue (P/E near 100 as we go to press); strong rumors and a large camp of true believers have kept ORA's price above 20 even in the face of declining cash flow and ballooning debt. Ormat is a beneficiary of Department of Energy (DOE) cash grants and American Recovery and Reinvestment Act loan guarantees for geothermal projects, but its need for these funds begins to cast doubts on the stability of future earnings. The company currently has 553 megawatts of operating capacity, all of it presently at full utilization. They expect to bring another 228 megawatts of capacity online in the next three years.

Geothermal plants are quite a bit more expensive to bring online than, say, a gas turbine plant. A geothermal plant will cost approximately $2,500 per kilowatt installed versus $1,000 per kilowatt for a gas turbine facility. Operating costs are where the geothermal plant shines—generation costs are in the range of one to three cents per kilowatt hour. Coal, the next cheapest alternative, yields costs of two to three cents per kilowatt hour. Geothermal plants are also extremely reliable, with 24/7 availability and near 98 percent uptime, with very little maintenance and near zero environmental impact. Coal plants, on the other hand, average about 75 percent availability. These geothermal plants are very good solutions for particular needs in particular locations, but cannot be plopped down just anywhere as they require a source of geothermal heat. Fortunately, the DOE estimates there are a large number of potential sites in the western United States.

How's Business?

The company has warned that it will likely lose money in the first half of FY2011. It expects the full year will be profitable, however. New capacity is coming online and some enhancements to existing facilities are expected to make the differencc.

Upside

- Unique technology
- Demonstrated success in narrow segments
- Governmental tailwind

Downside

- Emerging markets
- Large investment compared to alternative sources
- Debt will require attention

Just the Facts

INDUSTRY: **Electric Utilities**

BETA COEFFICIENT: **1.15**

5-YEAR COMPOUND EARNINGS-PER-SHARE GROWTH: **11%**

	2006	**2007**	**2008**	**2009**	**2010**
Revenues (Mil)	269	296	345	415	373
Net Income (Mil)	34.4	27.4	49.8	68.9	10.4
Price: high	43.9	57.9	57.7	44.1	38.8
low	25.1	33.5	21.8	22.8	23.0

Ormat Technologies, Inc.
6225 Neil Road, Suite 300
Reno, NV 89511
(775) 356-9029
Website: ***www.ormat.com***

AGGRESSIVE GROWTH

Overstock.com

Ticker symbol: OSTK (NASDAQ) ❑ S&P rating: NA ❑ Value Line financial strength rating: C++ ❑ Current yield: Nil

Who Are They?

Overstock.com is an online retailer offering a wide variety of brand-name merchandise at discount prices, including bedding, home décor, appliances, watches, jewelry, electronics, sporting goods, clothing, and shoes. The company also operates a number of affiliated websites, including an online auction site, a car shopping site, and a real estate search site.

The concept is simple—customers shop online for bargains and other discounted merchandise, with the presumption that much of it is sold at bargain prices due to a manufacturer's overrun or other retailer's overbuy. Whether this is true for 10 percent or 90 percent of the products sold on Overstock's website is neither here nor there. It's a retailing operation that provides suppliers an alternative sales channel, and alternative sales channels are generally a good thing.

The company operates in two segments: the Fulfillment Partner Segment and the Direct Segment. As fulfillment partners, Overstock does not hold inventory but rather acts as a go-between for buyers and sellers. Sellers' products are listed on Overstock's site, which is effectively the seller's retail presence. Overstock has approximately 1,200 partners in this program with over 160,000 products. In the Direct Segment, Overstock sells directly to consumers from Overstock's leased warehouses, where owned surplus inventory is stocked and resold at a premium. The Fulfillment business accounts for 80 percent of revenue.

Why Should I Care?

Founded in 2001 and operated at a net loss until 2009, the company has started to turn the corner. Its big problem has been the rather large infrastructure it put in place to handle the enormous demand it anticipated for its service. Unfortunately, the enormity of the demand fell short of expectations, and the resulting high operating costs have erased the bottom line for most of the company's history. They've been able to cut costs over time and have gotten much smarter about their operating model. Still, this is a risky play. They're up against some very savvy competition, and the online retail business is not what it was when Overstock got started. The company has to pay for search positioning (see below), and many of its partners maintain their own online retail presence as well.

Overstock has built up a large core customer base who use the site as a primary shopping destination, not just a seasonal or "specials" site. The company has been able to retain these customers through its superior service policies—Overstock is ranked second in customer service among all U.S.-based online retailers.

How's Business?

The company learned the hard way that you don't fool around with Google. By offering a special discount program to university students and faculty, Overstock was able to get links to its sites to appear on thousands of sites with dot-edu domains (Harvard.edu, for example). Since Google's search logic applies a high level of trust to dot-edu domains, Overstock was able to move up to the top of the search listings for most of its items. Google has rules about manipulating search results in this way, and dropped the hammer on Overstock. Its listings were artificially lowered by Google for six weeks in early 2011.

Upside

- Improved profits forecasted for 2011—light/tunnel?
- Discounted vacations a new product
- Company nearly debt-free

Downside

- Internet sales tax?
- Large business risk—tread lightly
- Appeal may just be too narrow

Just the Facts

INDUSTRY: **Retail (Catalog & Mail Order)**
BETA COEFFICIENT: **1.50**
5-YEAR COMPOUND EARNINGS-PER-SHARE GROWTH: —

		2006	2007	2008	2009	2010
Revenues (Mil)		788	760	834	877	1,090
Net Income (Mil)		(-94.9)	(-41.1)	(-12.7)	7.7	13.9
Price:	high	35.0	39.4	29.6	18.0	26.5
	low	13.4	14.0	6.3	6.7	10.9

Overstock.com, Inc.
6350 South 3000 East
Salt Lake City, UT 84121
(801) 947-3100
Website: ***www.overstock.com***

AGGRESSIVE GROWTH

PACCAR Inc.

Ticker symbol: PCAR (NASDAQ) ❑ S&P rating: A+ ❑ Value Line financial strength rating: A ❑ Current yield: 1.6%

Who Are They?

Here's a company that would be unknown to most until you started naming some of its brands: Peterbilt, Kenworth, and in Europe, DAF and Foden. PACCAR owns them all, making them the second-largest manufacturer of heavy-duty trucks in the United States (behind Daimler AG), and third largest in the world. PACCAR also manufactures light/medium duty trucks under the Leyland brand in the United Kingdom, as well as occupational vehicles (dump trucks, tankers, etc.). The company's primary markets are North America, Western Europe and the United Kingdom, and Australia. In addition to truck bodies and chassis, PACCAR also manufactures many of the engines that are installed in the trucks—the company has been in the diesel engine business for more than fifty years and has produced over a million engines. It also produces several lines of industrial winches. The company also maintains a separate financing arm with assets of nearly $8 billion. PACCAR Financial Services primarily provides leasing services and credit for PACCAR's vehicle customers.

Why Should I Care?

The large-scale users of heavy-duty trucks, the fleet operators, regularly rotate older vehicles out of their inventory as maintenance costs increase and new features become available on new truck models. The recent economic downturn effectively extended the useful life on many fleets, as the miles were not being put on the vehicles. Fleet operators were also reluctant to commit to new assets until it was clear that an economic turnaround was in sight. Now that global economies are nearly in full recovery, capital budgets are freeing up for new truck purchases. The company anticipates a 40–60 percent increase in North American sales over 2010's numbers, or roughly 180,000–200,000 vehicles. European volume is expected to grow 20–30 percent, reflecting the continued economic recovery in the industrial sector there.

In addition, the U.S. government's mandated reductions in tailpipe emissions took full effect (up from 50 percent to 100 percent of sales) in 2010, requiring all engines sold to comply with the new strict standards. PACCAR's new MX engine design, built at its new dedicated facility in Tennessee, exceeds all applicable standards, and we anticipate an improvement in gross margins as the company's own engines are installed in a higher percentage of the vehicles sold.

PACCAR Financial Services (PFS) expects a 5–10 percent increase in earning assets, primarily from new business financing related to increased truck sales. In 2010, PFS financed 28 percent of all new truck loans worldwide. Historically, PFS contributes 20–25 percent to PACCAR's bottom line, but in a dismal 2009, PFS accounted for nearly half of the corporation's net income.

How's Business?

It's good to be in a recovery. Revenues in 2011 are expected to rise nearly 40 percent to $14.5 billion. Income is expected to increase 91 percent to $875 million, or *ten times* 2009's earnings. If the expected North American volumes materialize, the company will have recovered most of the 2 percent market share that was lost during the recession. Europe has no such concerns, and the company gained just over 1 percent market share over the past two years.

Upside

- Strong pent-up fleet demand
- Technology leader in a market that needs one
- Rising freight volumes worldwide

Downside

- New engine plant not fully utilized
- Pressure from rising commodity costs
- Early recovery momentum has pushed stock to high multiple

Just the Facts

INDUSTRY: **Auto & Truck Manufacturers**
BETA COEFFICIENT: **1.25**
5-YEAR COMPOUND EARNINGS-PER-SHARE GROWTH: **6.5%**

		2006	2007	2008	2009	2010
Revenues (Mil)		16,454	15,222	14,973	8,087	10,293
Net Income (Mil)		1,496	1,227	1,018	83.0	457.8
Price:	high	46.2	65.8	55.5	40.3	57.8
	low	30.1	42.2	22.0	20.4	33.4

PACCAR Inc.
777 106th Avenue NE
Bellevue, WA 98004
(425) 468-7400
Website: ***www.paccar.com***

AGGRESSIVE GROWTH

Panasonic Corp.

Ticker symbol: PC (NYSE) ❑ S&P rating: A+ ❑ Value Line financial strength rating: B++ ❑ Current yield: 0.8%

Who Are They?

Panasonic, founded in 1935 in Japan as Matsushita Industries, manufacturers electronic and electric products for a range of consumer, business, and industrial uses. The company consists of six segments: Digital AVC Networks (basically, home and automotive entertainment), Home Appliances, Panasonic Electric Works and PanaHome Corporation, Components and Devices, and Sanyo (Sanyo Corp. was acquired in December 2009).

Panasonic is perhaps best known in the United States for its consumer electronics products: televisions, audio systems, and mobile electronics. While this is the biggest single part of its business, it is also one of the largest manufacturers of heating, air conditioning, and refrigeration products in the world, and it is the number one brand for these products in many Asian markets.

Panasonic Electric Works and PanaHome manufacture, sell, install, and service electrical construction materials, home appliances, building products, electronic materials, and automation controls. The Components segment provides devices such as small and large-scale integrated circuits, image sensors, passive components, and a wide range of batteries.

The Sanyo segment manufactures and sells products in many of the same markets where Panasonic already operates: energy (solar cells and rechargeable batteries), environmental controls (commercial equipment, home appliances, and car electronics), and electronics (consumer electronics and semiconductors). The integration of Sanyo's organization and product line will play a large part in Panasonic's profitability over the next few years.

Why Should I Care?

As one of the largest consumer electronics manufacturers in the world, Panasonic's name should be well known to most investors. What may not be as well known is its presence in the industrial sector; Panasonic is one of the world's largest battery and power system suppliers. It manufactures and markets batteries of all chemistry types under its own name and produces batteries for OEM applications; its batteries are found in everything from watches to laptops to automobiles and electric cars. The battery business is thought to be one of the more profitable businesses in the company, given their volumes and the premiums paid for high-performance lithium and NiMH chemistries. The company's overall energy systems business ($6 billion in 2010) is targeted for $10 billion in sales in 2013. Over the same period, it plans to grow its consumer electronics (entertainment) business 10 percent per year from $18 billion to $24 billion.

How's Business?

Panasonic has 679 subsidiary companies, each with its own R&D, manufacturing, and marketing operations. Partly as a result, Panasonic's operating margins are less than half of the consumer goods industry average over the past five years. A continued emphasis on cost cutting is needed for Panasonic, and we hear all the right words from the CEO in this regard. If the follow-through on reorganization and cost cutting is there, earnings should get a nice free bump in 2012 and 2013. Given the overlap in Panasonic's product lines, the Sanyo integration should provide more than enough reason and opportunity for a much-needed streamlining of the organization.

Upside

- Sanyo acquisition to boost revenues, operating margin
- Top player in several high-growth markets
- Strong brands in the Chinese market

Downside

- Could take some time to turn this big ship
- Complex corporate structure
- Full extent of tsunami damage unknown, but appears to be minor

Just the Facts

INDUSTRY: **Audio & Video Equipment**

BETA COEFFICIENT: **0.85**

5-YEAR COMPOUND EARNINGS-PER-SHARE GROWTH: —

		2006	2007	2008	2009	2010
Revenues (Mil)		77,187	90,689	78,758	79,763	104,700
Net Income (Mil)		1,908	2,819	3,843	(-1,150)	1,345
Price:	high	25.1	21.7	24.4	16.6	17.2
	low	17.7	16.6	10.9	10.6	12.1

Panasonic Corporation
1 Rockefeller Plaza, Suite 1001
New York, NY 10152
(212) 698-1365
Website: ***www.panasonic.com***

AGGRESSIVE GROWTH

Peet's Coffee & Tea

Ticker symbol: PEET (NASDAQ) ❑ S&P rating: NA ❑ Value Line financial strength rating: B++ ❑ Current yield: Nil

Who Are They?

Peet's Coffee & Tea is a specialty coffee roaster and marketer of roasted whole bean coffee and tea. It sells coffee through multiple channels of distribution, including grocery stores, home delivery, office, restaurant and foodservice accounts, and company-owned retail outlets. As of January 2011, it operated 192 retail stores in six (mainly western) states. These stores account for approximately 60 percent of its net revenues.

The company was founded in 1966 and is widely considered the first ultra-premium coffee retailer in the United States and an inspiration for Starbucks and others. Peet's was purchased by two of the founders of Starbucks after it sold that firm in 1987 to Howard Schultz and other investors.

Peet's stores are designed to encourage the purchase of roasted whole beans through the sale of coffee beverages. Like Starbucks, Peet's stores have attractive environments and are effective gathering places for all walks of urban and suburban life.

In addition to sales through retail stores, the company sells products through nearly 9,000 grocery stores, including Safeway, Albertson's, Ralph's, Kroger, Publix, and Whole Foods Market. Peet's reps deliver directly to their stores anywhere between one to three times per week during which time they perform re-shelving, stock rotation, display management, and collect feedback from the retailer.

Why Should I Care?

With mergers, buy-outs, partnership deals, and lots of new product in the gourmet coffee space, Peet's seems content to stay on the sidelines. The stock has held its own, but little more than that. On the other hand, holding your own as a purveyor of discretionary goods during a recession is not all bad. We think it says a lot about the quality of the product and the loyalty of the customer base. Still . . . wouldn't it be nice to see Peet's participate in the single-serve "K-Cup" business? Wouldn't that be a terrific way for folks to get a taste of your product who might not have a chance otherwise? Wouldn't that help to drive grocery sales of your beans, which is where you've always said you wanted to focus? And how about a Peet's instant? Would a somewhat diluted blend really dilute the brand?

Okay, full disclosure: We like Peet's coffee. We're drinking some right now. It's a home team thing, and if we had a Peet's baseball hat, we'd be wearing it.

Honestly, though, the company has forecast single-digit EPS growth through 2012, so we're not sure this is the aggressive stock you're looking for. *If*, though, Peet's does come out with some new and interesting product that leverages its growing brand strength, then there's nowhere to go in these new markets but up.

How's Business?

The first quarter of 2011 had an upside surprise for Peet's. Per share earnings came in at forty-one cents, up 58 percent from the year-ago period and beating estimates by 20 percent. Revenue was up 9 percent largely on the strength of the specialty business, and particularly in grocery, where revenues were up 22 percent. Unfortunately, there was a downside surprise as well; significant increases in the cost of raw coffee beans over the past year caused the company to lower EPS guidance for the year by ten cents to a range of $1.43–$1.50.

Upside

- Strong growth in the more profitable segments
- Post-recession coffee habits unchanged
- Bean prices moderately hedged in 2011

Downside

- Retail store cost structure
- Retail revenues have tapered
- Bean prices may affect 2012

Just the Facts

INDUSTRY: **Restaurants**

BETA COEFFICIENT: **0.75**

5-YEAR COMPOUND EARNINGS-PER-SHARE GROWTH: **12.5%**

		2006	2007	2008	2009	2010
Revenues (Mil)		211	250	285	311	334
Net Income (Mil)		8.9	12.9	15.1	17.3	18.0
Price:	high	32.8	30.4	29.8	42.2	43.0
	low	24.3	23	17.8	19.3	31.5

Peet's Coffee &Tea, Inc.
1400 Park Avenue
Emeryville, CA 94608-3520
(510) 594-2100
Website: *www.peets.com*

AGGRESSIVE GROWTH

Penn National Gaming

Ticker symbol: PENN (NASDAQ) ❑ S&P rating: NA ❑ Value Line financial strength rating: B ❑ Current yield: Nil

Who Are They?

Penn National Gaming owns, operates, or has ownership interest in twenty-three gaming facilities (that's casinos and pari-mutuel horse and dog tracks to the uninitiated) located primarily in the eastern United States and Canada. The company was incorporated in 1994 strictly as an owner/operator of pari-mutuel facilities and in 1997 began a period of expansion into casino operations, primarily through acquisitions but also through green field development. The complete list of properties includes sixteen casinos (nine dockside, seven land-based), six pari-mutuel tracks (three thoroughbred, two harness, one greyhound), and it manages and operates Casino Rama in Ontario, Canada, without ownership interest. As of December 31, 2010, the company had a base of 27,000 gaming machines, 533 table games, and 2,000 hotel rooms.

Why Should I Care?

The gaming industry in the United States faces a number of challenges unique to the business. Obviously, they cannot locate a casino wherever they like. Gambling is highly regulated even in those jurisdictions where provisional license is granted to build and operate a facility. Even after a licensed facility is built, the owner is generally not free to substantially change the type of gaming or the number of gaming stations in the facility without first seeking approval from (typically) a board of state regulators.

On the other hand, most jurisdictions feel it's in the best interests of the community to restrict the number of outlets for gambling urges and so limit facility licenses by geography. Thus, Penn National finds itself with a monopoly in most of the areas in which it operates, including several of their largest installations. Lawrenceburg, Indiana (population 5,000), is one such location. Lawrenceburg isn't going to need more than the one casino, but it might need a new freeway to handle the traffic from nearby southwestern Ohio and Kentucky, where casinos are nonexistent.

The gaming businesses that Penn National operates are not resort destinations, by and large. Although there are hotel rooms available at some of its facilities (fewer than half), most of the casinos are day trips, just a short drive from major metropolitan centers. Chicago, for example, has three Penn National casinos nearby. As such, these casinos are not as exposed to the downturns in the economy as would be, say, a Las Vegas destination property. Penn's revenue has been flat but steady from 2006 through 2010.

Penn made several acquisitions in 2010, including the M Resort Casino in Las Vegas. This is Penn's first Las Vegas property. The resort was acquired essentially at the cost of its outstanding debt, around $250 million; compare this to the original land cost of $300 million and the construction cost of $1 billion and it would appear that Penn played their cards right.

The company plans to open two more casinos in Ohio (Columbus and Toledo) in 2012, adding 5,000 slots, 150 table games, and fifty poker tables to its existing base.

How's Business?

The first quarter of 2011 was very positive for Penn. Revenues were up 11 percent, driving an income increase of nearly 40 percent versus 2010. The company should return to profitability for the year overall with record revenue.

Upside

- Solid 2011 in sight
- Minimal carrying cost on M Resort
- Room for more acquisitions

Downside

- Potential regulatory delays in Ohio
- Vegas debut may have to wait until 2013
- Canadian contract up for re-bid this year

Just the Facts

INDUSTRY: **Casinos and Gaming**
BETA COEFFICIENT: **1.45**
5-YEAR COMPOUND EARNINGS-PER-SHARE GROWTH: —

		2006	2007	2008	2009	2010
Revenues (Mil)		2,245	2,437	2,423	2,369	2,459
Net Income (Mil)		136	160	153	265	59.5
Price:	high	43.8	63.7	59.8	35.2	37.2
	low	29.5	39.9	11.8	16.4	22.3

Penn National Gaming, Inc.
825 Berkshire Blvd, Suite 200
Wyomissing, PA 19610
(610) 373-2400
Website: ***www.pngaming.com***

AGGRESSIVE GROWTH

The Pep Boys—Manny, Moe & Jack

Ticker symbol: PBY (NYSE) ❑ S&P rating: B ❑ Value Line financial strength rating: C++ ❑ Current yield: 0.9%

Who Are They?

Okay, first of all, that really is the name of the company. It says so right on the 10K above "exact name of registrant as specified in its charter." For now, though, we'll just call them Pep Boys, because that's what it says on the signs above the 621 stores in the thirty-six states where Manny, Moe and Jack can be found.

Pep Boys is an automotive parts and accessories retailer. Founded way back in 1921 in Philadelphia, the company went public in 1946 and got its first "non-family" management in 1986, when it began a period of rapid growth. In 1991, it began adding service bays to its shops, paving the way for the company's current supercenter format. It now has over 6,500 bays, which account for nearly 20 percent of revenue. The supercenter stores also sell tires and provide a delivery program to support commercial customers.

Why Should I Care?

Pep Boys is often compared (unfavorably) with the other, far larger players in the automotive retail aftermarket: Autozone, Advance Auto Parts, and O'Reilly. Yes, the big three have much higher margins than Pep Boys and open far more stores per year. But we don't feel these are particularly useful comparisons, as Autozone, Advance, and O'Reilly are far more like one another than any of them are like Pep Boys. For one, none of them sell tires, and stocking tires would double the size of any of the smaller retail shops. For another, only Pep Boys has service bays and does service on site. Pep Boys is an automotive aftermarket retailer as well, to be sure, but its typical supercenter has less than a third of its square footage devoted to the typical high-density, pegboard retail products that drive margins at the big three.

For the more speculative among you, note the strong rumors early in 2011 about Pep Boys looking for and finding a buyer. There were reports of Bank of America brokering a deal, but nothing came of it. While Pep Boys does not have the best margins in the business, it does have the best price-to-cash flow, which probably makes it even more attractive as a purchase.

How's Business?

The Boys appear to have busted out the socket wrenches and gotten to work on the earnings situation. The fourth quarter and full year results for FY2010 were much improved over the prior year, with Q4 earnings more than tripling year over year and full-year EPS coming in at sixty-nine cents versus forty-four cents the year prior.

The company opened twenty-eight service and tire centers and seven supercenters in 2010. It plans to open fifty more tire and service centers and five more supercenters in 2011.

Upside

- Earnings can be fixed, cash flow less so
- Tire/service center concept working out
- New leadership

Downside

- Longer warranties on new autos
- Retail space could use some freshening
- In-house brands not particularly strong

Just the Facts

INDUSTRY: **Retail (Specialty)**
BETA COEFFICIENT: **1.35**
5-YEAR COMPOUND EARNINGS-PER-SHARE GROWTH: **Not meaningful**

		2006	2007	2008	2009	2010
Revenues (Mil)		2,272	2,138	1,928	1,911	1,989
Net Income (Mil)		6.6	2.4	25.2	21.0	36.6
Price:	high	16.5	22.5	12.6	10.8	14.2
	low	9.3	10.4	2.7	2.6	7.9

The Pep Boys—Manny, Moe & Jack
3111 West Allegheny Avenue
Philadelphia, PA 19132
(215) 229-9000
Website: ***www.pepboys.com***

AGGRESSIVE GROWTH

Perrigo Company

Ticker symbol: PRGO (NASDAQ) ❑ S&P rating: NA ❑ Value Line financial strength rating: B++ ❑ Current yield: 0.3%

Who Are They?

Perrigo is the world's largest manufacturer of over-the-counter pharmaceutical products for the store brand market. It also manufactures generic prescription pharmaceuticals, nutritional products, and active pharmaceutical ingredients (APIs).

The company operates in four segments: Consumer Health Care, Nutritionals, Rx, and API. Consumer Health Care is the largest segment, generating 62 percent of Perrigo's revenue thus far in FY2011. Perrigo employs internal R&D resources to develop product formulations and manufacture in quantity for its customers. It also develops retail packaging specific to the customer's needs.

The Nutritionals segment manufactures and markets infant formula, foods, and vitamin, mineral, and dietary supplements to retailers and consumers in the United States, Canada, Mexico, and China. As with the Consumer Health Care segment, this business markets products that are comparable in quality and effectiveness to the national brand products.

The "Rx" operations produce generic prescription drugs. The company's success in this segment depends on its ability to quickly manufacture and market generic equivalents to branded products as those products come off patent protection. The majority of these are topical treatments for skin and scalp conditions. The company markets approximately 300 generic prescription products with over 620 SKUs. The API division markets an assortment of active pharmaceutical ingredients to other drug manufacturers.

Why Should I Care?

The next time you're buying a store-branded or other generic over-the-counter medication, look at the packaging—there's a 70 percent chance the product (and the packaging) was made by Perrigo. Perrigo sells more than 1,300 store-brand products to over 900 customers, including Wal-Mart, CVS, Walgreens, Kroger, Target, Safeway, Dollar General, Costco, and other national and regional drugstores, supermarkets, and mass merchandisers. It is everywhere, and most people have bought and used its products at one time or another, but since the Perrigo name is never advertised alongside a product, most people don't make the connection.

There's a lot of appeal to these products. Store-branded versions typically sell for less than half the price of national brands, even though the product has an identical formulation in terms of the dosage and formula of the active ingredients. Retail stores do very well with these products, and Perrigo has also been doing very well.

Speculating a bit, Pfizer has openly discussed spinning off segments of the company, including the $10 billion (estimated value) generics unit. If this were to occur, it would create, at a minimum, an opportunity for market share expansion for Perrigo and perhaps a few select acquisitions should the spinoff wish to right-size itself. This is a development worth watching in any case, as Pfizer's generics unit is quite a bit larger than Perrigo and nearly two-thirds the size of Teva, the market leader.

How's Business?

In the fourth quarter of 2010, the company acquired PBM Holdings, Inc., the market share leader in store brand infant formulas and baby foods in most retail channels in the United States, Canada, Mexico, and China. The PBM acquisition, at a price of $808 million, will add nearly $350 million in net sales and to the full year's results. The exact contribution to earnings is less clear, but for the entire company, full-year earnings should come in at $340 million, up 45 percent over 2010.

Upside

- PBM purchase a good fit
- Improving cost structure
- Excellent cash flow growth

Downside

- Not well positioned for more acquisitions
- Shares pushing higher
- Distribution costs continue to rise

Just the Facts

INDUSTRY: **Biotechnology and Drugs**
BETA COEFFICIENT: **0.7**
5-YEAR COMPOUND EARNINGS-PER-SHARE GROWTH: **24%**

		2006	2007	2008	2009	2010
Revenues (Mil)		1,366	1,447	1,822	2,007	2,269
Net Income (Mil)		74.1	78.6	150	176	263
Price:	high	18.7	36.9	43.1	61.4	68.4
	low	14.4	16.1	27.7	18.5	37.5

Perrigo Company
515 Eastern Avenue
Allegan, MI 49010
(269) 673-8451
Website: *www.perrigo.com*

AGGRESSIVE GROWTH

Power Integrations

Ticker symbol: POWI (NASDAQ) ❑ S&P rating: NA ❑ Value Line financial strength rating: NA ❑ Current yield: 0.5%

Who Are They?

Power Integrations, a fabless semiconductor company, designs and markets specialized integrated circuits for a wide variety of electronic devices in the commercial, consumer, and industrial markets. Its products accelerate the design of complex power supply circuitry and provide simpler designs. The resulting product will have fewer parts, higher performance, and better regulatory compliance than an identical circuit implemented with discrete components.

The company was founded in 1988 and re-incorporated in Delaware in 1997. PI ran into some problems with its financial statements in the early 2000s as a result of options backdating and had to restate earnings for the 2001–2006 period, but the problem appears to have been limited to two individuals, both of whom are long gone.

Why Should I Care?

PI's secret sauce is the way in which it combines several semiconductor technologies into one device. This technique allows the users of its products to avoid many of the pitfalls and compromises inherent in the power supply design process. How valuable is this, really? Consider PI's first product, released in 1994, which introduced this technology. Seventeen years later, this product (in newer iterations) still forms the core of PI's profitable product line.

A coming trend in the electronics industry is a mandated push for efficiency. Power supplies built on older technologies can be very inefficient, wasting as much as 40 percent of the energy supplied to them. Modern designs can also be costly to run—it's estimated that as much as 10 percent of residential energy usage is consumed by recently designed devices operating in standby mode. Recent industry initiatives such as EnergyStar have set guidelines for efficiency in electronic products, but compliance with the standards set by the programs has been voluntary, with no consequences for non-compliance. That situation is changing, however. The California Energy Commission mandated a set of efficiency standards for external power supplies beginning in 2007 and in July 2008, the Energy Independence and Security Act of 2007 implemented those standards nationwide. Similar standards have been adopted in the European Union, Australia, and New Zealand. The EISA further mandates significant improvement to the efficiency of lighting systems beginning in 2012.

Fortunately, Power Integrations's products allow manufacturers to meet all current and proposed energy-efficiency regulations for electronic products, which puts PI in a very good position to capitalize on this rather enormous market opportunity. Going forward, we can expect to see EISA standards applied to many other classes of products, including televisions, audio equipment, and small appliances.

The semiconductor market tends to do very well during an economic recovery. Budgets are freed up to improve and modernize infrastructure and tools, and much of that spending is on new technology. New tech means new electronic devices, and all of those devices will require power supplies. We're in a recovery now, which is very good news for the semiconductor market in general, and the current focus on energy efficiency is particularly good news for PI.

How's Business?

The company's gross and net margins are approximately twice the industry average. Having proprietary products is as powerful in the semiconductor business as it is anywhere else.

Upside

- Well-regarded products and support
- The energy efficiency trend is your friend
- Modular design gaining momentum in supply business

Downside

- Attractive acquisition target
- Market development could be lengthy
- Costly IP protection

Just the Facts

INDUSTRY: **Semiconductors**
BETA COEFFICIENT: **1.38**
5-YEAR COMPOUND EARNINGS-PER-SHARE GROWTH: **41%**

		2006	2007	2008	2009	2010
Revenues (Mil)		162	191	202	215	300
Net Income (Mil)		9.43	26.6	1.8	23.3	49.5
Price:	high	27.6	34.4	34.3	36.4	44.7
	low	14.3	23.5	24.6	18.4	26.8

Power Integrations, Inc.
5245 Hellyer Avenue
San Jose, CA 95138
(408) 414-9200
Website: ***www.powerint.com***

AGGRESSIVE GROWTH

Power-One, Inc.

Ticker symbol: PWER (NASDAQ) □ S&P rating: NA □ Value Line financial strength rating: C++ □ Current yield: Nil

Who Are They?

Power-One is a leading supplier in the power supply and power conversion markets. Nearly every electrical device that you own uses a power supply of some variety. Power sources, such as batteries and the sockets in the wall, only provide power at a few select voltages. A device such as a home theater receiver or a personal computer, however, may require power at many different voltages to operate the different kinds of electronic devices in the unit. When you plug something into the wall, the first place the power goes is into the power supply where the 120-volt AC from the electric company is converted into something the device can actually use internally. Power-One makes a range of supplies that are designed to fit established industrial form factors and electrical outputs, primarily for high-value equipment like computer servers, telecommunications equipment, medical devices, and industrial equipment.

With the growing popularity of alternative energy programs such as photovoltaics (solar panels) and wind power, Power-One has capitalized on its expertise in converting AC (alternating current) to DC (direct current) and has created a range of products that go the other way: They convert the DC output from wind turbines and solar panels back to AC power suitable for use or for simply feeding back into the power grid. These products are called inverters.

Power-One thus operates two business units: its traditional power supply business, and its new renewable energy BU (inverters and power management tools).

Why Should I Care?

Governments in many European Union countries and the United States have provided strong tax incentives in order to subsidize the growth and development of "green" alternative energy programs like wind and solar. Every wind or solar installation requires an inverter to connect to the grid, and a number of smaller niche players produced inverters for the market that operated with varying levels of reliability. For an established tier-one supplier like Power-One, this market was essentially found money. It produced its first photovoltaic inverters in late 2006 and are now the second highest volume supplier of PV inverters in the world. In less than two years, it has grown from 3 percent market share to

13 percent, while revenues from its inverter business grew from $12 million in 2Q2009 to $260 million in 4Q2010. In 2010, it shipped over 2.6 gigawatts of inverter capacity, which is about the output of two mainline nuclear facilities.

How's Business?

The company's $148 million in earnings in FY2010 represents the first profits in the last nine years. The current management team, all new since 2008, have overseen a remarkable turnaround in the company's direction and fortunes. The company was barely breathing at the start of 2009, with no cash flow and an inventory value representing three months of sales. It now has one-third the debt, very healthy cash flow, greatly reduced inventory (even though revenue has doubled), and $200 million cash in the bank. Revenues for 2011 are expected to increase 25 percent with net margins holding steady at 10 percent.

Upside

- Right place, right time with respect to renewable energy
- Management making the correct calls
- Innovative products lead the way

Downside

- Share price may have lost momentum
- Tax incentives may not last much longer
- When do Chinese loss-leaders appear?

Just the Facts

INDUSTRY: **Electronic Instruments & Controls**
BETA COEFFICIENT: **1.55**
5-YEAR COMPOUND EARNINGS-PER-SHARE GROWTH: **NM**

		2006	2007	2008	2009	2010
Revenues (Mil)		338	512	538	432	1,047
Net Income (Mil)		(-14.6)	(-36.4)	(-17.5)	(-63.3)	148
Price:	high	8.2	7.8	4.1	4.8	13.0
	low	5.1	3.3	0.9	0.3	3.0

Power-One, Inc.
740 Calle Plano
Camarillo, CA 93012
(805) 987-8741
Website: *www.power-one.com*

AGGRESSIVE GROWTH

Powerwave Technologies, Inc.

Ticker symbol: PWAV (NASDAQ) ❑ S&P rating: NA ❑ Value Line financial strength rating: C ❑ Current yield: Nil

Who Are They?

Powerwave Technologies is a global supplier of products and technologies for wireless communication network infrastructures, including PCS, 3G, 4G, and cellular. The company designs, manufactures, and markets products such as antennas, boosters, cabinets, electrical filters, amplifiers, repeaters, and networks of these products for complete end-to-end hardware solutions. These products are most often sold to integrators (such as Alcatel, Motorola, etc.), which in turn sell to end providers of cellular and other wireless services (such as AT&T and Verizon), but Powerwave also sells individual components directly to end providers, typically for support as spares or repair.

Founded in 1985, the company's first products included radio frequency power amplifiers for use in analog wireless networks and the air-to-ground market, and then ultimately in digital cellular networks. The company's IPO in 1996 marked the beginning of a period of substantial organic growth and selective acquisitions, greatly expanding its product line and applications.

Why Should I Care?

The company made a number of acquisitions over the past decade that gained it entry to and strengthened its presence in a number of key markets (Europe, particularly), but which also burdened Powerwave with some extraordinary integration costs that negatively impacted its bottom line over multiple fiscal years. Complicating this situation was a multi-year downturn in orders from three of its primary customers: AT&T, Nokia, and Nortel. The result was a period of losses that drove the stock price into the sub-$1 range for several quarters. The company was able to maintain market share through this period while reducing costs through consolidation of manufacturing resources.

In mid-2009, as the general business environment began to recover from the financial crisis, Powerwave's customers started investing in new infrastructure and the company finally began to see the full benefits of their acquisition strategy. It is now on track to ship $720 million in 2012 with very strong margins.

In February 2011, the company introduced a new MIMO (multiple-input, multiple-output) tower antenna for the rapidly expanding mobile broadband market that nearly doubles the current standard coverage pattern and reduces power consumption by 40 percent. This will greatly reduce the operational costs for wireless broadband providers, allowing them to provide higher levels of coverage for a lower investment. At the same time, the company introduced proprietary technologies that will allow wireless operators to quickly deploy 4G services over existing 2G/3G wireless networks. The combination of the two should permit operators to selectively upgrade services in high-demand areas while enhancing service and coverage in adjacent areas without the burden of upgrading hardware in every tower.

How's Business?

The company recently confirmed analysts' estimates for FY2011 for revenues in the range of $650–$680 million, representing a 13.8 percent increase over FY2010. Earnings are expected to increase 136 percent to $40 million, a very significant recovery from the two consecutive years of losses in 2006–2007. Cash flow, which had been under pressure of late, has recovered to a healthy fifty-five cents per share and is expected to increase another 20 percent in 2012, more than enough to support its low debt service and maintain a reserve for strategic growth opportunities.

Upside

- Broad customer base
- Global presence
- "End-to-end" product line

Downside

- Tail of the wireless market dog
- Rapidly evolving technology
- No "killer" tech as yet

Just the Facts

INDUSTRY: **Communications Equipment**

BETA COEFFICIENT: **1.05**

5-YEAR COMPOUND EARNINGS-PER-SHARE GROWTH: **NM**

		2006	2007	2008	2009	2010
Revenues (Mil)		717	781	890	568	592
Net Income (Mil)		19.6	66.0	19.6	3.2	17.2
Price:	high	15.8	7.6	5.3	1.8	2.8
	low	5.9	0.3	0.2	1.0	2.5

Powerwave Technologies, Inc.
1801 East St. Andrew Place
Santa Ana, CA 92705
(714) 466-1000
Website: *www.powerwave.com*

AGGRESSIVE GROWTH

Radware, Ltd.

Ticker symbol: RDWR (NASDAQ) ❑ S&P rating: NA ❑ Value Line financial strength rating: NA ❑ Current yield: Nil

Who Are They?

Radware, founded in 1996, develops, manufactures, and markets computer networking products for the application delivery and network security markets. Its products consist mainly of internally developed applications that run exclusively on Radware's intelligent network switch. The switch and the applications are modular and upgradeable in response to the need for more ports, higher bandwidth, higher speed, or other considerations. It competes with all of the big players in this market (Cisco, 3Com/HP, Juniper, F5) but has established a beachhead by focusing on a specific set of needs common to small and midsized businesses. Its targeted applications include datacenter management, firewall and application gateway management, management of multiple wide-area networks, packet inspection, and traffic prioritization.

The company also provides intrusion prevention and other security products to protect against worms, bots, viruses, malicious intrusions, and denial of service attacks; a device that provides online network-based pervasive monitoring solution; and an appliance-based management and monitoring system.

Radware's primary customers include banks, insurance companies, manufacturing, retail, government agencies, media companies, and service providers worldwide.

Why Should I Care?

Radware's business addresses the two main concerns of businesses with regard to their networking infrastructure: delivery of service and data security. Delivery of service is a broad term, but it basically means that an ideal state is one in which all applications receive the level of service from the network that's appropriate for their needs. Some applications require high throughput, some require low latency, some require tight synchronization with other services, and some require all three and several other things as well. The goal of load balancing software and hardware is to provide optimum levels of service to all demands at all times, within the limits of external constraints. Radware's value proposition is the intelligence with which its products perform this optimization, its awareness of enterprise-wide resources, and its real-time response to threats to data security. Radware data security provides protection against threats on WAN storage, a feature that will become even more valuable as backup service moves to "the cloud."

All of these services can be run on the actual server itself, and in many cases, they still are. But going forward, for a number of sound technical and economic reasons, it often makes more sense to aggregate these activities in an intelligent switch, which is what Radware has done. And this is the key to the future of the company: As customers adopt Radware's proprietary hardware and software platform, the company creates lock-out potential. It's critical to establish a solid customer base as quickly as possible, and 2010's results are very encouraging in this regard.

How's Business?

After five years of losses, Radware turned the corner in 2010 with nearly $10 million in earnings. Its marketing strategy had been to build the brand recognition while developing support for the product concept. It was early to the party, and as other better-known players announced similar products, the market has warmed to the idea and Radware's sales have begun to meet expectations. Revenue was up 40 percent in 2010 and estimates are for another 20 percent growth in 2011, with per-share earnings of $1.31 (versus forty-four cents in 2010).

Upside

- Market support for the technology
- Relatively small share base (20 million)
- Solid financing and no debt

Downside

- Big, healthy competitors
- Dynamic technological battlefield
- Proprietary tech can also work against you

Just the Facts

INDUSTRY: **Communications Equipment**
BETA COEFFICIENT: **1.2**
5-YEAR COMPOUND EARNINGS-PER-SHARE GROWTH: **NM**

		2006	**2007**	**2008**	**2009**	**2010**
Revenues (Mil)		81.4	88.6	94.6	109	144
Net Income (Mil)		1.28	12.0	31.0	5.93	9.63
Price:	high	21	16.8	14.4	15.1	39.8
	low	11.6	12.3	5.2	5.4	15.1

Radware Ltd.
22 Raoul Wallenberg Street
Tel Aviv, 69710, Israel
972-3-7668666
Website: ***www.radware.com***

AGGRESSIVE GROWTH

Red Hat, Inc.

Ticker symbol: RHT (NASDAQ) ❑ S&P rating: BB+ ❑ Value Line financial strength rating: B+ ❑ Current yield: Nil

Who Are They?

Red Hat is the leading distributor of open-source Linux software. Linux itself is a free "Unix-like" operating system that runs on a variety of hardware platforms, including PCs, tablets, game consoles, servers, and mainframes. In fact, Linux runs on some of the most recent smartphones and runs the ten fastest supercomputers in the world. One of the very powerful features of Linux is its modularity and ease of customization—a builder can add or remove functionality as needed to meet the requirements of use, with the only common thread among these various installations is that they run the Linux kernel.

Red Hat builds configurations of Linux (called distributions), which are customized for the intended application: There are different builds for desktop users, workstations, and so on. Server bundles are optimized for the intended hardware and intended function—there are distributions specifically tuned for running SAP, for example.

Red Hat's business model is built around its subscription-based support services, although it also collects revenues on the initial sale of the distribution.

Why Should I Care?

Five years ago, an IT manager making a strategic commitment to a Linux-based platform for mission-critical applications would have met with resistance, or at least a great deal of skepticism from his peers. That's not the case today. Hotels, banks, airlines, national postal systems, railroads, telephone systems, hospitals . . . the list of real-time, transaction-intensive installations that rely on Linux (and Red Hat) is growing quickly, particularly in international markets. Red Hat, as the largest of the value-added distributors with the most highly developed support channels, will benefit as a result. These task-oriented machines are the strength of Red Hat's product line.

The Red Hat Enterprise Linux (RHEL) distribution is very well regarded against the competition and appears to be emerging as "the OS of choice for private cloud computing architectures," according to analysts. Cloud computing is a recent trend in information services in which pools of computing resources are dynamically allocated among users and applications. An application might draw computing resources from several different virtualized machines simultaneously, for example. Cloud computing's goal is to make computing resources more available, more flexible, and less expensive to acquire and use. Virtualization is an important first step in creating a cloud architecture, and RHEL's powerful virtualization tools make it an excellent platform on which to build cloud computing architectures. RHEL's virtualization tools also make it a favorite for data center application servers.

We like Red Hat's healthy cash balance and absence of debt. The company recently acquired cloud software developer Makara to supplement the company's own JBoss middleware platform. Additional acquisitions during the year would not surprise us.

How's Business?

Although revenues and deal volumes are clearly gaining momentum, the bottom line has not yet gotten the message. The current comps show welcome improvement (4Q2010 EPS up 42 percent over 2009), but on an absolute basis, seventeen cents per share and an 18 percent operating margin is not where we'd like to see a software/services company. We expect this to improve as the year wears on.

Upside

- Secure, high-performance OS
- Cost-effective versus Microsoft
- Persuasive virtualization story

Downside

- Mid-40s share price deserves scrutiny
- Competitors (HP, Oracle) are larger, better-established
- Top-line growing—operating margin, not so much

Just the Facts

INDUSTRY: **Software and Programming**
BETA COEFFICIENT: **1.1**
5-YEAR COMPOUND EARNINGS-PER-SHARE GROWTH: **56.5%**

		2006	2007	2008	2009	2010
Revenues (Mil)		401	523	653	748	900
Net Income (Mil)		59.9	76.7	78.7	87.3	104
Price:	high	32.5	25.3	24.8	31.8	49.0
	low	13.7	18.0	7.5	13.0	26.5

Red Hat, Inc.
1801 Varsity Drive
Raleigh, NC 27606
(919) 754-3700
Website: ***www.redhat.com***

AGGRESSIVE GROWTH

Riverbed Technology, Inc.

Ticker symbol: RVBD (NASDAQ) ❑ S&P rating: NA ❑ Value Line financial strength rating: C ❑ Current yield: Nil

Who Are They?

Riverbed Technology, founded in 2002, designs and markets hardware and software appliances that address some of the operational problems that arise when companies deploy wide area networks, or WANs. Most of its products are designed simply to speed up operations across the WAN by a variety or a combination of methods, including data compression, smart caching, and bottleneck identification.

Riverbed's products address networks for branch offices, mobile workers, private data centers, private clouds, and cloud computing. The company's hardware products include the Steelhead line and the Cascade line. Steelhead products are designed to accelerate application and data delivery through local caching, data compression, and other methods, while the Cascade line is a collection of network diagnostic tools for troubleshooting and monitoring network performance. An integrated solution, the Riverbed Optimization System (RiOS), consists of hardware and software products that address distributed computing environments. During 2010, Riverbed introduced solutions for the public cloud, including a cloud-intelligent WAN optimization solution and a cloud storage accelerator targeting back-up and select archive workloads. In October 2010, Riverbed acquired CACE Technologies, Inc., and in November 2010 acquired Global Protocols LLC.

Why Should I Care?

The core Internet protocols were designed at a time when the scope of most companies' IT infrastructure was a data center and bunch of attached terminals. The most distant user was perhaps 1,000 feet from the server and networks were often point-to-point, running proprietary protocols under proprietary operating systems. Today, it's not at all unusual for a company to have a far more robust and powerful IT service, even though the data center may be a bunch of wires and three metal boxes in a broom closet at remote, even international branches and two or three more boxes at headquarters. The core resource in this new model is the connection between the branches and headquarters and the Internet. Riverbed's products are not servers or traditional routing tools that make up the core of the data path, but rather adjuncts that optimize the utilization of those connections.

The company designs the products to be largely self-configuring and simple to use during operation. The products are really designed to provide the greatest benefit to those companies without the IT resources to configure and troubleshoot network problems with a dedicated IT staff, and to prevent companies from having to invest in those resources before deploying WAN technologies. In the case of the Cascade line, the troubleshooting expertise is built into the product, freeing up personnel resources and providing a comprehensive, updateable knowledge base for the entire network at one location. The Steelhead products reduce the load on existing links and can eliminate the need for higher bandwidth connections due to network traffic contention as the user base or application size increases. These are useful tools that work across networks of dissimilar hardware and software platforms and which can be installed at remote locations by untrained personnel.

How's Business?

Riverbed's earnings, while not stellar, are in the black, which is more than can be said for a lot of the hot tech stocks on the market. Perhaps more importantly, it has beat expectations in all five of the last five quarters. This will make you a darling of the analysts, and indeed this company is one of the most closely watched and (perhaps) overbid in the sector. The burden of high expectations is in place, so beware the arrival of the first disappointing quarter, as the share price will take a hit.

Upside

- Product positioned well for market trends
- Solid financing
- Management depth

Downside

- Tough competition
- P/E ratio 170+
- SG&A is 50 percent of revenue

Just the Facts

INDUSTRY: **Communications Equipment**
BETA COEFFICIENT: **1.60**
5-YEAR COMPOUND EARNINGS-PER-SHARE GROWTH: **NM**

		2006	2007	2008	2009	2010
Revenues (Mil)		90.2	236	333	394	552
Net Income (Mil)		(-15.8)	20.0	2.3	11.4	57.0
Price:	high	16.6	24.0	11.7	12.0	38.4
	low	8.4	13.2	4.2	4.9	11.2

Riverbed Technology, Inc.
199 Fremont Street
San Francisco, CA 94105
(415) 247-8800
Website: *www.riverbed.com*

AGGRESSIVE GROWTH

SanDisk Corporation

Ticker symbol: SNDK (NASDAQ) ❑ S&P rating: BB- ❑ Value Line financial strength rating: B ❑ Current yield: Nil

Who Are They?

SanDisk is one of the world's largest suppliers of the various types of "flash" memory products. Flash memory is a type of solid-state memory that, unlike standard random-access memory, retains the data written to it after its power has been removed. Growth in the market acceptance has largely paralleled the advances in the technology, with density (size) increasing 16,000-fold and speed increasing by a factor of ten since the introduction of the devices in the early 1990s.

SanDisk's products are distributed through retail and OEM channels. Its products are sold as stand-alone devices, such as removable memory cards, and as embedded devices such as packaged memory die and their associated controllers. Most of its products include memory and a controller; SanDisk produces the bulk of its memory components in venture relationships with Toshiba foundries, and designs its controllers in-house for production by third parties.

The flash memory market has generally been price-elastic—the lower the price per unit of capacity the higher the demand and the greater the number of new applications for the product. As such, SanDisk's strategy is to remain the highest-volume supplier, allowing it to open new markets and drive revenues with volume.

Why Should I Care?

Flash memory's distinguishing property—the non-volatility of its data—has enabled more new products and applications than almost any other single product in the semiconductor industry. Digital cameras, smartphones, portable music players, and many other electronic devices we now take for granted would be impossible to produce had it not been for the advent and rapid development of flash memory. A relatively new application, the solid-state drive (SSD), has the potential to become a very large revenue generator for flash manufacturers and SSD OEMs. The SSD is essentially a flash-based replacement for many applications where a disk drive is the current storage medium of choice. The dollars-per-gigabyte cost ratio for SSDs to disk drives is about ten to one, but SSDs' performance, particularly in use profiles with a high transaction rate (such as servers), far exceeds that of disk drives. As the cost of SSDs continues to drop due to density improvements, demand will reach some critical inflection points where their production economies of scale override the disk drive cost advantage and SSDs will become the dominant storage medium for sub-terabyte applications.

Flash memory is in its twelfth generation. There's room for perhaps four or five more generations before the memory architecture runs into physical limits beyond which it no longer scales. SanDisk is already working on alternative technologies to replace/augment flash in the market when flash can no longer scale effectively.

How's Business?

SanDisk, with over 2,800 United States and international patents, owns a large chunk of the underlying IP for the entire flash market. As a result, SanDisk's licensing is a significant part of its business: From 2008 through 2010, SanDisk generated $1.28 billion in revenue through license agreements, or roughly 11 percent of its total revenue.

Upside

- Popularity of "tablet" products
- Stock is very cheap at mid-40s
- Semiconductor boom cycle—hop on

Downside

- State-of-the-art fabs are not cheap
- Wide adoption of cloud streaming could reduce flash demand
- Solid competition in Samsung and Hynix

Just the Facts

INDUSTRY: **Computer Storage Devices**
BETA COEFFICIENT: **1.35**
5-YEAR COMPOUND EARNINGS-PER-SHARE GROWTH: **18.1%**

		2006	**2007**	**2008**	**2009**	**2010**
Revenues (Mil)		3,258	3,896	3,351	3,567	4,827
Net Income (Mil)		425	218	(-572)	415	1,100
Price:	high	79.8	59.8	33.7	52.3	53.6
	low	53.8	32.7	5.1	7.5	24.9

Sandisk Corporation
601 McCarthy Boulevard
Milpitas, CA 95035
(408) 801-1000
Website: ***www.sandisk.com***

AGGRESSIVE GROWTH

Schnitzer Steel Industries

Ticker symbol: SCHN (NASDAQ) ❑ S&P rating: NA ❑ Value Line financial strength rating: B+ ❑ Current yield: 0.1%

Who Are They?

Founded in 1906 as the Alaska Junk Company, Schnitzer Steel's operations now include fifty-seven scrap metals recycling facilities, fifty self-service automobile parts yards, and a furnace and rolling mill for the production of basic steel shapes. The company is one of the largest metals recyclers in North America, and its vertical integration has made it a low-cost producer of finished steel product.

The company's recycling facilities are located primarily in the three western states and British Columbia, Georgia, Alabama, and New England. The recycling business was responsible for 80 percent of Schnitzer's revenue in 2010 and sourcing good quality scrap in sufficient volumes is key to its success. As such, the recycling facilities are all located near major rail lines and highways. The company's main sources of ferrous and non-ferrous metals are automobile and truck chassis, railroad car bodies, home appliances, and demolition metal. These skeletons are fed into huge shredders that spit out compressed chunks of steel with the size and density appropriate for Schnitzer's customers, including its own foundry/mill. Smaller quantities of non-ferrous metal gained in the recovery process are sorted, graded, and sold to other recyclers.

Its automobile parts business is relatively new but is growing rapidly, adding eleven new facilities in the last three years.

Why Should I Care?

The company is primarily an exporter of processed scrap metal to mills and foundries in emerging markets. To support this business, Schnitzer operates seven deepwater ports on the east and west coasts of the continental United States, as well as in Hawaii and Puerto Rico. The ability to ship anywhere in the world allows Schnitzer to respond quickly to market opportunities.

Continued focus on the growth of the auto parts business could be very good for Schnitzer's bottom line. In 2010, the auto parts business turned in 21 percent operating margins, versus 6 percent for the recycling business and 8 percent for the company as a whole. The company recently sold off its Greenleaf full-service parts operations due to the poor geographic fit and other issues. Its Pick-n-Pull chain, however, is performing well and is well integrated in Schnitzer's overall model. Schnitzer's inter-corporate sales, by the way (such as Pick-n-Pull's sales of auto hulks to Schnitzer's recycling business), are all accounted for at market rates, so these margins would appear to be honest.

The company is doing well in its sector. Looking at the trailing twelve-month margins for Schnitzer, U.S. Steel, and Nucor, we see that Schnitzer's gross margins are nearly double those of its two largest competitors, and net margins are higher still. Some caution should be applied in these comparisons, as Schnitzer is primarily a recycler, while Nucor (also a recycler) has substantial production capacity.

How's Business?

Continued weak demand overall for finished steel products in the western United States led to another year of losses in Schnitzer's manufactured steel business. Average selling prices continued their decline in 2010, off another 5 percent versus 2009. If there's a good sign, it's that volumes were up 17 percent and the net loss was far less than in 2009.

Upside

- Rebuilding in Japan
- Good profitability in auto parts
- Strong demand in recycled metals, especially in China

Downside

- Weak pricing for finished steel
- Could be a late bloomer in 2012
- Acquisition costs will temper bottom line

Just the Facts

INDUSTRY: **Iron and Steel**

BETA COEFFICIENT: **1.55**

5-YEAR COMPOUND EARNINGS-PER-SHARE GROWTH: **1.0%**

		2006	**2007**	**2008**	**2009**	**2010**
Revenues (Mil)		1,855	2,572	3,642	1,900	2,301
Net Income (Mil)		105	131	249	(-32.2)	66.8
Price:	high	44.0	77.9	118.6	64.0	66.9
	low	29.8	33.3	16.5	23.3	37.0

Schnitzer Steel Industries, Inc.
3200 N.W. Yeon Avenue
Portland, OR 97296
(503) 224-9900
Website: *www.schnitzersteel.com*

AGGRESSIVE GROWTH

SeaChange International, Inc.

Ticker symbol: SEAC (NASDAQ) ❑ S&P rating: NA ❑ Value Line financial strength rating: B ❑ Current yield: Nil

Who Are They?

SeaChange International develops and markets digital video storage and distribution systems used to automate the management of video streams on multiple platforms. SeaChange's proprietary software runs on industry standard and custom hardware, allowing on-demand programming, movies, television content, and advertising all to be controlled through one interface. The company's products and services are marketed worldwide to cable system operators (Comcast, Cablevision, Cox Communications) and broadcast television companies (ABC Disney, Clear Channel, Viacom).

The company operates in three segments; Software, Servers and Storage, and Media Services. The Software segment is by far the revenue leader with 72 percent of the company's total sales. The Servers and Storage segment has been losing money recently and the company is in the process of restructuring that business to improve its profitability, primarily through offshoring a larger percentage of its manufacturing. The Media Services segment, created when the company acquired On Demand Group Limited and later expanded with the acquisition of Mobix, has been the growth leader of late, helping make 2011 the first year in which revenue from services exceeded revenue from product sales.

Why Should I Care?

SeaChange has a number of core competencies that will provide for great opportunities moving forward. It is the market leader in local spot ad insertions in national broadcasts, with 70 percent of operators using SeaChange's hardware and software. This is an important part of content delivery, as targeted ads generate higher marginal revenues per slice of bandwidth used, which translates into more money for less cost for the cable operator. This concept becomes even more important in the Brave New World of mobile content delivery, as smartphones and tablets grow in their importance as media platforms. And now we see a study out of Northwestern University that shows it's possible, with no application support on the user end, to determine an Internet user's location within half a mile. This is all done in the matter of a few seconds, completely in the background, using existing infrastructure. The implications for this kind of technique for a company like SeaChange could be profound. A hotspot user watching streamed content might be treated to ads not for an airline or a phone company, but for that Chipotle restaurant across the street, or the Barnes & Noble next door.

This localized, targetable advertising is just the kind of thing that broadcasters have been wanting for years, and now the platforms, infrastructure, and techniques appear to be in place to support it. SeaChange is in position to capitalize in this scenario with its recently developed Adrenaline platform, which combines its Axiom On Demand back office with a service architecture that supports "multi-screen" (television, PC, mobile device) video delivery.

How's Business?

The company is still struggling to maintain profitability in light of declining volumes for its hardware solutions. The cost-cutting measures taken recently will help, but frankly, we'd like to see it concentrate as much as possible on its software and services segments and let the customer provision their own industry standard storage and server hardware.

Upside

- Respected, widely used products
- Solid customer base
- Advanced technology

Downside

- Hardware dragging down earnings
- Comcast and Virgin account for one-third of revenue
- Tough competition from Cisco and Arris

Just the Facts

INDUSTRY: **Communications Equipment**
BETA COEFFICIENT: **1.0**
5-YEAR COMPOUND EARNINGS-PER-SHARE GROWTH: **Not meaningful**

		2006	2007	2008	2009	2010
Revenues (Mil)		161	180	202	202	215
Net Income (Mil)		(-8.2)	(-5.0)	10.0	1.3	13.0
Price:	high	10.6	11.0	9.8	10.0	9.5
	low	6.0	4.9	5.5	4.2	6.3

SeaChange International, Inc.
50 Nagog Park
Acton, MA 01720
(978) 897-0100
Website: ***www.schange.com***

AGGRESSIVE GROWTH

Smithfield Foods

Ticker symbol: SFD (NYSE) □ S&P rating: B+ □ Value Line financial strength rating: B □ Current yield: Nil

Who Are They?

Smithfield is the largest hog producer and pork processor in the world. Founded in 1936 as a family-run meatpacking operation, the company went on an acquisitions tear in 1981 that continues today. Over a dozen major acquisitions of rival companies has left it with over fifty different brands of pork products and more than 200 gourmet foods. Some of the more well-known brands in the United States include Morell, Eckrich, Armour, and of course Smithfield's own brand.

The company operates in four segments: Hog Production, Pork, International, and Other. Over the past few years they have restructured their Pork segment to reduce operating costs and improve ROIC. In 2011, it expects these efficiency improvements will yield $125 million in cost reductions.

The company has extensive international operations and partnerships. It has a 37 percent interest in Campofrio, the largest meat processor in Europe, and owns processors and hog production facilities in Poland, Romania, the United Kingdom, and Mexico.

Why Should I Care?

Concern in Japan about the quality and safety of their food supply has pushed the import demand for beef, chicken, and pork higher. Current importers such as Smithfield (Japan already represents 43 percent of Smithfield's export revenue) have been able to provide supply, but with inventories at normal levels the surprise demand has pushed prices higher.

In mid-2011 Smithfield is discussing taking a controlling interest (potentially 87 percent) in Campofrio. The move makes sense for Smithfield as it diversifies its product base and further reduces the effect on its bottom line of fluctuations in domestic feed prices.

Speaking of those feed prices . . . Smithfield's hog production insulates it from swings in the hog commodities market, but not the feedstocks markets. Nearly two-thirds of the cost of raising a hog is in its feed, and corn makes up 85 percent of a hog's diet. Corn prices are currently at record highs and the flooding along the Mississippi River in the spring/summer of 2011 is likely going to put additional pressure on prices. As a result of the high markets, acreage under corn is going to be way up this summer, but unfortunately, so is acreage under water.

Smithfield was heavily hedged on corn futures in 2008 during corn's prior spike and got burned when prices dropped precipitously. Since then, Smithfield's CEO claims the company has been buying feedstocks "closer to the cash market" and has curtailed its participation in the hog futures market altogether. The markets have been wary of SFD's shares for over a year now on sustained high corn prices, but Smithfield's financials have not really suffered from these higher input prices, largely due to its geographic distribution and vertical integration.

How's Business?

The company's operating margin, which was at 0.8 percent in 2008, shot to a record-high 9.0 percent in 2010, in spite of the volatility in corn prices. The company is guiding for lower margins in 2011, but expects a rebound to 8.0 percent in 2012.

Upside

- Current low-20s price is an excellent entry point
- Strong brand lineup
- Efficiency measures proven out in 2009

Downside

- Rising oil prices and ethanol subsidies causing corn to pop
- Campofrio buy coming at an iffy time for SFD debt
- Full effects of Mississippi River floods unknown

Just the Facts

INDUSTRY: **Food Processing**

BETA COEFFICIENT: **1.30**

5-YEAR COMPOUND EARNINGS-PER-SHARE GROWTH: **NM**

		2006	2007	2008	2009	2010
Revenues (Mil)		11,911	11,351	12,488	11,203	12,325
Net Income (Mil)		188	132	242	101	475
Price:	high	31.1	35.8	32.2	17.6	21.5
	low	24.9	24.4	5.4	5.6	13.3

Smithfield Foods, Inc.
200 Commerce Street
Smithfield, VA 23430
(757) 365-3000
Website: ***www.smithfieldfoods.com***

AGGRESSIVE GROWTH

Southwest Airlines

Ticker symbol: LUV (NYSE) ❑ S&P rating: A- ❑ Value Line financial strength rating: B+ ❑ Current yield: 0.2%

Who Are They?

Southwest is a major U.S. domestic airline, the largest in the world measured by passengers flown, and one of the largest by revenue. It provides primarily short-haul, high-frequency, point-to-point, low-fare service to destinations in the United States and, with the recent acquisition of AirTran, select cities in the Caribbean. Southwest flies the Boeing 737 series exclusively, serving sixty-nine cities in thirty-five states with 548 aircraft.

Southwest built its business on a "no-frills" principle: There are no first-class cabins, no meals, no wide-body aircraft, no piano lounges at the airport. The company has one of the most successful Internet sales programs in the industry—84 percent of sales are booked online, reducing costs and simplifying the ticketing process. The company has begun to offer some options to its programs in hopes of winning over business travelers, but has been careful not to damage the "convenient, low-cost transportation" message.

Why Should I Care?

In early May 2011, Southwest completed purchase of AirTran, opening up routes to a number of cities in the eastern United States, including the highly used primary gateways of Atlanta Hartsfield and Ronald Reagan in Washington, D.C. If the rest of the airline industry was built on the idea of overcharging the business traveler (who wasn't paying the bill anyway), Southwest was built around the idea that the rest of us have to fly as well, and we'd really prefer to spend our money at the destination rather than in the air. Over time, however, many business travelers have come to appreciate Southwest's commute-friendly schedules, frequent departures, and reasonable last-minute fare structure. The purchase of AirTran sent a fairly clear message to the industry: We're in this for growth, and we want the business traveler.

Business travelers prefer close-in airports, so Southwest has added LaGuardia, San Francisco, Denver, Philadelphia, and Boston in the last few years, and now two more key regionals in Atlanta and Washington, D.C. The AirTran deal also brings additional gates at LaGuardia, some of the most valuable in the country.

Southwest's fuel hedging program remains the most successful in the industry, with the over/under for 2011 set at a benchmark petroleum price of $102 per barrel. Though some have claimed the company is really running its fuel business as a profit center, speculating on oil prices rather than running a business hedge, the fact is their hedging program has had only one negative quarter in the last twenty years.

How's Business?

Fiscal 2010 was Southwest's thirty-eighth consecutive year of profitable operations in its thirty-nine-year history. In what it was hoping would be simply a respectable rebound year, Southwest had its highest revenue ever. And in a year in which jet fuel prices rose 25 percent, it turned in its second highest earnings on record. In the first four months of 2011, revenue passengers carried are up more than 4 percent and the load factor is up 2 percent. First quarter revenues increased by $473 million (18 percent) compared to the first quarter 2010, nearly all of it due to an increase in passenger revenues, the majority of that due to an 11 percent increase in average fares. By comparison, in the same quarter, its four biggest rivals lost a combined $1 billion. So it wasn't a rising tide that lifted this, umm, plane.

Upside

- AirTran instantly adds 25 percent to top line
- AirTran flies primarily 737s
- Learning how to capture business traveler, too

Downside

- AirTran integration costs
- Vacationers returning in full force?
- Fuel costs always a wild card

Just the Facts

INDUSTRY: **Airline**
BETA COEFFICIENT: **0.95**
5-YEAR COMPOUND EARNINGS-PER-SHARE GROWTH: **4.0%**

		2006	2007	2008	2009	2010
Revenues (Mil)		9,086	9,861	11,023	10,350	12,104
Net Income (Mil)		592	471	294	140	550
Price:	high	18.2	17.0	16.8	11.8	14.3
	low	14.6	12.1	7.1	4.0	10.4

Southwest Airlines Company
2702 Love Field Drive
Dallas, TX 75235
(214) 904-4000
Website: *www.southwest.com*

AGGRESSIVE GROWTH

Standard Register

Ticker symbol: SR (NYSE) ❑ S&P rating: NA ❑ Value Line financial strength rating: C++ ❑ Current yield: 6.1%

Who Are They?

Standard Register is best known for its business forms and printing business. It designs, produces, and distributes printed and electronic documents, label systems, data capture systems, document security, e-businesses, and consulting services. The company's products are ubiquitous: Surely everyone in the United States, at some point in their life, has touched a Standard Register document. The company also provides extensive document management solutions, particularly for the health care industry. Its customers include nearly all of the *Fortune* 500 and many federal, state, and municipal bodies.

Why Should I Care?

Say what? Standard *Register*? Yes, yes, calm down now. We know. The SR company car is a 1977 Buick LeSabre. We know. And although it hasn't been proven that Standard Register was the model for Dunder-Mifflin, the Pleistocene paper company in *The Office*, it very well could have been. We know. But hear us out.

Normally you'd expect to find another high-flying tech stock or fashionable consumer goods brand occupying this space. Standard Register is certainly neither of those. But SR has a lot more in common with a start-up than you might think. First of all, SR is in the midst of a strategic redirection unseen since Renee Richards. Two years ago, the company aligned its businesses into three market-facing units: Health Care, Commercial, and Industrial. These markets, SR's largest traditional customers, are the targets of the company's new corporate strategy, announced in late April 2011.

SR's new focus is on "advancing its customers' reputations" which, if we can say, is an unusual focus for a company whose own reputation lately has bordered on dull, crusty, and glacial. But perhaps this is how you kill two birds with one stone—you take what you learn about your own company during its transformation and you sell it to your customers to assist them with theirs. From an operational standpoint, we interpret this to mean SR will continue to provide the paper and electronic communications tools they always have, but will also take its hundred years of experience and market-specific expertise and use it to help its customers "operate more efficiently, build brand consistency, reduce risk and advance their company reputations." In other words, in their history of creating thousands of companies' day-to-day documentation, SR has learned a lot more about companies than just what color forms they're likely to want for the next few years. When you help to manage the context of a company's most mission-critical communications, you're managing part of the content as well, and you guide their business in a limited, but still fundamental way. The visual (non-textual) content of any communication is still part of the communication, and this visual content is in Standard Register's DNA.

Standard's message to its customers is that branding and corporate identity is everywhere, and we know a lot more about it than you might think. We're going to sell you on this concept over the next few years—this is our new strategy.

And this is why SR is one of our picks for an aggressive stock. This may not be a make-or-break moment for SR, but it'll do until a real one comes along.

How's Business?

Standard turned a small profit in 2010 and posted positive cash flow growth. Operating margins are firming up as the company has trimmed many of its non-contributing operations.

Upside

- Massive customer base
- Potential to streamline customer transactions; e.g., in the health care industry
- Okay, it's a nice dividend

Downside

- Massive turning radius
- Printing operations do not scale downward well
- Pension obligations still hanging around

Just the Facts

INDUSTRY: **Office Supplies**

BETA COEFFICIENT: **1.25**

5-YEAR COMPOUND EARNINGS-PER-SHARE GROWTH: **21%**

		2006	2007	2008	2009	2010
Revenues (Mil)		895	866	791	694	668
Net Income (Mil)		5.2	(-1.0)	6.8	0.9	2.6
Price:	high	18.4	14.7	11.9	9.3	6.6
	low	11.0	11.1	4.6	2.6	2.7

The Standard Register Company
600 Albany Street
Dayton, OH 45408
(937) 443-1000
Website: ***www.stdreg.com***

AGGRESSIVE GROWTH

Starbucks Corporation

Ticker symbol: SBUX (NASDAQ) ❑ S&P rating: BBB+ ❑ Value Line financial strength rating: A ❑ Current yield: 1.6%

Who Are They?

Starbucks Corporation, formed in 1985, is the leading retailer, roaster, and brand of specialty coffee in the world. The company sells whole bean coffees through its retailers, its specialty sales group, and supermarkets. The company has 6,769 company-owned stores in the United States and 2,081 in international markets, in addition to 8,025 licensed stores worldwide. Retail sales constitute the bulk of its revenue. Note that the company-owned store count is actually down, as the company went through a modest downsizing to close 600 low-performing stores, a gutsy move in the retail sector.

The company's retail goal is to become the leading retailer and brand of coffee in each of its target markets through product quality and by providing a unique Starbucks Experience, which the company defines as a third place beyond home and work. The "experience" is built on superior customer service and a clean, well-maintained retail store that reflects the personality of the community in which it operates, thereby building a high degree of customer loyalty.

The company just ended a long-term arrangement with Kraft Foods for distribution of its products into grocery chains and similar. The non-renewal of this arrangement has helped fuel rumors of a possible acquisition of Peet's Coffee & Tea, as Peet's Grocery distribution segment has outperformed for the past several years.

Why Should I Care?

Some of us had some doubts about this company a few years ago, but looking at the stock charts going back to 2006, we're now willing to concede two points: One, people still like their coffee, and two, Starbucks knows what it's doing. The company's stock was in decline well before the start of the recession as it had more stores than good locations. It had allowed operating costs to grow ahead of revenues, and by the time it got a handle on that problem, the recession had hit and there was nothing to do but close 9 percent of its retail stores. Well, Starbucks could have tried to muddle through, but closing the stores turned out to be the smart move. Coming out of the recession the share price has rebounded nicely, operating margin is at an all-time high, and the top line is 10 percent larger on a smaller store base. A lot of the companies in this book would say, "Pour me a cup of that."

Some might argue that the company is just too big to be included in a list of aggressive stocks, that it has saturated the mocha market and jumped the java shark. We would disagree—Starbucks got to where it is by plowing all its money into growth and expanding the market for its products beyond where anyone thought it could go. Is it really a different company now? It has completed several deals in the last two years to expand its markets even further—instant coffees, single servings, and (our personal favorite) expanding into China. Yes, Starbucks is selling tea (and coffee, of course) in China. This is how smart, aggressive companies leverage brand power.

How's Business?

Perky. Second quarter comps were up 7 percent, leading to higher operating margins and a per share earnings increase of 21 percent over 2010. Higher commodity costs, mostly for coffee but also for dairy, cocoa, and sugar reduced actuals by about four cents per share.

Upside

- Brand strength
- Continued attention to costs
- Product line expansion, China

Downside

- No grocery partner as yet
- Commodity costs uncertain, but likely increasing
- U.S. retail may be mostly foam at this point

Just the Facts

INDUSTRY: **Restaurants**

BETA COEFFICIENT: **1.15**

5-YEAR COMPOUND EARNINGS-PER-SHARE GROWTH: **14.5%**

		2006	2007	2008	2009	2010
Revenues (Mil)		7,787	9,412	10,383	9,774	10,707
Net Income (Mil)		519	673	525	598	982.5
Price:	high	40	36.6	21	24.5	31.3
	low	28.7	19.9	7.1	8.1	21.3

Starbucks Corporation
2401 Utah Avenue South
Seattle, WA 98134
(206) 447-1575
Website: *www.starbucks.com*

AGGRESSIVE GROWTH

Target Corporation

Ticker symbol: TGT (NYSE) ❑ S&P rating: A+ ❑ Value Line financial strength rating: A ❑ Current yield: 2.1%

Who Are They?

Target is the nation's second-largest general merchandise retailer, offering merchandise at a discount in a large store format. The company operates 1,750 stores in forty-nine states, including 251 "Super-Targets," which also carry a broad line of groceries. Target stores are concentrated in California, Texas, and Florida, with another clump in the upper Midwest. With the sale of Marshall Field and Mervyn's in 2004, the company has focused completely on discount retail in store locations and on the Internet.

In 2000, the company formed "target.direct," its direct merchandising and electronic retailing organization. The business combines the e-commerce team of Target with its direct merchandising unit into one integrated organization. The target.direct organization operates seven websites that support the store and catalog brands in an online environment, and produces six retail catalogs.

Target positions itself against its main competitor, Wal-Mart, as a more upscale and trend-conscious "cheap chic" alternative. The typical Target customer, with a higher level of disposable income, is courted with brand name merchandise as well as a number of (largely) successful house brands like Michael Graves and Archer Farms.

The company's revenues come from retail sales and credit card operations. Target is one of the few retailers that still finances its in-house credit operations, although this has given the company some problems in tougher times. The company has been looking to sell the receivables and financing operations while still maintaining operational control of the in-house credit name.

Why Should I Care?

Target closed a deal in January 2011 to acquire 220 stores from Canadian retailer Zeller's for $1.83 billion. Zeller's is a discount retailer, the second largest in Canada and part of the Hudson's Bay Company. Target plans to have approximately 150 of these stores ready and operating by 2013. The purchase is a smart move for Target. The biggest impediment to a move into Canada is the shortage of prime locations. Over 75 percent of the Canadian population lives within ninety miles of the U.S. border, and much of the retailing space is pretty well spoken for.

Good news: Target announced its intent to find a buyer for its credit card receivables portfolio, which as of November 2010 amounted to $6.7 billion. Yeah! The company is still flushing out the bad credit card debt; credit card expenses fell from $1.52 billion in FY2010 to $860 million in FY2011. Unfortunately, this reduction in expenses accounts for over 120 percent of the increase in EBITDA from 2010 to 2011. Boo! We're glad that Target is starting to get this problem down to a manageable level, but it underscores the need to either get this business under control or get it off the annual report.

How's Business?

Count on Target's EPS to be down a bit through 2011 due to retrofits of its grocery sections and costs associated with Zeller's acquisition. Should the sale of all or part of the credit card business go through, look for slower growth in income for 2011 as well. Calendar 2012 (Fiscal 2013 for Target) will be, as they say, another day.

Upside

- Retail sector showing good signs in first half of 2011
- Economic recoveries under way in most of Target's focus areas
- Strong reputation and brand with more affluent customers

Downside

- Record versus S&P index not stellar
- Moderate inflationary pressures on overseas suppliers
- Execution risk in Canadian expansion

Just the Facts

INDUSTRY: **Retail (Department & Discount)**
BETA COEFFICIENT: **1.0**
5-YEAR COMPOUND EARNINGS-PER-SHARE GROWTH: **10%**

		2006	**2007**	**2008**	**2009**	**2010**
Revenues (Bil)		52.6	59.5	63.4	64.9	63.4
Net Income (Mil)		2,408	2,787	2,849	2,214	2,488
Price:	high	60	60.3	70.8	59.6	51.8
	low	45.6	44.7	48.8	25.6	25

Target Corporation
1000 Nicollet Mall
Minneapolis, MN 55403
(612) 370-6735
Website: ***www.target.com***

AGGRESSIVE GROWTH

Temple-Inland, Inc.

Ticker symbol: TIN (NYSE) ❑ S&P rating: BBB ❑ Value Line financial strength rating: B ❑ Current yield: 2.3%

Who Are They?

Temple-Inland is the third-largest producer of corrugated packaging in North America and a low-cost producer of building products such as lumber, gypsum, MDF, and fiberboard. Its packaging segment is responsible for more than 80 percent of its revenues and its annual output of nearly 4 million tons of corrugated represents a 12 percent market share. Its building products operation is much smaller in the scheme of things, but produces a dozen or more standard and special purpose products.

The company has a fair degree of vertical integration but is no longer in the timber production business. It has long-term supply agreements for wood fiber as a result of the sale of their timber operations in 2007. Its fiber sourcing is split nearly equally between these long-term contracts and open-market sourcing. The synthetic and quarried gypsum used in its wallboard products are similarly purchased via long-term contract and the open market.

Why Should I Care?

Temple's packaging business has done very well over the past year. The construction materials business has not. Tied closely to the housing market, the construction materials segment has lost money in each of the past three years even as the company as a whole has shown steadily improving margins against fairly flat earnings. Cost-cutting measures implemented by the company over the last two years have included the closing of some facilities and the elimination of nearly 1,000 jobs. Further cost reductions are scheduled for 2011, which should have the effect of improving margins even further. The company is confident that the measures will bring costs in line with revenues; it has announced increases in the dividends and has hinted at repurchasing up to 6.5 million shares. Make no mistake, the company has profitability in the plans. It's just that it hasn't found revenue-generating uses for the earnings as yet.

Normally a company that's shuttering nearly 15 percent of its facilities wouldn't make the cut for this book, but the packaging business is a little different. Temple has seven plants that actually make the corrugated stock in standard sizes and another sixty facilities that accept this stock and cut it to suit customer's needs. When capacity is not required and the cost of consolidating production is favorable, customizing facilities can be turned off completely. When demand rebounds and business conditions improve, restarting a shuttered cutting facility is a fairly straightforward process—labor and tooling costs are not high and the product is non-perishable.

This is not Temple's first down cycle. We expect that a mild recovery in the construction market is in the offing for 2012 and beyond, which should push Temple well into the black in both of their operating segments.

How's Business?

Sales in 2011 will be above prerecession levels with improved cost models. Per share earnings of $2.00 (estimated) in 2012 should price the shares in the $40–$50 range. If the construction sector shows any real signs of life next year, these estimates could prove to be fairly conservative.

Upside

- Flexible input pricing
- Good upside on construction segment
- Structural improvements will pay off well beyond 2012

Downside

- We're iffy on dividends here at *100 Best Aggressive*
- This year's sales somewhat inflated by restocking
- Check out that big beta!

Just the Facts

INDUSTRY: **Paper and Paper Cyclicals**

BETA COEFFICIENT: **1.9**

5-YEAR COMPOUND EARNINGS-PER-SHARE GROWTH: **-15%**

		2006	2007	2008	2009	2010
Revenues (Mil)		4,389	3,926	3,884	3,577	3,799
Net Income (Mil)		366.2	69.4	11.3	77.6	100
Price:	high	47.9	66.3	21.7	25.0	26.2
	low	37.8	18.0	2.3	2.4	15.5

Temple-Inland, Inc.
1300 MoPac Expressway South
Austin, TX 78746
(512) 434-5800
Website: *www.templeinland.com*

AGGRESSIVE GROWTH

Textron Inc.

Ticker symbol: TXT (NYSE) ❑ S&P rating: BBB- ❑ Value Line financial strength rating: B ❑ Current yield: 0.3%

Who Are They?

Textron is a global, diversified industrial company with four large manufacturing-based operations and a large finance segment. It sells a broad range of manufactured goods into the consumer, commercial, industrial, and military markets. The manufacturing segments include: Cessna (general aviation and business jets); Bell (commercial and military helicopters, V-22 Osprey); Textron Systems (military vehicles and general systems, including weapons); and Industrial (automotive systems, test equipment, hand tools, turf maintenance equipment, golf cars).

Its finance arm (Textron Financial Corporation) provides financing services primarily to Textron customers and primarily in the United States, but Bell helicopters and Cessna aircraft are also financed worldwide.

The company is heavily invested in advanced technology, specialized manufacturing systems and methods, and state-of-the-art product performance and safety. It has more than 32,000 employees in twenty-five countries.

Why Should I Care?

It makes golf carts and cluster bombs—where's Bill Murray? Textron undoubtedly has some of the most interesting factory tours around.

Textron shares in early 2008 were trading very near $75. Post-recession, the company, which is essentially unchanged, has seen its stock helicoptering around $25. The bad news, of course, has been the cratering of the commercial aircraft market. Although industry-wide non-military aircraft orders in 2010 were a 65 percent improvement over 2009, orders at the end of the year were off sharply (sharply, as in a 97.2 percent drop in the month of December). Cessna's backlog dropped by half from 2009 to 2010, and the company has had to reduce headcount in its Cessna manufacturing operations. On the other hand, the military's V-22 program—which had been a target for cancellation not that long ago—is now safe through 2012. In addition, Pentagon officials associated with the program have said they will request an additional five-year extension. Bell's backlog has increased 16 percent, further softening the blow.

China, which now has 115 billionaires, has only 200 private planes in the entire country, compared to 11,000 in the United States. Dozens of new airports are under construction there, and the executive jet market (personal, lease, and corporate ownerships) is expected to soar in the near future. How much of this new wealth finds its way to Cessna's sales office is hard to predict, but it's certainly an encouraging sign.

How's Business?

Although net margins in 2011 will be off some 60 percent from their peak in 2007, operating margins should be 80 basis points higher. Free cash flow, already at 7 percent of sales, should be up some 30 percent over 2010. The company's marketing and R&D will be well funded, and component costs appear to be under control. Unused capacity at Cessna is the issue here, but analysts at J. P. Morgan have claimed to see a light at the end of the commercial aircraft tunnel and have raised their current (4/11) target price to $30. Further, there are rumors that tax incentives for the commercial aircraft industry will be extended through 2012.

Upside

- Industrial segment profiting from automotive rebound
- Bell backlog rising
- Stock price fully cleansed at $25

Downside

- Cessna will be taxiing for a while
- Military spending coming under focus in United States
- V-22 program still dodging political AA fire

Just the Facts

INDUSTRY: **Conglomerates**

BETA COEFFICIENT: **1.65**

5-YEAR COMPOUND EARNINGS-PER-SHARE GROWTH: **15.5%**

		2006	**2007**	**2008**	**2009**	**2010**
Revenues (Mil)		10,692	12,350	14,246	10,500	10,230
Net Income (Mil)		706	946	790	160	195
Price:	high	49.5	74.4	70.1	21.0	25.3
	low	37.8	43.6	10.1	3.6	15.9

Textron, Inc.
40 Westminster Street
Providence, RI 02903
(401) 421-2800
Website: ***www.textron.com***

AGGRESSIVE GROWTH

Tiffany & Co.

Ticker symbol: TIF (NYSE) ❑ S&P rating: NA ❑ Value Line financial strength rating: A ❑ Current yield: 1.7%

Who Are They?

If you have to ask who they are, you can't afford them. Okay, that isn't a Tiffany quote, but we couldn't resist. Technically speaking, Tiffany and Co. is a holding company for the various operations of its subsidiaries, the largest being its namesake retailer, Tiffany and Company. Sales are via the company's 225 retail stores, its catalogs, and Internet sales. It also has smaller B2B and wholesaling operations.

In addition to retailing a broad line of luxury goods, Tiffany also designs and manufactures much of its branded jewelry. The jewelry is the big story, obviously, representing as it does over 90 percent of the company's sales. That means, however, there's still a healthy $300 million in sales of watches, silverware, china, crystal, stationery, fragrances, and general gift items. The Tiffany cachet raises margins on these items without significantly diluting brand strength, while at the same time driving store visits higher.

Of note, the sales from one store, the home store in New York City, account for nearly 10 percent of the company's entire revenue.

Why Should I Care?

The Asia-Pacific region is an area of focus for Tiffany. In the past four years, store growth in this region accounted for 36 percent of all store openings for the company. In 2011, the company plans to open another eight stores in the region (a 17 percent increase), making it the second largest and fastest growing region for the company. What's particularly attractive about the region is that it includes the enormous amount of new wealth in China, India, the oil-producing regions, and other newly industrialized areas. Traditional high-end brands are very popular in these areas, and Tiffany is a brand that carries instant recognition. Interestingly, the region also has by far the highest percent of sales of what the company calls "statement" jewelry, its high-end pieces with average selling prices of $4,500. The Asia-Pacific region also has a very high percentage of engagement and wedding jewelry sold (with $3,400 average selling prices), far higher than in the United States. U.S. jewelry sales are skewed far more toward the lower-end lines, where average selling prices are in the $200–$500 range. So even though the Asia-Pacific region currently accounts for only 18 percent of the company's sales, revenues from this region grew 29 percent in

2010 (versus 14 percent for the company overall) and the prospects for significant growth in the sales of high-margin items there seems clear.

Sales of Tiffany's relatively new branded lines of handbags, watches, and accessories should continue to accelerate through 2011. Unfortunately, we missed out on its recent sale of eight diamond-encrusted $134,000 cell phones.

How's Business?

The company has recently gone through a significant cost-cutting exercise, which included the closing and divestiture of two underperforming retail brands. As a result, operating and net margins have improved significantly in 2010 and should do so again in 2011. Assuming the expected 10 percent increase in revenues for 2011, earnings per share should approach $3.25, indicating a reasonable expectation of shares reaching $68.

Upside

- Brand strength
- Terrific momentum in the Asia-Pacific region
- Reduced cost structure

Downside

- Volatility in precious metals prices
- Foreign currency exposure to 48 percent of sales
- High unemployment in its largest market

Just the Facts

INDUSTRY: **Retail (Specialty)**

BETA COEFFICIENT: **1.25**

5-YEAR COMPOUND EARNINGS-PER-SHARE GROWTH: **10.5%**

		2006	2007	2008	2009	2010
Revenues (Mil)		2,648	2,939	2,860	2,710	3,085
Net Income (Mil)		254	322	294	266	368
Price:	high	41.3	57.3	50.0	44.5	65.8
	low	29.6	38.2	16.8	16.7	35.8

Tiffany and Co.
727 Fifth Avenue
New York, NY 10022
(212) 755-8000
Website: ***www.tiffany.com***

AGGRESSIVE GROWTH

Titanium Metals Corp.

Ticker symbol: TIE (NYSE) ❑ S&P rating: NA ❑ Value Line financial strength rating: B+ ❑ Current yield: Nil

Who Are They?

Titanium Metals is a vertically integrated U.S.-based producer of raw and processed titanium products. The company's production process begins with ore extraction and ends with the distribution of its processed titanium products. The bulk of its revenue comes from melt (ingots and slabs) and mill (bar, plate, and sheet) titanium, and nearly all of its customers are in the commercial aerospace, military, and industrial sectors. TIE is also the largest U.S. producer of titanium sponge (raw titanium for reprocessing).

Titanium is traditionally used in demanding applications such as jet-engine turbines and other high-load aircraft components because of its strength, corrosion resistance, and light weight. As such, the company is highly dependent on the aerospace industry. Its contracts with customers such as Boeing, United Technologies, and their parts suppliers accounted for 55 percent of revenue in 2010.

Why Should I Care?

The greatly reduced cost of raw materials in recent quarters has improved TIE's financials substantially. Operating margin in 2010 was up 500 basis points and should increase as much as 250 basis points more in 2011.

Both Boeing and Airbus are looking at greatly increased production levels beginning in 2012. Boeing (fingers crossed) expects to begin full production of its Dreamliner in late 2011, with nearly 850 orders on the books. Airbus is also accelerating its schedules for a number of projects, including its A350 airframe. Largely because of these developments, shipment volume for melted products was up 90 percent in 2010 versus 2009, and the company entered 2011 with a 32 percent higher backlog versus the prior year. The projections are very promising: Industry analysts suggest that Boeing and Airbus will ship an aggregate of between 1,200 and 1,300 airframes per year between 2012 and 2015.

Titanium is widely used in the commercial aerospace business and is a strategic material in many defense-related programs. As such, western governments are protective of their sources, and the U.S. government shields its domestic titanium industry with a 15 percent duty on all imports. TIE is the only titanium producer with major production facilities in both the United States and Europe and so benefits from this arrangement.

How's Business?

The outlook for TIE in 2011 and beyond is decidedly brighter than the recent past. Revenues and earnings (and share price) took a drubbing in 2009 as major customers delayed orders and titanium prices increased fourfold. TIE's customers require long-term contracts, and with $1 billion in backlog and no opportunity to pass through the full weight of the cost increases, TIE's bottom line was left exposed. Going forward, raw materials prices are expected to be far less speculative.

TIE's revenues for 2011 should rise some 20 percent, with margins up significantly over 2009 levels. Due to the increased competition, we can't see a return to 2006's net of nearly 24 percent, but 12 percent is not at all out of the question.

Upside

- Resumption of deliveries to major aerospace customers
- Growth in TIE's industrial customer base
- Growth in titanium applications

Downside

- Growing use of composite materials in new airframe designs
- Import duty will not last indefinitely
- Nascent competition with lower labor costs

Just the Facts

INDUSTRY: **Metal Mining**
BETA COEFFICIENT: **1.9**
5-YEAR COMPOUND EARNINGS-PER-SHARE GROWTH: **-12.25%**

		2006	2007	2008	2009	2010
Revenues (Mil)		1,183	1,279	1,152	774	857
Net Income (Mil)		281.3	251.6	149.5	34.5	80.6
Price:	high	47.6	39.8	26.8	13.2	22.9
	low	15.6	25.3	5.3	4.0	10.5

Titanium Metals, Inc.
5430 LBJ Freeway, Suite 1700
Dallas, TX 75240
(972) 934-5300
Website: *www.timet.com*

AGGRESSIVE GROWTH

Tractor Supply Company

Ticker symbol: TSCO (NASDAQ) ❑ S&P rating: not rated ❑ Value Line financial strength rating: A+ ❑ Current yield: 0.7%

Who Are They?

Tractor Supply Company is the largest operator of retail farm and ranch stores in the United States. Its target market includes recreational farmers, ranchers, and those who enjoy the rural lifestyle, as well as tradespeople and small businesses. Its stores, located mainly in towns outside major metropolitan markets and in rural communities, operate under the names Tractor Supply Company and Del's Farm Supply. Representative merchandise includes supplies for horses, pets, and other farm animals; equipment maintenance products; hardware and tools; lawn and garden equipment; and work and recreational clothing and footwear. As of December 25, 2010, TSCO operated just over 1,000 retail farm and ranch stores in forty-four states. The company does not plan to grow Del's Farm Supply significantly beyond its current size of twenty-seven stores.

It owns and operates its own distribution network, with warehousing located in Indiana, Georgia, Maryland, Texas, Nebraska, and Washington, representing a total capacity of 2.9 million square feet. No warehousing expansions are needed or planned for 2012. Tractor Supply Company also sells a subset of its store goods online.

Why Should I Care?

TSCO serves a growing, specialized niche in geographies often ignored by other retailers. It carries a specialized mix of merchandise that occupies a broad space—part big-box hardware, part garden shop, and part feed store. Its unique target market nonetheless has broad geographic distribution, and its fiscally conservative customer base has retained their purchasing power through the financial crisis. TSCO has no direct national rivals in this space, and it is three times the size of the next five largest privately held farm stores. It plans to add another eighty to eighty-five stores in 2011, with further plans to add 10 percent per year out to 1,800 units.

This is a stock with momentum-share price that has more than doubled over the past twenty-four months. The company's financial fundamentals are rock solid. Revenues are not nearly as seasonal as most retailers, and the company carries zero debt. Tractor Supply is well funded for expansion, with nearly $200 million in cash at the end of FY2010, and it has proved itself more than capable of aggressive, self-funded organic growth. Since 2004, it has opened over 450 new stores and closed only four.

At this point, there's not a lot holding it back, but TSCO's growth is bound to attract competition; the sooner it can build out to its target size, the better it will be able to protect margins. If attractive financing and an aggressive competitor come together in the right way, TSCO will have to respond. Given the state of its finances versus the rest of the field, we wouldn't be at all surprised to see Tractor Supply make a few tactical acquisitions.

How's Business?

Tractor Supply followed up on its solid 2009 with an outstanding year of growth and profitability in fiscal 2010. Net sales increased 13.5 percent, with particular strength in the fourth quarter, which saw a nearly 20 percent increase. Earnings were up a whopping 45 percent on a 100 basis point increase in net margin. The company declared its first-ever dividend in 2010 of twenty-eight cents per share and has already raised the dividend for 2011 to thirty-six cents per share.

Upside

- Strong niche dominance defined by geography
- Loyal customer base
- Strong cash flow

Downside

- Stock valuation
- Limits to expansion
- Rising commodity costs (mainly in animal feed and ag products lines)

Just the Facts

INDUSTRY: **Retail (Home Improvement)**
BETA COEFFICIENT: **0.9**
5-YEAR COMPOUND EARNINGS-PER-SHARE GROWTH: **14%**

		2006	2007	2008	2009	2010
Revenues (Mil)		2,370	2,703	3,008	3,207	3,638
Net Income (Mil)		91	96.2	81.9	115.5	168.0
Price:	high	33.8	28.8	23.8	27.3	48.8
	low	19.4	17.5	13.4	14.3	24.6

Tractor Supply Company
200 Powell Place
Brentwood, TN 37027
(615) 440-4000
Website: ***www.tractorsupply.com***

AGGRESSIVE GROWTH

Trex Company

Ticker symbol: TREX (NYSE) ❑ S&P rating: NA ❑ Value Line financial strength rating: B ❑ Current yield: Nil

Who Are They?

Trex is the country's largest manufacturer of non-wood decking. It recycles wood pulp and plastics into a wood-polymer composite, which is then formed into standard lumber sizes for use in decking surfaces (it does not make structural components). From the same material, it also manufactures outdoor furniture and accessories such as downspouts, lighting fixtures, trim, railing and fencing. All the products are sold under the Trex name to contractor-oriented lumberyards via wholesale distributors located throughout the United States, and to the major home improvement warehouse chains.

Trex products provide the look and benefits of standard wood materials without the need for regular maintenance or the additional cost of sealers, paints, or stains. The material does not discolor, warp, or rot, and can be recycled and re-used.

The company, formerly a division of Mobil, was founded in 1996 and went public in 1999.

Why Should I Care?

You'd be hard-pressed to find a societal trend more widespread lately than that of "going green" and Trex has a very good "green" story. At first glance, many would question the green credentials of a deck made largely from plastic, but when it's understood that all of the materials in Trex products are waste or industrial scrap that would otherwise end up in landfills, people come around to Trex's way of thinking. In fact, the company is thought to be the world's largest buyer of recycled grocery bags and plastic milk cartons.

The story gets better when one considers that over its typical lifespan, a wood deck requires new wood (from trees), waterproofing (several gallons every few years), gallons of stain, and potentially gallons of fungicide and termite treatment. At the end of their lives, the wood components of a deck are typically tossed out, creating an additional environmental burden, compounded if the wood began as pressure-treated lumber. Trex material, on the other hand, can be recycled or simply re-used on another project.

The company's move into accessories, lighting, and furniture is a good one, in our view. Customers who have made the decision to use Trex decking material have already taken the big step, from a marketing perspective, away from wood. They're already favorably disposed to Trex and are likely to be similarly persuaded when considering railing and furniture. Whether the decision to use Trex was based on the economics of the materials or a commitment to green principles, being able to offer a broad line of products with the same attractive characteristics can only help to reinforce both the company's message and the customer's purchasing decision.

How's Business?

The home-improvement market is driven largely by the housing market, as new home owners are those most likely to be buying appliances, building decks, etc. The housing market is starting to recover from a dismal couple of years during the recent mortgage crisis, and the turnaround is good news for Trex. Orders are up across the board, with 2011 expected to show another 10 percent top-line growth to go with 2010's 16 percent gain. The two production facilities are not inexpensive to run, and the improved capacity utilization should do wonders for profitability.

Upside

- Strong positive trend in margins
- Good cash flow
- There are a lot of rotted old decks out there

Downside

- Recent share price recovery
- Price competition from upstart Veranda
- Health of housing market still suspect

Just the Facts

INDUSTRY: **Forestry & Wood Products**
BETA COEFFICIENT: **1.4**
5-YEAR COMPOUND EARNINGS-PER-SHARE GROWTH: **31.6%**

		2006	**2007**	**2008**	**2009**	**2010**
Revenues (Mil)		337	329	329	272	318
Net Income (Mil)		2.3	(-75.9)	13.6	1.0	10.1
Price:	high	32.5	27.7	21.7	21.2	26.5
	low	20.3	5.3	6.4	5.1	15.4

Trex Company
180 Exeter Drive
Winchester, VA 22603
(540) 542-6300
Website: *www.trex.com*

AGGRESSIVE GROWTH

TTMI Technologies

Ticker symbol: TTMI (NASDAQ) ❑ S&P rating: BB- ❑ Value Line financial strength rating: NA ❑ Current yield: Nil

Who Are They?

TTM Technologies is the largest printed circuit board manufacturer in North America and the fifth largest in the world. A printed circuit board (PCB) is the platform onto which integrated circuits and other electronic components are mounted in order to build a functioning product like a PC motherboard or any of thousands of other electronic products. Building a PCB is a rather specialized process requiring customized fabrication equipment and, in the more exotic applications, unique design expertise. The vast majority of PCBs are manufactured by companies like TTM, rather than by the companies that assemble the finished circuit board.

The company is based in the United States, with fifteen specialized facilities split roughly equally between the United States and China. The Chinese facilities, acquired in the 2009 purchase of Meadville, are focused primarily on high-volume products for the consumer electronics market, while the U.S. facilities build mainly lower-volume designs for the networking and military markets.

Why Should I Care?

If you've read anything about the electronics industry in the past twenty years, you may be thinking: "North America? I thought all this stuff was built in China." You would be mostly right, as only 8 percent (by revenue) of world production is U.S.-based. Still, this is a $3.9 billion market, while TTM's China facilities have close access to the $28.6 billion market there.

What makes the U.S. market attractive is the product mix: The U.S.-based production addresses customers who need more complex designs with specific performance characteristics. As products reduce in size and increase in operating speed, the connections between the electronic components become more and more critical to the operation of the product. If you've ever looked inside an iPhone, you've probably seen examples of these rather exotic PCB technologies. The trends toward further miniaturization, higher speed operation, and higher circuit complexity will only accelerate the demand for improved interconnect performance.

TTM also supplies the companies that build electronic gear for the U.S. military. These contracts are only available to a small number of qualified suppliers, most often based only in the United States. The technologies employed in some of TTM's products are very sophisticated and difficult to manufacture, but are irreplaceable in many of the military's designs. Military PCBs also are typically "ruggedized" for operation in extreme environmental conditions and often have unique form factors. These state-of-the-art PCBs are just the sort of product that TTM specializes in, and these products are, on a per-unit basis, far more profitable for TTM than the higher-volume, consumer grade designs built in its facilities in China.

The company also provides extensive quick-turn capability, delivering prototypes quickly and offering fast ramps into production volumes. This service is valued highly in competitive bid cycles and time-limited market opportunities.

How's Business?

TTM's acquisition of Meadville was a bit of a surprise, given TTM's closing of three facilities due to the economic downturn, but the move looks as if it will pay off brilliantly. The price was very reasonable, the debt was attractively priced, and the effect on the income statement has been impressive. Meadville also gives TTM a much broader customer base and access to lower-cost labor with which to quote on more competitive North American business.

Upside

- Very broad technical capability
- Volumes adequate to compete on cost
- Big fish in the profitable military market

Downside

- Cyclical businesses
- Somewhat speculative price
- Manageable, but significant debt

Just the Facts

INDUSTRY: **Electronic Instruments & Controls**
BETA COEFFICIENT: **1.7**
5-YEAR COMPOUND EARNINGS-PER-SHARE GROWTH: **Not meaningful**

		2006	2007	2008	2009	2010
Revenues (Mil)		369	669	681	582	1,180
Net Income (Mil)		35.0	34.7	(-36.9)	4.9	71.5
Price:	high	16.5	14.0	14.7	12.4	15.3
	low	10.7	9.5	4.2	4.3	8.4

TTM Technologies, Inc.
2630 South Harbor Boulevard
Santa Ana, CA 92704
(714) 241-0303
Website: ***www.ttmtech.com***

AGGRESSIVE GROWTH

Ultratech Inc.

Ticker symbol: UTEK (NASDAQ) ❑ S&P rating: NA ❑ Value Line financial strength rating: NA ❑ Current yield: Nil

Who Are They?

Ultratech is a semiconductor process equipment manufacturer based in San Jose, California. The company, founded in 1979, was a subsidiary of General Signal until 1993, the same year the company had its IPO as Ultratech Stepper.

The company's main product lines are steppers, packaging equipment, and laser processing tools. Steppers are machines that expose silicon wafers with the patterns that create integrated circuits on the surface of the silicon. The packaging equipment is not for boxes and such, but rather for the placement of minute connectors directly onto the surface of the silicon die. These connectors are later attached to external metal pads, allowing the die to be integrated onto a circuit board. The company's laser processing tools are used to enhance the performance of a finished circuit, a process that benefits a number of mainstream applications.

The company designs and manufactures its products in California, with a fair amount of subassembly work handled by subcontractors. The company's marketing activities are headquartered in California, with eight sales and marketing offices in technology centers worldwide.

Why Should I Care?

We tend to think of high-tech companies as being either on the leading edge or failing. This used to be closer to the truth, but as highly capable processors and other circuit blocks have come way down in price and are showing up in modestly priced consumer goods, the tools used to produce them have formed a stratified market, from machines that cost as much as some companies themselves, to machines that simply get the job done. Ultratech's main line of products, their photolithography tools, are not state of the art in terms of feature size. They are not used to build the incredibly dense and advanced dies of the latest CPUs from Intel or the high-density memory used in modern servers and PCs. The optical design they employ would not permit it. What they give up in terms of ultimate resolution, though, they gain in ease of use, flexibility, and overall cost of ownership. You wouldn't lease a stable of Ferraris to deliver the bread, and you wouldn't use the latest thirty-two nanometer IC process to make inkjet print heads. Horses for courses is the game here, and Ultratech's workhorses are the machines used to make print heads, thin-film heads for disk drives, laser diodes, and LEDs, as well as digital integrated circuits. It's a good business to be in, as Ultratech's fairly steady revenues and remarkably stable stock price have shown.

In 2004, however, the company advanced the state of the art with an interesting new process it calls Laser Spike Annealing. LSA is a variation on an established process that uses highly localized heat during the IC fabrication process in order to improve the performance characteristics of certain structures in the circuit. It has been shown to provide benefits in customer designs all the way down to 45 nanometers (so far) and has been well received in the market overall.

How's Business?

Over the past five years, revenues have been fairly steady, although earnings have been somewhat spotty. High R&D and SG&A costs in 2007–2008 affected the bottom line, but these appear to have been addressed in 2009 and 2010.

Upside

- Bump packaging becoming more widely adopted
- LED volumes increasing
- Ultratech one of the lowest cost suppliers

Downside

- Competition for laser process arriving soon
- Used equipment competes in Ultratech's market
- Earnings highly volume sensitive

Just the Facts

INDUSTRY: **Semiconductors**
BETA COEFFICIENT: **0.5**
5-YEAR COMPOUND EARNINGS-PER-SHARE GROWTH: **NM**

		2006	2007	2008	2009	2010
Revenues (Mil)		120	113	132	95.8	141
Net Income (Mil)		(-8.97)	(-1.04)	11.8	2.13	16.8
Price:	high	24.5	14.4	17	15.7	20.8
	low	11.2	11.4	9.0	10	12.8

Ultratech Inc.
3050 Zanker Road
San Jose, CA 95134
(408) 321-8835
Website: ***www.ultratech.com***

AGGRESSIVE GROWTH

Under Armour, Inc.

Ticker symbol: UA (NYSE) ❑ S&P rating: NA ❑ Value Line financial strength rating: B++ ❑ Current yield: Nil

Who Are They?

Under Armour is one of the up-and-coming brands in the popular sports apparel market. Founded in 1996 to develop and market a line of special moisture-wicking clothing to be worn under traditional sports apparel, it has grown the catalog to include footwear and accessories. Its apparel line has grown as well, and it now markets its products as a "performance alternative" to traditional sports and athletic gear. The company remains focused on its core value-add of its proprietary performance-based fabrics, which are used in all of its apparel products and many of its accessories.

The company generates about 75 percent of its revenue via wholesale distribution through sporting-goods chains such as Dick's and Sports Authority, which together account for 27 percent of the company's revenue. The remaining 25 percent of revenue is derived through direct sales (web-based and via the company's fifty-four factory outlets) and licensing of the company's brand to third parties.

Why Should I Care?

As it turns out, moisture management (for serious lack of a better term) is pretty important to the dedicated athlete. Sweat is critical to anyone engaged in exercise for extended periods. Without the cooling effect of the evaporation of the water in sweat, regulation of body temperature would be impossible and the athlete would quickly find him- or herself down for the count.

Sweat only works when it evaporates, however, and when there's an excess it actually acts as an insulator, trapping heat in and preventing the sweat closest to the skin from evaporating. Under Armour's products are designed to pull excess sweat away from the body and provide a free path for air to reach the skin. In the process, the excess sweat is given a large surface area in the fabric of the garment on which to evaporate, increasing the cooling effect on the body. In theory (and in practice, as it turns out), wearing the garment actually causes you to sweat less because you're cooling more efficiently, which is something the athlete finds pretty cool, indeed.

In the end, though, selling sports apparel is less about the thermodynamics of sweat and more about the dynamics of marketing. Under Armour plays in the same space as Nike, Adidas, and other marketing monsters many times its size. Under Armour's strategy in the marketplace is a familiar one: Find a successful, visible, and attractive athlete and dress them in your products. This is a time-tested strategy and Under Armour has its share of exclusives among the top players in major sports. It also has an impressive number of sponsorships for participant events at the high school, collegiate, and serious amateur levels. Its brand is well regarded among those who buy gear for performance rather than appearance or recognition.

How's Business?

UA has done remarkably well during the recovery, we suspect due to a lot of pent-up demand. Customers delayed purchases of new gear during the recession, as this class of apparel is very much a discretionary purchase. Revenues in 2011 are expected to climb another 25 percent, while earnings should follow suit.

Upside

- Discretionary spending on the rebound
- Good brand identity
- Europe still largely untouched

Downside

- High multiple—any earnings miss will hurt
- Cotton prices continue to advance
- Share momentum could be running out of breath

Just the Facts

INDUSTRY: **Apparel/Accessories**
BETA COEFFICIENT: **1.3**
5-YEAR COMPOUND EARNINGS-PER-SHARE GROWTH: **NM**

		2006	2007	2008	2009	2010
Revenues (Mil)		431	607	725	856	1,064
Net Income (Mil)		39.0	52.6	38.2	46.8	68.5
Price:	high	54.0	73.4	47.2	33.3	60.1
	low	25.8	41.4	16.0	11.9	23.7

Under Armour, Inc.
1020 Hull Street
Baltimore, MD 21230
(410) 454-6428
Website: ***www.uabiz.com***

AGGRESSIVE GROWTH

Valero Energy Corp.

Ticker symbol: VLO (NYSE) ❑ S&P rating: BBB ❑ Value Line financial strength rating: B++ ❑ Current yield: 0.7%

Who Are They?

The largest independent petroleum refiner and marketer in the United States, Valero Energy owns and operates fourteen refineries and ten ethanol plants in the United States, Canada, and the Caribbean. Its refineries produce a variety of petrochemical distillates, including conventional gasoline, jet fuel, asphalt, lubricants, diesel fuel, and various premium products such as ultra-low sulfur diesel and special formulations of CARB-compliant gasoline. It sells branded and unbranded product on a wholesale basis in the United States and Canada, and supplies branded products though its network of over 5,800 retail and wholesale outlets in the United States, Canada, and Aruba.

In response to continued decreased demand, in June 2010 the company sold its shutdown Delaware City refinery and associated pipelines, and in December 2010 shut down its Paulsboro refinery and associated inventory.

Why Should I Care?

Many of the companies covered in this book have already experienced at least a moderate recovery in share price since the end of the recession. Valero is one of the few whose shares are still trading well under half of their prerecession peaks. Why? Mostly due to the continued high prices in petroleum feedstocks, even in the "sour" (high-sulfur) crudes that Valero specializes in with its technically advanced refineries. Is this a problem? Not if you're looking for an undervalued company.

Valero is a refining company and, as such, is always a bet on reduced petroleum prices. The current and continued political instability in Libya appears to be having an effect on prices out of proportion to its effect on actual production, and we anticipate that as that situation is resolved (in whatever form that resolution takes), the price of crude will begin to decrease. Oil demand growth projections from the International Energy Agency are holding steady throughout 2011, and the increased prices of late appear to be having little impact on economic recovery. It's possible, then, that lower prices may not be critical to Valero's FY2011 results—it may end up with pricing power sufficient to offset the higher price of feedstocks.

The demand for diesel fuel is projected to grow at twice the rate for gasoline and diesel prices remain higher at the pump. With its many refineries, more advanced diesel production technology, and flexible production capability, Valero is in a better position than most to capitalize on the changing demands of the market.

How's Business?

The company returned to profitability in 2010 after two consecutive years of losses. This kind of swing in the bottom line is not at all unusual for a refiner during a recession. When demand drops below the economic break-even point for these large operations, losses pile up quickly. On the plus side, when times are good they tend to be very, very good. In terms of its current situation, Valero (and some other refiners) are in a bit of a holding pattern at the moment; demand is definitely rising, but crude prices are still relatively high, impacting margins.

Upside

- Reduced cost basis via sale of two refineries
- Captive ethanol sources for blending
- Improved debt structure and strong cash position

Downside

- Lack of vertical integration leads to earnings instability
- Speculators control over 80 percent of market in crude futures
- Continued instability in oil-producing regions

Just the Facts

INDUSTRY: **Oil and Gas Operations**

BETA COEFFICIENT: **1.25**

5-YEAR COMPOUND EARNINGS-PER-SHARE GROWTH: **Not meaningful**

		2006	2007	2008	2009	2010
Revenues (Bil)		91.8	94.5	118.3	67.3	82.3
Net Income (Mil)		5,251	4,565	(-1,131)	(-352)	923
Price:	high	70.8	78.7	71.1	26.2	23.7
	low	46.8	47.7	13.9	15.3	15.5

Valero Energy Corp.
One Valero Way
San Antonio, TX 78249
(210) 345-2000
Website: ***www.valero.com***

AGGRESSIVE GROWTH

Valmont Industries

Ticker symbol: VMI (NYSE) ❑ S&P rating: BBB- ❑ Value Line financial strength rating: B++ ❑ Current yield: 0.6%

Who Are They?

Valmont Industries was founded in 1946 as a supplier of irrigation products and became one of the classic post-war industrial success stories, growing along with the baby boom and the need for increased farm output. It was an early pioneer of the center-pivot irrigation systems, which enabled much of that growth and which now dominates high-yield agriculture. These machines remain a mainstay of Valmont's product line, but the company also makes non-agricultural infrastructures such as light poles, cell phone towers, and those familiar high-tension electric towers that crisscross the landscape. The company also sells its metals coating services to those in need of galvanizing, electroplating, and powder coating for very large structural pieces.

In 2010, Valmont completed a $420 million acquisition of Delta plc, a maker of infrastructure products closely matching the Engineered Support Structures product line in the United Kingdom. The company also has very large holdings with suppliers of manganese and manganese dioxide, used in the manufacture of specialty steels and batteries. The company has operations in Australia, New Zealand, the United States, China, South Africa, and throughout Southeast Asia.

Why Should I Care?

Among the basic requirements for growth in every developing nation, few are more fundamental than food, roads, and electrification. Valmont has made a good business of supplying the needs of farmers, utilities, and municipalities in the United States for more than sixty years and now it's time to take the show on the road. The Delta acquisition gives Valmont some much-needed exposure to developing economies and to the overall growth of international markets while at the same time helping to reduce the risks of relying entirely on growth in the U.S. economy, said growth having been anything but steady over the past decade. The first three quarters of results from Delta have been as advertised, with solid sales and earnings growth.

Valmont's acquisition of Delta's customer base is the bonus that makes the deal most attractive, though, and Delta's Australian locations are a strategic platform for expansion into the rapidly growing Asian markets.

A long-delayed U.S. highway bill now appears to have support from both parties, but the funding is still foggy. A recent proposal of $556 billion for a six-year bill has little chance of getting past conservatives, but both parties agree that continued extensions of the current bill are unworkable.

Being both a buyer of steel and a supplier to the steel industry also gives it some measure of protection from the inflation in that market, but is it enough?

How's Business?

Fair. Comparisons to first quarter 2010 require pulling out the Delta numbers, which for the first quarter 2011 were $133 million in sales and $6.2 million in operating income. Absent that contribution, a big bump came from Irrigation, where sales were up 39 percent.

The Engineered Infrastructure Products segment had a rough quarter. Accounting for 30 percent of revenue, its earnings were only 2 percent of the quarter's total. Although sales were up 54 percent year over year (the Delta acquisition), operating income was actually down 16 percent. Greatly increased prices for steel and other commodities are the culprit here, which forced an additional $7 million LIFO expense.

Upside

- Smart acquisition of Delta
- Surprisingly strong rebound in irrigation
- Steel prices and Aussie floodwaters will subside

Downside

- Acquisition has temporarily bloated corporate expenses
- Fairly high street expectations
- Need a good sub-$100 entry price

Just the Facts

INDUSTRY: **Construction—Supplies & Fixtures**
BETA COEFFICIENT: **1.30**
5-YEAR COMPOUND EARNINGS-PER-SHARE GROWTH: **32.5%**

		2006	2007	2008	2009	2010
Revenues (Mil)		1,281	1,500	1,907	1,787	1,976
Net Income (Mil)		61.5	94.7	132	151	110
Price:	high	61.2	99.0	120.9	89.3	90.3
	low	32.8	50.9	37.5	37.5	65.3

Valmont Industries, Inc.
One Valmont Plaza
Omaha, NE 68154
(402) 963-1000
Website: *www.valmont.com*

AGGRESSIVE GROWTH

VMware, Inc.

Ticker symbol: VMW (NYSE) ❑ S&P rating: NA ❑ Value Line financial strength rating: B++ ❑ Current yield: Nil

Who Are They?

VMWare is the world's largest supplier of virtualization software, platforms, and tools. Virtualization is a growing trend in IT that encompasses many concepts, with the benefits being mainly a higher utilization of expensive hardware, improved security, ease of administration, and improved data integrity.

VMWare's products are widely used across many industries. They are present in all of the *Fortune* 100 companies, and in 96 percent of the *Fortune* 1,000. Their economic benefits are quickly realized in use.

The majority of its sales are through indirect channels, including software distributors, hardware bundlers, and other value-added resellers. VMware also develops custom solutions in collaboration with manufacturers such as Intel and Cisco to optimize performance on its hardware.

Why Should I Care?

In VMWare's virtualized architecture, the operating system no longer controls the hardware directly. In between the operating system and the hardware is a platform called the Hypervisor. This "middleware" is the basis for the virtualization scheme, as it permits access to the hardware from not only the operating system you're currently using, but from other operating systems and applications being used elsewhere. In most user environments, Windows would only permit one user at a time to be logged on to a machine, but in a virtualized environment, many applications can have access to the CPU and memory of that machine, putting to economic use what would otherwise be sitting idle. Market intelligence specialist International Data Corporation (IDC) estimates that the typical Intel server is utilizing only 10–15 percent of its capacity. With virtualization, a single server could then reasonably be expected to do the work of six to ten servers, generating enormous cost savings in multi-machine environments.

The coming wave of "cloud" computing environments, by the way, relies on virtualized architectures as a foundation. You can't have a cloud without it. Anyone who wants to take their current dedicated hardware and implement a cloud configuration must first virtualize their hardware and operating systems.

VMware's revenues come from licenses (the initial sale of the software and other proceeds) and services, which includes support, training, etc. As late as 2007, revenue from services was less than half of that from licenses. In 2008, however, service revenue began to increase far more quickly than license fees. In 2010, revenue from services exceeded licenses for the first time. Since 2006, service revenue has increased sevenfold. This bodes very well for steady revenue in the future, given VMware's large installed base and rapidly consolidating position as the dominant player.

How's Business?

As widespread as VMware is at the moment, the potential for growth is still there. Every new machine installation, whether it's in a Windows, OSX, or Linux environment, is a potential VMware seat. On top of that, a great many datacenters are still running dedicated hardware, and these all represent potential sales waiting to happen. The company's finances are exceptionally strong, with $3.3 billion in cash, zero short-term debt, and rock-solid net margins in the mid-teens.

Upside

- Nearly 80 percent market share
- Ten year lead on Microsoft
- Oracle, HP . . . all pushing cloud architectures

Downside

- Shares won't be cheap
- Hard to capture more market share
- Revenue is 65 percent international—currency exposure

Just the Facts

INDUSTRY: **Software and Programming**

BETA COEFFICIENT: **1.15**

5-YEAR COMPOUND EARNINGS-PER-SHARE GROWTH: **33.2%**

	2006	**2007**	**2008**	**2009**	**2010**
Revenues (Mil)	704	1,326	1,881	2,024	2,857
Net Income (Mil)	85.9	218	290	197	357
Price: high	—	125.3	86.9	45.6	91.9
low	—	48.0	17.3	19.2	41.1

VMware, Inc.
3401 Hillview Avenue
Palo Alto, CA 94304
(650) 427-5000
Website: *www.vmware.com*

AGGRESSIVE GROWTH

WebMD Health Corp.

Ticker symbol: WBMD (NASDAQ) ❑ S&P rating: NA ❑ Value Line financial strength rating: B++ ❑ Current yield: Nil

Who Are They?

WebMD is actually a group of three main Internet portals serving different audiences and purposes. The Consumer Network provides information to individuals who are looking for tips on managing their own health, advice on lifestyle, and relevant condition information. Information is presented in an attractive, convenient, searchable format with timely content quickly presented. The WebMD Professional Network offers physicians and other health care professionals access to clinical knowledge, medical opinion, current medical research and findings, and information on patient care and treatments. The WebMD Private Portal service is a secure gateway to a client employer's health care system, permitting individuals access to their personal health information, with the goal of making informed benefit, treatment, and provider decisions.

WebMD collects advertising and sponsorship revenue on its public portals, while its private portals are contractual services where no advertising is allowed.

WebMD also maintains an ad-supported publications service for complementary health and reference content.

Why Should I Care?

Is there a better web destination for a nation of hypochondriacs? We go there just to see if there's anything new and interesting that might be coming our way. Just kidding. The site does draw a great deal of traffic, however. During 2009, the WebMD Health Network had an average of 61 million users per month and generated approximately 6 billion aggregate page views (over 7 billion in 2010). Affiliated sites owned by WebMD accounted for nearly 95 percent of the users and 98 percent of the page views, critical measures for a business where ad revenues flow to the page owner. The numbers make WebMD the big kid on the block in terms of health care portals, and by a large margin. It has developed a winning formula and has tremendous momentum. Six years ago, it didn't exist, and now it has bought up and integrated nearly every viable competitor. When professionals in every field need quick access to current information, they generally prefer to have one commonly used, well-vetted, and trusted resource, and for a very large number of practicing health care professionals, that resource has become the WebMD portal. The portal is obviously available worldwide, but a significant amount of the content (and the advertising) is necessarily localized to the United States. The company has already developed custom content for England and is working on European localization as well.

The company notes that the majority of its advertisers are pharmaceutical, biotech, and medical device suppliers. Traditionally, these companies have spent freely on the marketing of their products, and WebMD feels strongly that the percentage spent on online media will increase as companies recognize the particular advantages to be gained in reach and breadth.

How's Business?

WebMD is one of those rare companies that maintained revenue growth throughout the recession. Margins were certainly affected, but sales momentum was maintained. Since mid-2009, margins have rebounded nicely and revenue growth has accelerated—the company expects top-line growth of 16–18 percent in 2011 and 2012, with net margins increasing 540 basis points over the same period.

Upside

- Well-heeled advertiser base
- Should fare well as health care technology evolves
- Clear value in market leadership

Downside

- Shares are not cheap—P/E in the 40–50 range
- Impact of health care reform unclear
- Uncertain costs of future acquisitions

Just the Facts

INDUSTRY: **Computer Services**
BETA COEFFICIENT: **0.8**
5-YEAR COMPOUND EARNINGS-PER-SHARE GROWTH: —

		2006	2007	2008	2009	2010
Revenues (Mil)		254	332	383	439	535
Net Income (Mil)		2.5	62.4	54.3	15.4	57.7
Price:	high	47.3	63.5	42.0	39.0	52.8
	low	28.5	38.7	13.6	19.4	37.6

WebMD Health Corporation
111 Eighth Avenue
New York, NY 10011
(212) 624-3700
Website: ***www.wbmd.com***

AGGRESSIVE GROWTH

Western Digital Corp.

Ticker symbol: WDC (NYSE) ❑ S&P rating: NA ❑ Value Line financial strength rating: B+ ❑ Current yield: Nil

Who Are They?

Western Digital is the largest hard disk drive (HDD) manufacturer in the world (or should be by the time we go to print). It is one of only two vertically integrated HDD manufacturers, the other being its chief rival Seagate. WDC began as a supplier of controllers, the interface between the HDD and the rest of the computer. The controller business turned out to be a bit more profitable than the early HDD business though, and as HDD manufacturers one by one bit the dust, WDC found itself in good position to expand its business through acquisition. With the market exits of Quantum, Maxtor, and later, IBM, WDC and Seagate were left as the only two U.S.-based HDD suppliers. Now with WDC's purchase of Hitachi, that leaves only WDC, Seagate, Toshiba, and Samsung, and the rumor is that Samsung is looking for a buyer.

In addition to disk drives, WDC also designs and manufactures HDD-based products such as external storage products, home entertainment devices, and a powerline networking product line.

Why Should I Care?

If there were one thing we'd add to death and taxes on the list of inevitables, it would have to be increased demand for fast digital storage. Every Goliath of the online world—Google, Amazon, eBay, plus all the thousands of wannabe Goliaths, plus all the video servers like Netflix, Comcast, the Dish network, plus all of the current and planned "cloud" services . . . all of them, everywhere in every market in every country on the planet—rely on the continued availability of fast, cheap, hard drive space. Count on WDC being a major supplier for all of these applications.

One might think a company that can double revenue and quadruple earnings over a four-year period might get some attention in the form of higher share price, but WDC's stock has struggled for as little as a 25 percent increase. The problem is that this is the tech market, and the tech market has long treated the HDD as a commodity item with very little speculative value. So WDC does what a smart company does in a commodity market: It develops vertical integration and attempts to acquire market share through any means possible. In early 2010, WDC announced a deal to buy Hitachi Global Storage, whose volumes were roughly equivalent to both WDC and Seagate. Assuming the deal goes through, WDC will be the clear market leader in terms of revenue and volume and will have acquired a very important toehold in the enterprise storage market, which has been its only weak spot in terms of market share. WDC will now be the dominant player in the overall HDD market, with only Seagate's presence in enterprise keeping them from leading all the product categories as well.

Western also has its own solid-state drive technology as well, with their SiliconDrive controllers and SiliconEdge drives.

How's Business?

The acquisition of Hitachi will add some sparkle to what might otherwise have been a solid, but not spectacular year. A flat PC market forecast has depressed revenues somewhat, but the addition of Hitachi will be immediately accretive to earnings starting in Q3.

Upside

- Picking up Hitachi and IBM tech in one purchase
- Solid financial ground—room for more acquisitions
- HDD market pricing environment should improve

Downside

- Earnings reliability, not so much
- Significant SSD earnings still a few years out
- Tablet sales displacing traditional PCs

Just the Facts

INDUSTRY: **Computer Storage Devices**
BETA COEFFICIENT: **1.25**
5-YEAR COMPOUND EARNINGS-PER-SHARE GROWTH: **34.5%**

		2006	2007	2008	2009	2010
Revenues (Mil)		4,314	5,468	8,074	7,453	9,850
Net Income (Mil)		359	438	976	574	1,382
Price:	high	24.7	31.7	40.0	45.0	47.3
	low	15.9	16.2	9.5	11.5	23.1

Western Digital Corporation
20511 Lake Forest Drive
Lake Forest, CA 92630
(949) 672-7000
Website: *www.wdc.com*

AGGRESSIVE GROWTH

Whole Foods Market, Inc.

Ticker symbol: WFMI (NYSE) ❑ S&P rating: BB ❑ Value Line financial strength rating: A ❑ Current yield: 0.8%

Who Are They?

Whole Foods Market is the largest organic and natural foods grocery retailer in the world, with more than 300 stores in the United States, the United Kingdom, and Canada. Founded in 1980 in Austin, Texas, Whole Foods has shown doubters that organic/natural foods can be sold to the mainstream public, as long as the product is presented in a pleasant, attractive environment by a knowledgeable, helpful staff.

Why Should I Care?

Whole Foods is the largest certified organic grocery chain in the United States. Come to think of it, it may be the only grocery chain that's certified organic, but that's probably beside the point. The point is that in their space, Whole Foods is an army of one. There are no other major players with the organic street cred to move into an area and instantly steal market share. And not just any market share—Whole Foods customers are at the top of the income scale. They pay full price for most products either because it can't be found anywhere else or because they're buying in small quantities. They visit the store frequently and spend a fair amount of time wandering. These are the people you want in your grocery store.

In some ways, the current Whole Foods resembles the early growth stages of Starbucks. At the time, many thought the Starbucks concept (boutique coffee?) had limited appeal among only a few well-heeled and rather snobby coffee geeks. What Starbucks proved, though, is that people are willing to pay more if they feel they're getting more in return. In the case of Starbucks, what they got was a good cup of coffee, a pleasant retail experience, and a branded product with some cachet. We'd submit that Whole Foods is traveling the same path with its grocery stores that feel more like a giant delicatessen—not only do you get a can of tuna, but you get to choose among three or four different kinds of tuna from places you've never heard of, plus you get your karmic ticket punched for buying dolphin-safe tuna. For many, this is a better shopping experience than braving the fluorescent lights of the local supermarket to pick out a can of the brand their parents bought thirty years ago. What Starbucks brought to coffee, Whole Foods brings to groceries; a sense that you're getting a better-quality product, one that you don't mind paying a little more for.

Whole Foods has just over 1 percent of the retail grocery market, so there's plenty of room for growth. We'd like to see it not get overextended as it did in 2007, though.

How's Business?

We were worried that when consumer spending was down during the recession, the typical Whole Foods customer might start shopping at Safeway and forget to come back when things picked up. Happily for Whole Foods, that appears not to be the case. Revenues are well above prerecession levels (okay, there was a rather large merger in there) and operating margins are clawing their way back up. Per share earnings, already at record levels, should increase another 20 percent in 2011.

Upside

- The flock has returned
- Finances greatly improved
- Upside prospects encouraging

Downside

- Concept proven sensitive to downturn
- Comps maxed out?
- Wild Oats acquisition pricey

Just the Facts

INDUSTRY: **Retail (Grocery)**
BETA COEFFICIENT: **1.0**
5-YEAR COMPOUND EARNINGS-PER-SHARE GROWTH: **0.5%**

		2006	2007	2008	2009	2010
Revenues (Mil)		5,607	6,592	7,954	8,032	9,006
Net Income (Mil)		204	183	115	147	246
Price:	high	78.7	53.7	42.5	34.4	51.8
	low	45.6	36.0	7.0	9.1	26.9

Whole Foods Markets, Inc.
550 Bowie Street
Austin, TX 78703
(512) 477-4455
Website: ***www.wholefoods.com***